THE VIOLENCE OF THE LETTER

THE VIOLENCE
OF THE LETTER
Toward a Theory of Writing

Melanie McMahon

University of Michigan Press
Ann Arbor

Published in the United States of America by the
University of Michigan Press
Printed and bound by CPI Group (UK) Ltd, Croydon, CR0 4YY

First published September 2023

A CIP catalog record for this book is available from the British Library.

Library of Congress Cataloging-in-Publication data has been applied for.
ISBN 978-0-472-07591-1 (hardcover : alk. paper)
ISBN 978-0-472-05591-3 (paper : alk. paper)
ISBN 978-0-472-90323-8 (OA)
DOI: https://doi.org/10.3998/mpub.12406894

The University of Michigan Press's open access publishing program is made possible thanks to additional funding from the University of Michigan Office of the Provost and the generous support of contributing libraries.

FOR TERRY

There is, I feel, an age at which an individual man would want to stop. You will seek the age at which you would want your species to have stopped. Dissatisfied with your present state for reasons that portend even greater grounds for dissatisfaction for your unhappy posterity, perhaps you would like to go backwards in time. This feeling should be a hymn in praise of your ancestors, the criticism of your contemporaries, and the dread of those who have the unhappiness of living after you.

—JEAN-JACQUES ROUSSEAU, *DISCOURSE ON THE ORIGIN OF INEQUALITY*

Contents

Digital materials related to this title can be found on the Fulcrum platform via the following citable URL https://doi.org/10.3998/mpub.12406894

Prelude

In Arthur C. Clarke's short story, "The Sentinel," on which the film *2001: A Space Odyssey* is based, millions of black monoliths have been dispersed throughout the universe. Their aim is to locate evidence of advanced intelligence. In the original story, there is no monolith sent to this planet, because terrestrial life-forms are far too rudimentary. What Clarke calls "the peoples of the dawn" passed by "our own Earth" because it was "peopled with crawling, mindless things."[1] In the film version, however, the monolith acts as a kind of "teacher"[2] who bestows *techne*, and sets in motion the Zarathustrian path from worm to ape to man to overman.

Within the filmic present the monolith, a massive unmarked black slab, appears on the Earth's surface to a simian creature called "Moon-Watcher." It is 3,000,000 years in the past. The presence of the monolith is accompanied by a sound, not unlike a swarm of insects or an inorganic hum, though it slowly reveals itself to be a dense weave of human ululation. The weft of sound also contains instruments and an unremarkable name—it is the Kyrie movement of a Requiem mass, though who or what has died? György Ligeti's use of micropolyphony compresses the sounds into something hardly reminiscent of music at all.[3] It is described in the screenplay as a sound the apes "could not possibly have identified, for it had never been heard before in the history of this planet."[4] Apart from the occasional primate bark or shriek, a heavy silence cloaks the land, as the tapirs move about noiselessly. The quavering of instruments and vocal cords awakens Moon-Watcher and his companions. As the Ligeti track grows louder and more frenzied, the apes grow more agitated in turn. Emboldened, they draw close enough to touch the mammoth stele and inspect it. Kubrick cuts to a worm's-eye view from the base of the monolith, with the camera facing upward toward the sun, which crests over the peak of the dark object and burns there, echoing both the "dawn" of the title-card and Clarke's original mention of the "blue-white iridescence as the sunlight flashes . . . and leaps again from world to world."[5] Abruptly the Ligeti track stops, and Kubrick cuts to black.

The next scene centers on the solitary Moon-Watcher, who crouches in the dirt amidst the dried tapir bones, scratching the earth for insects. His gaze is arrested by something the viewer cannot see. Kubrick cuts again to the worm's-eye view of the monolith, placing the viewer at its base, herself the worm-ape looking up to the cresting sun, along the length of the towering object. We cut once more to Moon-Watcher, except that in the duration, his empty vision ("watcher") has become somehow purposeful. As the early hum of Strauss's tone-poem becomes audible—its opening section fittingly entitled, *Sonnenaufgang* ("Sunrise")—we detect in the creature a new fixity of gaze. Animals, we imagine, look but do not see. Kubrick indicates cortical activity, this proto-thinking, with a tilt of the simian head to the right, to the left, slowly to the right and to the left again, signifying an emergent process of cogitation. His gaze is still attached to the bone, which he registers and isolates. In the interim, between Strauss's sustained double low C and the fanfare of the trumpets, it comes into focus—into existence—for the first time. The bone is, suddenly, a "means," the basis of the projection of some future state in which the newly individuated, newly seen thing, will become *of use*. In her article, "Kubrick's Obscene Shadows," Susan White uses the word "fantasy," stating, "At the moment of becoming human, of picking up the bone tool and striking the dried bones of the dead tapir, the ape-man violently fantasizes about killing its prey."[6]

Kubrick shifts to a worm's-eye angle yet again. The creature has risen onto its haunches, affirming André Leroi-Gourhan's conjecture that the beginnings of the human "lie in the adoption of the upright stance."[7] Grasping the bone, it lifts it high overhead and sends it plummeting, crashing into the pile of bones until they rebound. Though played out in slow motion, these acts convey frenzy. Kubrick cuts to a medium close-up of the ape salivating as it engages its new sport. He intercuts shots of live tapirs with shots of their skeletal remains. Fallen animals drop from their off-screen blows, and in a final sequence of destruction, Moon-Watcher trains his gaze on the skull in the foreground, lifts his tool-weapon high, and implodes it with a single, furious crack. And then he smashes it some more.

Once Moon-Watcher "sees" the weapon amidst the pile of dried bones, it can no longer be "unseen." The course is set. Hence the famous transition, the transformation by way of the tool itself: the bone-club thrown upward toward the clouds becomes, in a three-million-year time-lapse, the spacecraft cruising the skies. As Michel Chion argues, this transition forces the viewer to connect the bone with the vehicle, whether in terms of a causal connection or simply as an analogy of form, that is, a "rhyme." He writes, the audience "will make the same leap of abstraction that the apeman makes in inventing the tool. This edit is the very act of abstraction, since it constitutes a definitive, irrevocable leap into language, into the symbolic."[8] Perhaps it is significant that the object floating beside a sleeping Dr. Heywood Floyd on board the Pan Am Space Flight, which must be retrieved and re-secured by the stewardess, is a pen.

At the beginning of Kubrick's "Dawn of Man" sequence, the apes and tapirs jostle one another, ignore one another, and otherwise appear to coexist. When the tapirs annoy the apes by trying to feed on the same vegetation, the latter can only grunt and gesticulate. Only menace, not death, can be inflicted on the mute tapirs. Neither can death be reliably prevented, as in the scene when the great cat pounces on the ape from above. At the first waterhole scene, prior to the arrival of the monolith, one troop of apes can do nothing to discourage the approach of another, apart from leaping and shrieking in the hope of intimidating them into a retreat. After the arrival of the monolith, however, when Moon-Watcher and his troop arrive at the waterhole a second time, outfitted as they are with bone-clubs, they have gained a certain mastery over death. As one of the members of the rival troop charges, Moon-Watcher delivers a blow to its head. The ape twitches on the ground. His fellow proto-humans take the chance to wield their own weapons, pummeling the prone creature. The rival troop retreats.

It is here that the human is invented.[9] Moon-Watcher and his troop arrive at the waterhole, freshly armed, though there is no threat of bodily harm from the others. These others have not, after all, discovered weapons. The armed troop is well fed. We have already seen the tapirs collapsing into slabs of meat. The cats can be fended off. Why then go to the waterhole with arms? The infliction of violence—not for nourishment or self-defense, but simply because one can—would appear to be the "Dawn" Kubrick signals.

This dawn entails acts of violence which are strictly unnecessary for survival—so they are not, in other words, animal.[10] The scene at the waterhole is violence effected for its own sake, that is, for dominion. It is this combination of technology (tool-use) and a new transformative category of violence, and not simply spontaneous evolution, that spawns the figure of Man.[11]

Kubrick places tool-use, violence, and the human at a site of mutual emergence. Heidegger reminds us that Nietzsche, too, required this of "evolving" man, when he wrote, "The question is: is man, as man in his nature till now, prepared to assume dominion over the whole earth?"[12] Kubrick stages this drama in the affirmative. He also escorts us to its culmination: the temporal and spatial exhaustion of this particular human course as encapsulated by the (disabling of the) HAL 9000 computer. The evolutionary confluence of man and (the artificially intelligent) tool is rendered by Kubrick as a failed, if not disgraced, path: "*Homo machinus* turns out to be an evolutionary wrong turn; and the mistake must be corrected before the genuine man of the future—that is, the superman—can arise."[13]

Kubrick's choice of the tone-poem by Richard Strauss, "Thus Spake Zarathustra," alludes, of course, to Nietzsche's work of the same name in which the titular "teacher" points the way for the transformation from "worm to ape to man to overman."[14] Yet in his commentary on the work, Heidegger points out that the operative quality of this dominion must be horror. If you have failed to recognize the horror, he writes, then you have understood nothing of Zarathustra:

> Zarathustra must first of all *become* who he is. Zarathustra recoils in horror from this becoming. That horror pervades the entire work presenting his character. That horror determines the style, the hesitant and constantly arrested course of the entire book. That horror stifles all Zarathustra's self-assurance and arrogance from the very outset. One who has not previously and does not constantly perceive the horror in all the discourses—seemingly arrogant and often ecstatically conducted as they are—will never know who Zarathustra is.[15]

2001: A Space Odyssey, despite moments of great magnificence and beauty, is itself replete with strains of horror. One need only recall the shots of Dave Bowman's misshapen face as he hurtles through the wormhole; the sudden and bloodless deaths of four astronauts by the resolutely calm HAL; or the piercing, ear-splitting signal emitting from the lunar monolith.

The dawn of techne is continuous with the dawn of man, because it extends the range of "life" by granting a temporary dominion over death. Yet techne or the apparent mastery over death occurs overwhelmingly in relation to other creatures, and more often than not, at their expense. Tapirs change into meat, big cats change into formidable challengers rather than guarantors of death, and other apes become competitors. Ape-men turn into indiscriminate killers (as HAL 9000 is a killer): killers of tapirs, big cats, other apes, and eventually, other humans. Violence, not language, according to Friedrich Kittler, turns apes "into Superapes, that is, human beings."[16] He draws a direct line from the appearance of the monolith in the "prehistoric, fractal desert of Africa," which "falls from space like a marble wonder" to the alphabetic conquests of Magna Graecia.[17] One can easily continue the line from Magna Graecia all the way to the death-throes of HAL 9000, who resists extinction up to the end: ("I know everything hasn't been quite right with me, but I can assure you now ... very confidently ... that it's going to be all right again ... I feel much better now ... I really do").

The mention of Magna Graecia is appropriate because there is no computer without the Greek alphabet. It is the original code, the code of codes, a master-code, from which all others derive. The efficiency of computational media, moreover, when compared with the original twenty-four letters of the Greek and twenty-six of the Roman alphabets, is such that it only requires two signs—or indeed *only one*—the sign or its absence: 1 or 0.[18] Of HAL 9000, it is said that he "exemplifies near-perfect indoctrination in the form of programming."[19] But of course all of us, Dave Bowman included (though he is the only one who exceeds this programming, who dies to him-self, and is reborn as the star-child) are produced in the form of programming, as products of the code.

The monolith brings the code. The monolith is writing.

Introduction

In his remarkable travelogue about the Brazilian interior and its inhabitants, *Tristes Tropiques*, Claude Lévi-Strauss recounts an unusual experience.[1] It has been remarked upon in the scholarly literature at length.[2] It is one of only a handful of texts through which Jacques Derrida elaborates his major concepts in his most-read book, *Of Grammatology*.[3] Referred to as "A Writing Lesson," what makes the encounter exceptional is less the unfolding of the event itself than Lévi-Strauss's reaction to it, the magnitude of which seems to surprise and confuse even him. At first glance, it would appear to be nothing more than another example, so characteristic of early to mid-century anthropology (its colonial roots still very much intact), of a European who bears a technology and a "native" to whom it is astonishing. Though this would be far too simplistic a reading for one such as Lévi-Strauss, it is commonly rendered in precisely such terms. One can gather that something much more is at stake for him, if only judging by the tone of its delivery. For one thing, the lesson is enframed by multiple mentions of infection, and in a manner of speaking, Lévi-Strauss is made unwell by its occurrence.

On the occasion in question, the French crew have been seeking to engage a nearby people, the Nambikwara. Their primary aim, according to Lévi-Strauss, is to establish a reliable census. He opens the chapter with an explanation of sharp demographic decline. Figures have plunged from the already tenuous "thousands" in the late 1920s to as few as four or five in some locations a mere decade later. Lévi-Strauss insists on conducting this meeting at all costs, despite the profound misgivings of his hosts, the

Utiarity people, and the reluctance of the Nambikwara themselves. Even the journey to the site is fraught. The route proves treacherous, nearly impassable. The reader gets the strong sense that this assignment, however well-intentioned, will go badly, and indeed, Lévi-Strauss describes the situation afterward as a "grotesque interlude"[4] and an "abortive meeting."[5] One wonders what compels him then, in the middle of a self-described "dangerous situation"[6]—in which neither he nor his hosts "feel safe"[7]—to introduce his ethnologist's game. As if he cannot help himself, he takes out pencils and paper and distributes them to all present, perhaps expecting to ease the tension in this way—for if the Nambikwara were to respond as had the Caduveo, for whom the game-playing was a source of curiosity and amusement, all would have passed without incident. What happens next, he describes in painful detail.

In brief, the Nambikwaran leader proceeds to copy the wavy lines of alphabetic writing onto the page. He then pores over them, and begins to make declamations, as though based on the information gathered there. He even goads a certain acquiescence from the ungainly Frenchman, who having been caught off guard, participates against his better judgment. The Nambikwaran leader immediately recognizes, in other words, the entanglement of writing with an excess of power. He intends to siphon this power from the white interlopers and in so doing increase his esteem among the others. The Caduveo, by contrast, had regarded the writing objects as mere instruments, that is, as neutral tools. Arguably, Lévi-Strauss, too, prior to the encounter, saw writing and its implements in the same light, as transparent and disinterested modes of communication. It is as if in being party to this scene and witnessing his and the Nambikwaran's charade, he estranges himself just enough from writing to observe it for the first time. But it is only a glimpse. The experience produces tremors of disturbance throughout his lifetime that he will struggle to recognize and to name. What is clear is that he never saw writing in the same way again. As this book argues, neither should we.

On the way back to camp, Lévi-Strauss becomes separated from his party. His attention is focused on struggling with his mule whose mouth is full of ulcers. He cannot locate the route through the forest by himself and becomes lost. He circles endlessly and fears he will die there—"at any moment expect[ing] to be pierced by a shower of arrows."[8] In time he is rescued, but on returning to the encampment, he discovers there has been an outbreak of "putrid" gonorrheal ophthalmia.[9] The virus and its most acute symptom, blindness, has afflicted both the Utiarity people and Lévi-

Strauss's crew. Shortly thereafter, his wife, who had accompanied him to conduct her own research, must return to France, as her blindness threatens to become irreversible. The entire section of "A Writing Lesson" reads like a fever dream, despite the author's complaint of insomnia: "Being still perturbed by this stupid incident, I slept badly and whiled away the sleepless hours by thinking over the episode."[10] Excerpted from fieldwork undertaken in the 1930s, Lévi-Strauss imports this section, virtually unchanged, into the *Tristes Tropiques* decades later. He learns that during this expanse of time the Nambikwara have been reduced from roughly two-thousand to just eighteen people, several of whom live with skin infections, syphilis, a "scaly disease cover[ing them] head to foot," and another rendered "deaf and dumb."[11]

Upon inheriting the Chair from Marcel Mauss at École Pratique des Hautes Études in 1954, Lévi-Strauss changes the name of the department from "*Religions des peuples non civilisés*" to "*Religions comparées des peuples sans écriture.*"[12] It is the operative phrase, *sans écriture*, that hearkens back to the episode and provides a descriptor that he attributes, not unreasonably as we shall see, to indigenous peoples such as the Nambikwara. Yet to make such a distinction—*those who write, those who do not*—has been roundly condemned across multiple disciplines. It is also this phrase, *sans écriture*, that will launch Derrida's fifty-page diatribe against the "Writing Lesson" in *Of Grammatology*. Lévi-Strauss supplies a kind of foil against which Derrida poses his own theory of *arche-writing*, the notion of a "writing" before "writing," a "writing" which is always already operating within speech. A total human writing, in other words, that functions as a precursor to speaking. This "alleged derivativeness of writing,"[13] Derrida states, relies on the false notion of a speaking that comes before writing, not the other way around.

For Walter Ong, if we were to call by the name of writing all forms of inscription or marking, we would confound its meaning. By including *any* "visible or sensible mark with an assigned meaning," including a footprint, an animal's deposit of feces or urine, or those only interpretable to the ones who make them, then indeed, we might date "the antiquity of writing with the antiquity of speech," as does Derrida.[14] A more precise formulation is necessary, though to argue as much is to indulge in what Spivak terms "sentimental ethnocentrism." She summarizes Derrida's position as follows:

> [He] criticizes Lévi-Strauss for conceiving of writing only in the narrow sense, for seeing it as a scapegoat for all the exploitative evils of 'civilization,'

and for conceiving of the violent Nambikwara as an innocent community 'without writing.'[15]

To Lévi-Strauss, who connects writing with alphabetics, Derrida will inquire "up to what point it is legitimate *not to call by the name of writing* those 'few dots' and 'zigzags' on [the Nambikwara's] calabashes, so briefly evoked in the *Tristes Tropiques*."[16] What the anthropologist might call art, artisanship, embellishment, etc., Derrida insists on calling writing. In so doing, Derrida (and through his influence, postcolonial studies) sees himself as restoring the integrity to the Nambikwara that Lévi-Strauss withdrew when he refused "the dignity of writing [. . .] to nonalphabetic signs."[17]

Nowhere, however, does Lévi-Strauss imply that alphabetic writing is "dignified"—and by extension, non-alphabetics undignified—but rather that the imposition of alphabetic writing entails a violent intrusion, one which is more or less synonymous with, and indeed inextricable from, European colonization. Derrida argues that this false claim is an extension of Lévi-Strauss's "ethnocentric oneirism"[18]:

> No reality or concept would therefore correspond to the expression 'society without writing.' This expression is dependent on ethnocentric oneirism, upon the vulgar, that is to say ethnocentric, misconception of writing. The scorn for writing, let us note in passing, accords quite happily with this ethnocentrism.[19]

Derrida maintains that there was no "forced entry of the West," because there was no terrain of "an innocence and non-violence"[20] on which the Europeans purportedly trod. There can be no "Occidental intrusion," he states, when the culture in question is already violent, which is to say, already writing.[21] Derrida does not deny the violence of the letter. Instead, he argues that this violence existed well before the incursions of anything so formalized as an alphabet or anything so systematized as colonialism. His project in the *Grammatology* is to show

> why the violence of writing does not *befall* an innocent language. There is an originary violence of writing because language is first, in a sense I shall gradually reveal, writing. 'Usurpation' has always already begun.[22]

The European west cannot "introduce" something, as Lévi-Strauss would have it, that was already there; neither are they responsible for occupying, expropriating, or "usurping" something, when this process had already been well underway. We cannot underestimate the extent to which this claim informs the entirety of his philosophical project, especially in the charge of *phonocentrism* that follows each attempt to consider orality apart from the alphabetic.[23]

The trivialization of the alphabet is a ubiquitous postcolonial strategy, one which understands itself as correcting ethnocentrism. This approach is evident in Lydia H. Liu's work on writing as an imperial technology, where she rejects the differentiation between "metropolitan literacy and native orality in postcolonial studies of the modern world" as well as "the presumed dichotomy of writing and orality [which] often relies on a flawed, representational view of writing that is phonocentric to the core, à la Derrida."[24] We should recall that Spivak both introduces Derrida's approach to the Anglophone world, and so does she help initiate a discipline that is founded on his methods.[25] In other words, the paradigm most common in postcolonial studies accords with the approach laid out in the *Grammatology* as elaborated by Spivak: a) every human culture always already writes; b) no script or writing system is different in kind from any other; and c) colonization is not primarily a violence but rather a space of negotiation between equals, that is, cultures that are *equally written, and thus equally violent.*

When scholars such as Liu deliberately minimize the alphabet in order to demonstrate the refusal of Eurocentrism, they only succeed in erasing violence. Liu fails to recognize *the rupture* that is the Greek alphabet, using the word "alphabets" plural, and thus denying, as most historians of writing do, that the Greek invention is *sui generis*. She includes the alphabet within some two dozen other scripts and writing systems, describing it in the most casual language possible. They merely "adapted the conventional Phoenician Semitic consonantal alphabet and Cypriot syllabary" by importing these foreign scripts and fashioning "a Greek writing system."[26] Why the Phoenician system is an alphabet, but the Cypriot is a syllabary, is not explained. Rather, she presents this as analogous to the way in which the Devanagari script is used in India for the Hindi, Nepali, and Marathi languages. There is and never has been, Derrida and Liu reassure us, a culture "'without writing.'"[27]

Eric Havelock and Walter Ong have been conspicuously omitted from postcolonial studies, by contrast, presumably because Ong's major work is entitled *Orality and Literacy*. That all aspects of life change profoundly and irrevocably with the introduction of the Greek alphabet is a thesis—propounded by both Havelock and Ong—that has also been derided as ethnocentric. Havelock's and Ong's premises are diametrically opposed to

Derrida's in that they suggest that prior to the invention of the alphabet, everyone everywhere was always already "oral"—by which they mean simply non-alphabetic.

Havelock and Ong contend that the Greeks are as thoroughly oral as everyone else in the world, for this does not preclude the use of cuneiform, hieroglyphs, Linear B, counting systems, token systems, syllabaries, or indeed any other means of preserving and encoding cultural memory.[28] "Orality" does, however, preclude the use of the alphabet. The alphabet is not comparable to other such systems. It emerges at the relatively recent date in human history of roughly 800 BCE, and it does so only *once*. Every culture is oral, they stress, which is to say non-alphabetic, until that point in time when the Greek alphabet emerges, not as the result of innate Western genius, but as a kind of historical aberration.[29]

A note on terminology is in order. In tracking the effects of the Greek alphabet from the Mediterranean basin across Europe (and from there the wider world in various colonial iterations), I sometimes use the term "oral" culture for brevity. "Orality" is problematic because it places undue emphasis on the voice alone—which is itself a literate formulation—and so it is inaccurate and misleading. For the purposes of avoiding confusion, I use it here as the term to suggest a cultural formation that is faced by an alphabetic imposition. I speak of "writing" in what Derrida calls "writing in the narrow sense," by which I mean those behaviors related to using the Greek alphabet. I employ the term "literacy" to mean a fluency, by varying degrees, in the use and manipulation of the alphabet. Some have argued that this, too, is ethnocentric and that one should speak instead of literacies plural in a manner indicating various cultural competencies, with or without the use of an alphabet. This, to my mind, is simply another iteration of the postcolonial thesis that everyone everywhere always already writes.

The Greek alphabet is inextricable from the ascent of the European West. While more general assertions about "writing and civilization" are, as Liu herself points out, somewhat commonplace, this book concerns itself with a highly specific technology. It is one which would not consolidate itself fully until the Roman period. Its movement across the European continent was slow, uneven, and staggered in terms of its codification and entrenchment. Not surprisingly, perhaps, it is the printing press that most dramatically facilitates its solidification, standardization, and spread. Here we consider how the European West used the "recent accident" of the alphabet to effectively transpose its own version of civilization, with varying degrees of penetration, nearly everywhere in the world.

So, while the alphabet is indeed an imperial technology, and postcolonial studies would seem to be the area most germane to its investigation, for the reasons discussed above the discipline is unsuited to addressing these questions and, in many ways, discourages them from being asked. Yet the encirclement and penetration by alphabetics—and following on from this, the other *conversionary* codes it enables, such as capitalism and monotheism—goes on. It has often spelled certain death for cultures such as that of the Nambikwara. We must take issue with Derrida when he argues that this process *is not a violence.*

Lévi-Strauss attempts to redeem the debacle later, using "A Writing Lesson" to produce a kind of fable-like recapitulation of the European destruction of indigenous peoples. Derrida recognizes this mood: "The entire 'Writing Lesson' is recounted in the tones of violence repressed or deferred, a violence sometimes veiled, but always oppressive and heavy [. . .]. What can a relationship to writing signify in these diverse instances of violence? Penetration in the case of the Nambikwara [. . .]. Penetration, therefore, into the 'lost world' of the Nambikwara."[30] Apropos the quotation marks, we might ask in what sense the world of the Nambikwara is not lost? In that section of the *Grammatology* called "The Violence of the Letter"—from which this title is taken—the word "violence" is used with irony, if not mockery. It is directed against Lévi-Strauss's premise of an exogenous (i.e., colonial) violence. Though it is piecemeal and incomplete, Lévi-Strauss produces, following his "grotesque interlude," the rough outline of a new theory. The theory in question—that which is the object of Derrida's derision—is what Lévi-Strauss describes later in an interview with *Nouvelle critique* as his "Marxist hypothesis on the origins of writing."[31] He states,

> My hypothesis, if correct, would oblige us to recognize the fact that the primary function of written communication is to facilitate slavery. The use of writing for disinterested purposes, and as a source of intellectual and aesthetic pleasure, is a secondary result, and more often than not it may even be turned into a means of strengthening, justifying, or concealing the other.[32]

There is something about writing that continues to haunt Lévi-Strauss, impressing itself as both critical and yet fundamentally elusive.

My aim in this book is to begin to elucidate what he glimpsed as a young researcher in the rainforest but remained unable—partly because of his own alphabetization—to fully identify. Our profound epistemic limitations in this regard should not be minimized. Without an intensive, years-long form of apprenticeship, the alphabet cannot take hold in the brains of young users. (It is the Romans, more thoroughly than the Greeks, to whom it occurs that this is best undertaken in small children.) Yet so does such extensive programming actively foreclose other (nonalphabetic) ways of knowing since alphabetization becomes inseparable from, and indeed is mutually constituted with, the organ of cognition and perception itself. What is doubly problematic is that in response to this impossibility of "seeing" one's own alphabetized cognitive schema, she is likely to conclude that she is therefore not using one—indeed, that she is free to read or not to read as she chooses, and that most of the time, there is no alphabetic apparatus in operation at all (especially insofar as she is watching something rather than reading it). Yet "watching" (i.e., seeing, saccading, scanning) is an integral part of alphabetics from its inception. (The shift to a predominantly visual register with alphabetic literacy is discussed at length in the work of Marshall McLuhan.) Though we have removed the suffix for writing (*graph*) from common usage, still and moving images (photograph, cinematograph, etc.) are simply late forms of writing enabled by—if not direct expressions of—the alphabet, the dynamics of which are already present in its earliest iterations, including its context-free format and thus its autonomous or self-contained nature; its hallucinatory or "virtual" aspects; and its anonymizing functions, to name a few.[33]

Furthermore, the alphabet functions to obscure itself. This is complicated by the fact that the inability to discern the workings of the alphabet is not coincidental but fundamental to the system itself. We effectively see *through* alphabet writing (and onto fields of hallucination), as opposed to the markings themselves, for if we did not, we could never read anything. We would simply be confronted with meaningless blocks of "black squiggles"[34] set in relief upon white backgrounds. To put it another way, if a person were intent upon doing so, she would struggle to notice the apparatus rather than the hallucination. The alphabet is the only writing system that erases itself as part of its effective operation. One can easily eclipse writing from her awareness because writing eclipses itself.[35]

Another way to think of this is in terms of the alphabet as a code rather than a transcriber of language. Whereas language is meant to consist of statements, whether constative or performative, a code is executable, which is to say *it runs*.[36] It is undoubtedly difficult to develop a theory about a system or a program that one is in the midst of running. McLuhan says something to the effect that, whosoever has a theory of water, one can be sure it will not be a fish. And according to Friedrich Kittler, "Understanding media—despite McLuhan's title—remains an impossibility precisely because the dominant information technologies of the day control all understanding and its illusions."[37] There is also a sense in which alphabetic reading and writing are drawing to some kind of close. Why construct a theory of writing now in the era of its ostensible twilight?[38] Because it has been suggested that a form of media must be in the process of being replaced, that is, in its death throes, before it is possible to appreciate what it was. Only when we are becoming digital can we fathom what becoming typographic or becoming chirographic entailed.

At the same time, I would argue that we are not entering the death of writing so much as a state resembling super-writing. Though most of us make "black squiggles on white paper" less and less and compose almost exclusively on lighted screens, we are without question creatures who are written and who write. Even technologies that appear non-scriptural—or perhaps anti-scriptural—such as podcasts, YouTube videos, and other streaming content, are only made possible *because of* writing. More importantly, all of these media already presume an alphabetized (or in the case of children, an alphabetizing) subject.

Let us call the following book a continuation of Lévi-Strauss's unfinished theory of writing, where we will attempt to restore the title, *The Violence of the Letter*, to its literal sense, that is, to its literality. For literal—from the late Latin "letter for letter"—is what we must always face, what we are constantly obliged to encounter, and what we have with which to construct the world. (All that I am, or ever could be, to paraphrase Mallarmé, is down to twenty-six letters.)

Lévi-Strauss, meanwhile, registers this violence but also struggles to locate its mechanisms, and so fails to wholly overcome the self-occulting nature of its effects. Lévi-Strauss's difficulty is also our own. He cannot approach the thing without using the thing to approach it. This work takes upon itself the formidable task of proposing a new theory of alphabetic writing. Through a variety of historical, literary, filmic, and theoretical readings, it attempts to substantiate the famous words: "Writing is a strange invention."[39]

1

A Brief Technical Detour

Both crude and ruthless . . . the phonetically written word sacrifices worlds of meaning and perception.

—MARSHALL MCLUHAN[1]

As alphabetics emerged, sometime near the end of the eighth century BCE, the Greeks did not foresee the impact of their invention, nor could they have. Roughly three thousand years after its development, Vico expressed sympathy with the common person's assumption that the alphabet had sprung from the hands of God himself.[2] Not so much due to its perfection as to its utter improbability. As we will see, even the Greeks regarded the technology in this way—that is, as fundamentally "alien"—despite its evident autochthony. We are inclined to believe that *alpha beta*, as it was originally called, would have appeared within every human society in time, that it is somehow a rational progression all cultures ultimately attain. Yet the fact remains that the alphabet "occurred under unique circumstances which have never recurred, and in the nature of things *never could recur.*"[3] Before describing the mechanisms of this deviation itself, let us first consider a demonstration of its difference, including a brief consideration of its colonial implications. Afterward, we consider (and correct) several misconceptions regarding the manifestly unusual features that make the alphabet what it is.

Most historians of writing will argue that the invention of the alphabet consisted in a minor modification of the Semitic syllabaries. If this were the case, one could accept why Havelock's insistence on a rupture inaugurated by the Greek system might strike many scholars as overstated. The description of the alphabet as having merely "added vowels," however, is misleading. A consonantal system does not require vowels in order to achieve its purposes. If the alphabet were simply the first system to make this adjustment, then indeed, the development could be considered inconsequential if not superfluous. The absence of vowels in the Semitic system does not impede understanding to any significant degree.

The ability to decode a text using a syllabary had been confined to a small community of initiates—those likely responsible for the keeping and care of religious texts. Decoding would have been simplified by the relatively few number of such inscriptions. In the case that a text proved unfamiliar, its restricted uses, as well as the pre-formed expectations of the reader, would still have made the process unproblematic. A syllabary relies to a great extent on prior knowledge. One readily compensates for the absence of vowels because she has already anticipated the content. A syllabary user was in the habit of reading texts, in other words, the source, function, and content of which, she *already knew*. On the uncommon occasion of being presented with something new, and thus possibly ambiguous, the text would still belong to the same universe of purpose in which other, more familiar texts, existed.

The signs of a syllabary contain "triggers" of the memories of oral sound—as does the alphabet, though very differently, as we shall see—and with them, those pre-formulated utterances, or "whole meanings," that is, both "sounds and arrangements of sounds," which are "previously known and recognized" by the decoder.[4] For someone raised Catholic, for example, a text of the "Our Father" would require only the slightest prompt from a syllabary to trigger the memory of its entire sequence of words, as well as to distinguish it in length and content from other like texts, such as the "Hail Mary." Again, one can read without the vowels from a syllabary because in effect, she knows beforehand what message is to be imparted. Adding vowels then (i.e., OURFATHER instead of RFTHR), would not have been a radical departure, because it would not even have been necessary. Most historians of writing leave it at that.

Let us now attempt to read the following, which is written according to the principles of a consonantal (syllabary) system: "LTLBP." (The aids of spacing and lowercase afford higher levels of readability, but these will not be common until the advent of printing; they are typographic conveniences rather than chirographic features.) My presumption is that the reader struggled, at least for a time, to decipher the line. If I were to offer the second line in an attempt to provide additional clues, I would probably confuse rather than clarify matters: "LTLBP / HSLSTHRSHP." Yet the lines become perfectly, which is to say automatically, readable if I provide you with the information that it refers to a nursery rhyme about a female child and her misplaced flock. Had I mentioned this before presenting the line, it would have been far easier for you to decode. And the line that follows, though more complex, will be relatively uncomplicated to understand, in part because in all probability, you already knew it was coming.

We can see why vowels are extraneous for readers who are equipped with sufficient prior knowledge of the text, though we may also note that this is not the case for readers without it. A reader who was not familiar with the nursery rhyme—who was, in effect, reared outside the cultural context in which it was a fixture of childhood—would likely find the message impenetrable. Therefore, in a syllabary, the signs must trigger not only the memories of oral locutions, but also those "arrangements of sounds" that obtain from longstanding cultural embeddedness, including rhymes from childhood, for instance, or passages from scripture, in order to be legible. If one lived outside of this culture, she would have no point of entry for decoding the script. Conversely, a literate person from within that culture would have almost no difficulty. The point is that a syllabary is very much tied to a cultural context. One result of this is that it is overwhelmingly opaque to persons outside that milieu.

It is not enough to know the category or genre of the information (i.e., nursery rhyme). One must also have grown up in the culture for which it is a representative staple. So, while I do not need vowels to read the lines above, this is because I was raised in the Anglophone west, and with some basic orienting information, I read (without reading, in a sense; that is, without needing to) with relative ease. To put it another way, the syllabary functions as a mild prodding of the recesses of my memory, and my brain supplies the rest. Yet supposing I encounter a text written in a syllabary-like system from a culture in which I have not been reared. In that case, the text would give me no information and no prompting whatever, because the memories are not there to be retrieved. Let us imagine I am presented with a common nursery rhyme from Bengal. To facilitate the example, let us use one that has been translated into English. Even though the syllables are derived from my native language, and even though I am aware of the genre, I would still be quite unable to decode it, because I was not born into a context in which hearing, singing, reading, or saying it were common experiences. Consider the first line of this rhyme, rendered according to a syllabary principle: "RCKRCKRLLCKYGRL." I am even informed that, very much like my first example, it concerns a girl-child and would be expressed in "a sing-song voice."[5]

Given enough time, I might be able to make out the general tenor of its meaning. Yet the process of doing so would be halting rather than auto-matic and labor-intensive rather than effortless. My interpretation would always be tinged with doubt as opposed to relative certainty. And again, the addition of a second line offers me no assistance: "CMBNYRPRTTYHD." Though I have used an admittedly crude example, my aim is simply to indi-cate the issues surrounding a system that uses syllabary principles and the limitations such a system imposes upon either a foreign reader or an unini-tiated reader from within the same cultural context.[6] Let us consider how much understanding can be gathered from the full stanza—rendered into a consonantal system, according to a syllabary principle—for those of us who were not raised in the appropriate setting:

Rck rck rllcky grl,
Cmb n yr prtty hd
Grm wll cm prsntly
T tk y wy n jffy
Why d y cr yrslf hrs?
Ndrstnd yrslf
N whs hs y dwll.[7]

One of the words is complete ("Why") and several others are easy to discern ("prtty," "Ndrstnd"). Even with the benefits of spacing, punctuation and the other orthographic cues I have included—as well as its translation into English—I might still be a mere thirty percent certain of what the text was meant to convey. With time and diligence, I might even be able to dou-ble that percentage to a generous sixty or seventy percent. Let us conclude that eventually I could read roughly sixty-five percent of the syllabary lines with relatively low levels of ambiguity. Now let us read the same lines ren-dered into an alphabet:

Rock rock rollicky girl,
Comb on your pretty head

Groom will come presently
To take you away in a jiffy
Why do you cry yourself hoarse?
Understand yourself
In whose house you dwell.[8]

Even if I have no idea what genre of text I will be presented with before-hand, and even with an utter dearth of information about the culture from which it issues, I can nevertheless decode this text nearly *instantaneously* and with very little guesswork. As opposed to a syllabary or any other type of system, an alphabetic inscription provides the only instance in which I can read something immediately that a) I have never seen before, and b) the purpose of which I do not know beforehand. "Why do you cry yourself hoarse?" is perfectly readable, whether or not I am familiar with the cultural norms it expresses and whether or not I know it is from a nursery rhyme. I do not even need to know it is Bengali, for it might just as well have been Nambikwaran. For one who is alphabetically literate, a text is readable *every time, from the first time*, and provided it is written in my language, I can read literally *anything* that has been thusly recorded. No anticipatory expecta-tions, no limitations of genre or purpose, no cultural knowledge, *nothing* is required of me beforehand to facilitate a full decoding of the message. Not only that, but I can do so with a near-simultaneity in which mere sighting is equivalent to the act of decoding. I may not understand it—as, for exam-ple, with a paragraph in a chemistry textbook or the nuances of a Bengali rhyme—*but I can still read it.*

I hope the implications for colonial knowledge construction have begun to present themselves—for they are innumerable—and while I will illustrate a series of them in explicit terms throughout this book, it is important first of all to grasp how the alphabet accomplishes this dramatic difference. I request the reader's patience while I undertake this brief technical detour, which, while somewhat tedious, is unavoidable for explaining all that fol-lows. For as Havelock notes, "The usual answer given is that the Greek sys-tem invented signs for the five vowels. But this cannot be the real answer."[9] The separate vowel signs alone do not explain the departure inaugurated by the Greek alphabet. Among the many misconceptions, let us consider the following.

A. THE ALPHABET DOES NOT REPRESENT SOUNDS.

This is perhaps the most difficult to grasp. The idea that it does so is deeply ingrained; to my knowledge, Havelock is the only scholar to have identified this misunderstanding at all, much less sought to disabuse us of it. And even he did so sparingly and with an inconsistency that suggests he did not fully grasp what he had uncovered.

Virtually all mammals make noise by expressing air from the lungs and through the larynx, causing vibration. This vibration is emitted as sound. An alphabet does not attempt to record this or any process, but rather conceives of a singular object. Following Havelock, we refer to this object (generated by non-mute animals in the course of their vocalizing) as a "vibrating column of air."[10] The vibrating column of air neither warrants nor requires a mark, as it is simply the invented precondition of the alphabet's operation, and as such can remain invisible or simply presupposed. Upon this vibrating column of air, one must arrange and apply distinct and complex orofacial movements in order to modify the column and (ultimately, hypothetically) to produce sound. *Which* orofacial movements to apply to the vibrating column in order to produce any given hypothetical sound in a language is referred to as a phoneme. A phoneme represents the specific biomechanical positionings required of each hypothetical sound. It can be thought of as a set of imaginary instructions that inform the reader what a mouth would do if it were to make this sound. It is the recipe for making the sound, not the sound as such. Every set of instructions (i.e., every phoneme) is ideally assigned its own identifying mark. Each mark should indicate which orofacial movement is being demanded—though many require an entire sequence of such movements, rather than a single instance of positioning, such as lifting the back of the tongue; involving the nasal cavity; restricting the throat; pressing the lips; and so on. The Greeks invent not only the vibrating column of air but also the multiple, semi-discrete, bodily actions required to modify it, each of which is assigned a separate mark, the category we know today as letters.

In putting things in this way, have I not unnecessarily complicated matters? Am I not, in my circumlocutory and abstruse way, simply saying that the Greek invention, albeit along a tortuous path, nevertheless *represents sounds*? That the answer is resolutely negative has been overlooked, but for reasons that will become clear, this point cannot be overemphasized.

The alphabet functions not through representations of sound but through representations of its potential and its absence. *Potential* and *absence* correspond to the Greek inventions of "vowel" and "consonant," respectively. (Syllabaries are considered "consonantal" only in retrospect because these categories did not exist before the alphabet.) Let us put aside for the moment the utter improbability of devising a system of marks that has no relationship to actual noises but only to their possibility and to their obstruction. By now the field of linguistics has developed new and finely honed gradations of such classification, but let us turn to one of its founders, Ferdinand de Saussure, to appreciate what is meant by potential and absence.

We begin with his "occlusive" "p" as an example. "'P,'" he writes, "is formed by complete closure, the airtight but brief sealing of the oral cavity."[11] The action of the pressing of the lips—deliberately but gently, "airtight but brief"—and thereby the sealing of the oral cavity is definitionally a consonant because it traps, blocks, or otherwise occludes the flow of the vibrating column of air, hence the name occlusives. All consonants in the Greek system trap air in the oral cavity. Usually, we would be inclined to assume that the "p" is *not* the result of the pressing of the lips alone, but that this is only the first "step" of "p," as it were. "P," we believe, takes place in the *release* of the trapped air that occurs just after the pressing, not in the pressing itself. We imagine that expelling the trapped air is what creates the sound we identify as "p." But "p" does not exist on its own as a sound. The freeing of the vibrating column of air which has been trapped by the orofacial placements required of "p" necessitates a vowel. It is impossible, in other words, to avoid making one or another vowel-sound upon releasing the sealed oral cavity, because the shape of the mouth as it opens will determine what sound is uttered. What originates as "p," in other words, becomes "pu," "pa," "pi," "po," or "pe," depending on how the mouth is arranged. There is no way to produce only the "sound" of "p," because "p" represents strictly the pressing of the lips (or the sealing). "P" is no more than the blueprint that indicates its particular mode of trapping air (i.e., "complete closure, the airtight but brief sealing of the oral cavity"). Still, we conceive of consonants as producing something forceful or commanding, as in the word, *kick*. And yet consonants are not explosive. They are the opposite of explosive: they make no sound at all. Plato had already recognized this: the consonant, he noted, is non-sound.[12] Havelock, following Plato, designates a consonant as "an abstraction, a non-sound, an idea in the mind."[13]

If a consonant is the blocking of air and thus the absence of sound, then a vowel is the potential or possibility implied by which sound will be released according to the various positions the mouth could form as the vibrating column escapes the body.[14] To make the sound "ohh," for instance, one must tense one's lips to form a rounded shape. In order to read the (imagined) sound "po," one would see, in effect, the instructions: "Press the lips and seal the oral cavity; (expel the vibrating column of air); position the mouth to form a circle." For the literate person, these directions are condensed into the letters "p" and then "o."

B. "LETTERS" DO NOT PREEXIST THE GREEK SYSTEM; THEY ARE INVENTED BY IT.

In *The History and Power of Writing*, Henri-Jean Martin describes one of the alphabet's most direct precursors, the Egyptian-influenced West Semitic syllabary. This system employed the principle of acrophony, which functions by using a picture of an object to stand in for the first sound of its name. We retain something of this feature when we teach children to read, as with—"A is for apple; B is for boat; C is for cat,"—except that with acrophony there is no accompanying shape "A" but only the graphic likeness of an apple. The acrophonic principle follows this pattern throughout, so that one views a series of pictographs, with the initial sound of the object's name functioning as the audial memory trigger. The word bat, for instance, would be written with the pictographs, boat apple toad. In the West Semitic system, *Aleph* was signaled by a picture of a house and pronounced *alph*; the sign for *beth* was an egg, and so on.[15]

Two differences between a syllabary and an alphabet emerge here. "Aleph" and "beth" remain confined to the readership of this (Egyptian/West Semitic) universe. They cannot easily move outside of it in order to encode other languages, for example. Not only that, but these shapes—*house, egg*—contain additional resonances unrelated to the initial sound of the words they are meant to evoke. In this way, the shapes are already encumbered by prior associations, which is to say, they are shared or half-borrowed from the outset. By contrast, the alphabet fabricates "visible shapes" out of thin air, so to speak. These "visible shapes" are neither composites (of houses, boats, so on) nor symbols; they are not asked, as Havelock puts it, to do double duty, as is the case with an acrophonic system.[16] These visible shapes become letters, and letters are unique in that they include no cultural or linguistic anchors of any kind; they are deliberately meaningless. Some of them are derived from the Phoenician script, but these are turned upside down to ensure they are completely arbitrary. The only cultural residue preserved in the Greek system (and it is not Greek cultural residue) is in the names of the letters themselves—though to "name" letters is itself new, and these names must be equally arbitrary. In an acrophonic system, conversely, there is no "name" separate from the object its grapheme is meant to resemble (Aleph is the "name" of the sign as well as the object to which it refers). But because Aleph does not mean a dwelling place in Greek, nor beta an avian embryo, the Greeks retain these words as names for their own letters, hence alpha, beta, and so on. In this way, these "visible shapes" with non-sense names come to fulfill the new requirements of an alphabet. Letters are chosen and fashioned according to principles of randomness, precisely because they have neither meaning within, nor attachment to, the Greek cultural linguistic inheritance. In part Kittler calls these arbitrary shapes, "squiggles," so as to emphasize their contrived nature.[17]

C. THE ALPHABET INSTANTIATES UNIVERSALISM.

Greek "phonemes," as completely ideated units, solve a problem we may not have realized we had. Before the alphabet, I could not use, for example, my writing system to encode an appreciably different language, because the sounds in the respective languages are so dissimilar that many—if not all—of the symbols used for one would be quite useless for the other. And not only are the *symbols* confined to the culture in which they have meaning (i.e., house, egg), but so are the individual sounds they evoke too different for devising a means of interchange or transliteration between them. In other words, my system is resolutely tied to its cultural context for its symbols, on the one hand, and by the particular sounds of my language on the other. A syllabary, as the name suggests, captures the syllables of a given language. Phonemes are distinct from syllables because they are theoretic rather than observational.

Phonemes are often defined as the smallest discriminable unit of a speech sound, yet they are also defined as *indiscriminable*, because (as we have been exploring) they represent non-sound, or more precisely, its potential and its absence. As one linguist explains, "a phoneme" is a theoretical unit, whereas a "phone" is an observational unit.[18] It is important, he argues, to distinguish theoretical terms from observational ones, particularly in a field such as linguistics, and yet these are very often conflated. (Arguably this is another reason why we harbor so many misconceptions about what an alphabet is and how it works.) The meaning of a phoneme as theoretical or hypothetical tends to be confused with the adjective "phonetic," a term relating to actual speech sounds, that is, observational units, despite the fact that "a phoneme itself cannot be heard, since the realization of a phoneme is a phone."[19] A phone represents a sound—it is an "observational entity" that we can hear and record[20]—whereas a phoneme, we might say, is that which comes *before sound* (and is therefore non-observational). A "phoneme" is manifested in a phone, but that they are distinct entities should remain uppermost in our minds. Albertine Gaur speaks of "the elusive phoneme" as one of the most frequently used but most poorly understood terms in all of contemporary linguistics.[21] Linguists continue to define phonemes as the smallest possible elements of sound in a language—as do elementary school teachers—though we also know that "it is not a real but an imaginary sound underlying spoken language." Gaur echoes the insistence that "phonemes must be carefully distinguished from physical sounds" since "a phoneme cannot be produced as a sound. It is simply an abstract concept which can be made real only visually (as a letter) but not acoustically."[22] Can there be such a thing, then, as a phonetic alphabet as opposed to a phonemic one? The answer would seem to be no, and yet the phrase is regularly used.

We should regard phonemes not as small (the smallest) units of sound but rather as the bodily positionings that *precede* them. As noted earlier, phonemes are indicators of the placements of the human vocal apparatus (tongue, teeth, lips, glottis, alveolar ridge, palate, velum, uvula, etc.) that would accompany a sound *if it were to be made* and *if it were to be applied* to a hypothetical column of air. In this sense, the alphabet represents what a human anatomy *would* do—hence, hypothetical or theoretical—if intending to produce sound in an "actual realm." (The theoretical need never *become* the actual and oftentimes, it never does, but rather stays on the hypothetical plane, which is where we arguably spend most of our time.) We have seen how phonemes are biomechanical approximations, instructions to trigger an anonymous "speaker" who does not actually speak and whom we do not actually hear. You may notice that in reading the previous paragraph, you have not been accosted by actual sounds in the process; they have not come upon your person, in other words, or physically entered your ear canals. They are only "sounds" you hear with imaginary "ears" inside of your head—

and they are absorbed through your eyes, no less. When Havelock calls the Greek system "beyond language and beyond empiricism,"[23] it is to such oddities that he refers.

In creating an alphabet, the Greeks took aspects of the actual realm (ears, soundwaves) that they reconfigured into instructional blueprints (orofacial placements, non-sounds), which they then transferred to the hypothetical plane (where they are correlated with meaningless shapes). When we read alphabetic writing, there is no sound either being emitted or received, yet we experience a hallucinatory human source who is, again, making such sounds in our heads. The "voice" is neither mine, nor yours, nor that of anyone specific, but rather some form of featureless composite of my memories of having heard these sounds repeatedly before. We may or may not always be conscious of hearing a voice when we read—perhaps because this voice is not one that can be easily described, since, like the letters that invoke it, it is singularly *without qualities*: it has no gender, accent, timbre, pitch, volume, or any other modifier we might associate with a voice. (It is a hypothetical voice created by hypothetical units, operating on a hypothetical plane, triggered by context-free shapes.) One of the major consequences of the alphabet is that it removes sound from the physical or "actual" register (in which there are soundwaves and ears) and shifts it onto a hypothetical or noetic plane, where there are none.

We now have orofacial instructions and a vibrating column of air on the one hand, and a sizeable store of fully "neutral" squiggles with non-sense names on the other. Perhaps we can begin to see how one (anatomical instructions) cannot exist without the other (completely unknown shapes). With regard to the latter, we have seen how cultural symbols contain semantic residue and therefore interfere with an already demanding cognitive process. Once they are combined (phoneme + letter), *the principle can be adjusted to accommodate any language whatsoever.* Every other writing system is restricted in its ability to spread and to coopt other languages of other regions; syllabaries are confined to their environments. An alphabet, being without sounds and without cultural anchors, lends itself to circulation *outside* the sphere of its emergence. The Greek alphabet provides a matrix with which to transcribe all languages (since all human speech implies a vocal apparatus and its positionings). It effectuates a shift from the sounds in a particular language (i.e., Semitic dialects in the Mediterranean basin, for instance) to the biomechanics of *any* language—which is to say, any discernible noise the human vocal system can utter.

Primarily oral cultures exist within relatively circumscribed space and a culturally rooted sense of time. An Egyptian hieroglyph is confined to an Egyptian context; likewise with Chinese characters, Japanese kanji, Semitic consonantal scripts, and so on. There had been no such thing as a universal vantage point at this stage of history. But through the alphabet there becomes such a thing as any sound, any language, any people—which also means all sounds, all languages, all people.

And so we come to the last stage of the technical detour.

D. THE ALPHABET INVENTS "LANGUAGE."

The invention of phonemes is the invention of what we now know to be "language" as uniquely *sound-driven*. In pre-alphabetic cultures, there would have been no cause and no occasion to fixate on the vocal aspects of language alone. Some have suggested that the alphabet does not encode language but rather instantiates "a theory of language."[24] Havelock argues as much when he calls the alphabet an "analysis" of language rather than a form of its transcription. The alphabetic analysis, that is, language as metalanguage, consists in the following: there is a unifiable object ("language") that is transmitted through a voice. Prior to the alphabet, sound *or* voice would be only one of a multiplicity of facets comprising language. Sound combines not only with tone, pitch, timbre, and volume, but also with ambient sounds, bodily comportment, gestures, proximities, facial expressions, movement, relationalities, environmental factors, cultural norms, non-human elements, and so on, all of which contribute to the production of meaning. The Greek system isolates the vocal from all other dimensions of meaning-making and refers to it as "language." The alphabet then backdates language as something presumptively singular that it now seeks to duplicate. In other words, "language" is projected backward in order to become that preexistent material the alphabet sets itself the task of capturing. Alphabetic writing invents the very concept of "language" it purports to record.

Consider Walter Ong's description of a nonalphabetic culture as abiding in an "insistent actual habitat,"[25] rather than one stripped of all context, that is, as denuded of everything that is not vocal. Ong uses the term "habitat" rather than "context" because the latter notion, meaning *with text*, is not available in a pre-alphabetic setting. The alphabet works by disposing of context. Instead of text and *with text*—or the inscription and what surrounds the inscription, as it were—the surroundings have been operationally removed. It becomes possible to eradicate the "with," because the text is self-supporting by design. Its meaning is putatively inherent in the text itself, and it could not function otherwise. The difficulty intrinsic to removing the circumstances or surroundings is that the universe of orientational cues is now gone. Instead, one has a text that endeavors to contain all of its own orientational cues. But these can only ever be *other words*, that is, other portions of the text, and those portions will themselves be without circumstances. There is no text and context, but only text and text. In fact, there never was text and context, because once text is operational, context is irrelevant. (We will consider the problems following on from this contradiction in the next chapter.)

Non-alphabetic cultures do not rely strictly upon the verbal element, which is to say, words, and words are not defined by reference to other words. Words, in fact, are only small pieces of otherwise complex constellations. If we belong to a non-alphabetic culture, and I have a message to impart, the vocal component will only be one, and perhaps not even the most important, aspect of the process. Vocal content, in other words, combines with dozens of other overt and subtle relational cues, all of which the alphabetic theory of language removes. This means that once a society becomes fully literate, even *speaking*—not just writing—entails an alphabetic orientation because both partake of the same theory of language. The alphabet conditions us to pick up on non-specific, non-embodied voices, that is, voices with no context or circumstances, most of which arrive from a page or a screen. Even when we are having a conversation in person, we still concentrate on words and voice, largely deemphasizing the body or ignoring it altogether. This is a literate behavior, not an oral (i.e., non-alphabetic) one. For these reasons, Ong's hope that we might reinstate the positive aspects of non-alphabetic culture through telecommunications (and digital platforms such as Zoom) and so create a "secondary orality" is, in my view, misguided. Everything that is not the voice is called "non-verbal" and even the negative prefix confirms the preeminence of the verbal. "Non-verbal communication" is always at best considered an adjunct to the real matter of listening to and for words. In such ways, the "actual realm" becomes a projection of the hypothetical realm. The actual realm is subsidiary if not extraneous to the message because the message is self-contained in words. Voices can be delivered through my eyes (by reading), or through my ears (through hearing), but these have become different only by degrees.

Speaking, or orality, is understood as other-than-writing and "writing" becomes other-than-speaking. Together they conspire to constitute "language." In this respect, "language" can never be separated from writing (nor orality from the absence of writing) because it is a product of the alphabet. That colonial cultures conceive of themselves as opposed to indigenous groups along these lines is a matter not to be discarded or erased but investigated and properly understood. Ong writes, "We—readers of books such as this—are so literate that it is very difficult for us to conceive of an oral universe of communication or thought except as a variant of a literate universe."[26] Indigenous cultures thus become variants of a literate universe in which they are missing something crucial. That this "lack" can be used to the advantage of the colonizer is worth more exploration.

Once again, the alphabet is the only mode of writing that has no context, that is uniquely decontextualized. But because of its removal, a number of discursive cues must come to fill the "contextual" vacuum; context must be painstakingly supplied within the alphabetic document itself. It must provide its own context since it constitutively has none. The transposition of one "theoretic concept" (phoneme) with a second "theoretic concept" (letter) signals a new level of unprecedented abstraction. That the Greek system has no intrinsic context is another way to say it is operative *in every context*. To reiterate, phonemes are not sounds but blueprints, that is, instructions for bio-mechanical placements that encode non-observational behaviors (rather than their observational units). "Letters" are fully shorn of cultural context. Because phonemes do not belong to any particular language, and neither do letters, they can conceivably contain them all. The combination of the two in the construction of the alphabet is extreme in its ability to allow its users a) to exit their own contexts and b) to encode any other language in existence.

The mystery persists: why did the Greeks not create a system *for Greek*? Why and how did they create instead a universal system for any and every language, that is, a universal encoder? That which emerges entirely through a hypothetical plane, one could argue, is no longer hampered by the inherent restrictions of bodies and environments. By combining the two ideated units (phoneme and letter) and engineering both as distinctly *without qualities*, the alphabet becomes the code of all codes. A code that begets all other such codes is "universal" and universalizing. Its uniquely decontextualizing function features heavily in the movements and transplantations that characterize settler colonialisms. Even though everyone is apprised of the alphabetic principle now, this was not always the case. The use of the alphabetic principle over and above other groups conferred an imperial advantage to the European west of considerable magnitude for centuries.

2   *The Trauma of Literacy*

It is difficult to appreciate the magnitude of change brought about by the diffusion of the new alphabetic technology in Greece. Those scholars to whom it appears as an unmatched historical achievement, nevertheless understand its entry as "schizophrenia-inducing"[1] as well as an "invasion"[2] and a "trauma."[3] Some argue that the genre of tragedy itself arises as a means by which to accustom the Greek people to the upheavals brought about by writing.[4] Tragedy is replete with destruction, mourning, grief, and grotesquerie, but more importantly, perhaps, those elements are resolved by the end of the play. At its conclusion, Oedipus has accepted his fate, resigned himself to its panoply of horrors, and no longer feels the need to struggle against it. Either this, or tragedy provides the kind of public, ritual expulsion of these things that Aristotle will go on to theorize as catharsis. Whether a play ends by staging the dignified resignation of its hero or some other form of collective purgation, its elements in both cases become normalized. The menace itself, and the sources thereof, go unchallenged; what is presented are means of responding to such discord. This chapter explores two examples of the attempt to ameliorate alphabetic ruptures, through oracular consultation as a proxy "reading" situation on the one hand, and a new interpretation of the *Oedipus Tyrannus* on the other.

THE ORACLE AT DELPHI AS PROXY TEXT

The oracle at Delphi provides a form of primer through which the Greeks become acclimatized to a newly literate order. She retains some features of the non-alphabetic cultures from which she emerges, but these are minimal. For example, a speaking body is familiar. But a speaking body that is ventriloquizing a god's voice much less so. She occupies that halfway point between orality and literacy, because though she has a body, it "speaks" with someone else's voice. There is speculation about when the Pythia was introduced, as she is not mentioned in the "Homeric Hymn to Apollo," the first recorded description of the oracle at Delphi.[5] The appearance of the Pythia marks an important transition—that from primarily inductive divination, such as the reading of objects as omens, to a new type of messaging from the gods, that of "intuitive" or "inspired prophecy."[6] The oracle at Dodona had once consisted of an oak tree; that it will be replaced by a Pythia shows this shift from augury, often related to signs in the natural world and usually appropriate to "yes" or "no" questions, to the far more "word-based" character of prophecy.

"Inspired" is a suitable adjective, because it originally meant connected to the breath. The Pythia serves as the vessel into which the *pneuma*— variously translated as "wind," "air," "breeze," "breath," and "inspiration,"[7] of the god—will enter her body, as some early Christians who disapproved of the practice argued, through her vagina.[8] While sitting astride a tripod, itself perched over a cleft in the stones that may or may not have expelled inebriating fumes,[9] the Pythia spoke in Apollo's voice. She is a medium in both senses of the word: she "channels" the voice of Apollo as with a "spirit medium," though she is likewise a medium in the sense that stylus and stone are media. She provides no content herself but only serves as the material incarnation and the mode of transmission for Apollo's prophetic words. Though not exactly disembodied, the body of the Pythia is put out of commission, so to speak. Media are not meant to play a role in communicational content, but only to vehiculate the voice of another. The reduction of Apollo's message to "voice" alone is already indicative of an alphabetic orientation. Though Apollo uses her vocal cords, the Pythia's other senses and her body more generally are rendered inert.

In alphabetic terms, she is a blank slate waiting to be filled. Thusly empty, she is then able to become *full of god*. Hence, "The Pythia became *entheos, plena deo*: the god entered into her and used her vocal organs as if they were his own [. . .]. That is why Apollo's Delphic utterances are always couched in the first person, never in the third."[10] The Pythia in repose is the as-yet-unfilled. When Apollo speaks, however, she becomes "possessed" by his breath and words. She is the "'mouthpiece' through which the god could speak to mortals."[11] It was surely unnerving to behold a woman substituting her body for the form of Apollo in his ritual seat, emitting a voice that belonged to him, but which spoke through her voice box—though no less unnerving perhaps than an inanimate object such as a slab that "spoke" as though throwing its voice into one's head. (By the 4th century, Athens had begun to "publish" its decrees by inscribing them "literally in public in the open on stone.")[12]

For persons of a certain class, the alphabet had ceased to be an esoteric technology or literacy a rarefied skill. For the others, there are the public spectacles of the plays, which in themselves teach not literacy but how to negotiate and accept an environment organized around it. Once Sophocles writes the *Oedipus* around 430 BCE, alphabetics has made appreciable inroads in Athenian society, where an "archive mentality" and a "document mentality" had already begun to prevail.[13] Alphabetic methods were becoming the rule in matters concerning the state, bureaucracy, and policing.[14] Once such voice-throwing actions are thoroughly commonplace, the need for a Pythian intermediary, who still has a living and breathing form reminiscent of oral-cultural norms, will recede.

The Pythia at Delphi was originally a bewitching virgin. The legend went that she was so desirable, Echecrates of Thessaly became smitten with her, stole her away, and raped her. Because the ordeal threatened to destroy the functioning of the temple, the Delphians stipulated changes about her replacement. She had to be of "advanced" years, someone beyond the age of reproduction—no younger than fifty. Though past mid-life, she was required to wear the garb of a maiden, "in memory of the original virgin prophetess."[15] Clad in the dress of a child, she would retain the aura of "purity," of non-contamination, required of the solemnity of ritual. With her body now rendered presumably "sexless," she could no longer pose a distraction, or otherwise skew the proceedings by tempting the suppliants. The medium of inscription or transmission—either alphabetic or oracular—cannot be conspicuous. Otherwise, it threatens to upset the smooth process of communication. The contrived neutrality of the Pythian body—both unsullied and unnoticeable—is crucial to facilitating the prophecies and avoiding interference in the delivery of Apollo's message. Shorn of sexualized characteristics, the materiality of the Pythia's body becomes largely undetectable. Symbols in other (non-alphabetic) writing systems, we may recall, are not fully stripped of associations with the culture to which they are beholden and in which they remain embedded. They can never be arbitrary enough to prevent the reader from being pulled in separate and competing directions during the act of decoding. The "clutter" of pre-committed signs will prevent the act of spontaneous recognition. Likewise, the reformed Pythia in her de-sexualization, itself a kind of erasure of the body, can no longer distract the next Echecrates from attending to the word of god. Instead, she fades from view so that the voice of Apollo can resound unencumbered. The alphabet erases itself as part of its own apprehension.

Moreover, the Pythia is an "orphan" as Plato suggests of the alphabetic text. He refers to the autonomous piece of writing—this "bastard one"—as being "bandied about,"[16] since it has no context to which it belongs, no source of power or protection; its "father" is nowhere to be found. Though Plato means to criticize the helplessness of the text in the face of interrogation, the Pythia is similarly removed from the network of kindred relations that would have secured her place and imbued her with social "meaning." In taking up her role as Pythia, she is not permitted to maintain any associations or attachments. She is expected to abandon her husband and children in strict pursuit of her oracular duties, which are life-long, and which include rigorous exercise and permanent chastity.[17] Both celibate, and either literally or effectively childless, she has neither the opportunity to seduce nor preserve her cultural embeddedness. The Pythia mimics the featureless qualities and the non-attached nature of the alphabetic text. Though originally associated with a place where the prophecy was delivered (i.e., Delphi), the prophetesses would go on to form "a distinct class of persons, independent of any locality."[18] Being both sexually and socially neutered, they are better able to detach and circulate. Without a body and without a place, the Pythia becomes a proto-alphabetic text, which "speaks" but has no permanent context, and this makes her "without circumstances"—ideal for the Pythian vocation.

For the Greeks, the Pythia no more produced her own prophecy (or modified it at will) than a stone conjured its own inscriptions. Rather through the Pythia "you shall know the plans of the deathless gods."[19] The daughter of a poor farmer, "irreproachable" in reputation, she will have sprung from humble means, and she will have had "little education or experience of the world."[20] She must not be canny enough to add, for instance, her own interpretive flourishes or embroider anything. It would be imperative that when she "fulfills her prophetic role she does so quite artlessly and without any special knowledge or talent."[21] Plato remarks that when the prophetess of Delphi delivered inspired prophecy, she "conferred many splendid benefits upon Greece both in private and in public affairs, but few or none" when returned to her own devices.[22]

As letters provide biomechanical instructions for sealing, releasing, and altering the "vibrating column of air," so does the Pythia direct the (entry and) escape of *pneuma* from her living form. Apollo "writes" his prophecy though it is the Pythia who speaks with his voice. Bodies that do not speak in their own voices, and voices cut loose from any human body whatever, as with the Athenian decrees—these would seem to signal a level of disorder, if not mayhem. Words, and the disembodied voices that speak them, are the basis of the new form of prophecy; recall that the emphasis on *words* is the crucial difference between "inductive divination" and "inspired prophecy." *You will kill your father and you will marry your mother* would not have been a prophecy transmitted by augurs or other means of sortition.

Consultations at Delphi were indicative of the nascent cultural struggles to accept and internalize new forms of (mediated) "speaker" and "listener"—which is to say, "author" and "reader." If both require a measure of interpretation, the latter involves far more complex degrees of ambiguity, both for the poor approximations and reduced numbers of phonemes on the one hand, and the reduction of contextual cues to effectively zero, on the other. Whereas Greece remains residually oral in many respects, it is also noticeably affected by the profound changes brought on by incipient literacy, not to mention the drastic reorganization of the social order based on its exigencies.

Once the alphabet is domesticated, the conceit of a bodily (biloquial) source is no longer necessary. The experience of encountering a voice without a (human) body has ceased to be disturbing. Though still far from full literacy as we have come to understand it, the Greeks were nonetheless accustomed to a literate orientation by the time Plutarch laments the "total disappearance of all but one or two" oracles, and these "so utterly weak."[23] The Pythia as a waystation unto literacy obsolesces as soon as her purpose has been filled, whereupon Plutarch notes, "silence has come upon some and utter desolation upon others."[24] Just as the encroachments of the new technology become commonplace, Plutarch bemoans the frailty of the oracle and the growing disinterest in her prophecies.

A NOTE ON AMBIGUITY

As we have seen, the alphabet assigns each phoneme a distinct letter. Yet phonemes themselves are not "distinct"; they are but imperfect semblances, as well as "units" both "indiscriminable" and "non-observable." Phonemes are attempts to make instructional blueprints for those physical manipulations required to make each sound as separably and as accurately as possible. Yet the English language alone has at least forty-four phonemes.[25] There are far too many sounds and likely too many subtle movements of the vocal apparatus in any language to encode them all with complete precision. Whatever correspondences can be created, there will be a series of exclusions that are just as numerous. In the case of English, there is nearly a one-to-one correspondence between selected phonemes and discarded phonemes.

It is impossible to cover the total range of sounds in any spoken language, in other words, because the number of letters must be confined to very narrow limits, which Havelock sets at roughly twenty to thirty.[26] Otherwise, their proliferation will overburden the interplay of long-term and working memory required for the act of decoding. The dilemma is formidable: the letters must be numerous enough to cover the widest possible array, and to trigger the correct phonemic adjustments *each time*, rather than force the reader to hazard guesses, as had been the case in more conjectural systems, such as those without vowels. If the visible shapes are too few, they cannot exhaust the spectrum of phonemes. If they are too many, they will overwhelm memory "with the task of mastering a large list of them before the process of recognition, that is of reading, can even begin."[27] Too many signs compromise the commitment to long-term memory in childhood and thus subverts the whole process. It is not enough to remember the names of the letters and the pre-sound each one ostensibly makes. Learning the names, the pre-sounds, and the order may not take long in and of itself, but we must bear in mind that after this period, a child must recognize the letter when it is *out of order*. That is, she must recognize each separate phoneme, not singly, or as part of a fixed series (*a-b-c-d-e-f-g*...), but within infinite numbers of arrangement. Even with a limit of 26, this task is nearly impossible; it takes the entirety of childhood to accomplish it (at a minimum). In other words, a reader must recognize letters, correlate them to appropriate phonemes, and then *decode their limitless combinations:*

It is to be remembered that it is not enough for the brain to catalogue the shapes with precision. It is also required to associate them with a corresponding series of sounds [sic] and to be prepared to recognize the connection not in the tidy, constant sequence of letters of a memorized alphabet, an "abecedarium," but in the thousand eccentric combinations which make up words and sentences.[28]

A multiplicity of signs is not in itself insurmountable. The Chinese system has well over fifty thousand characters. While some of them are hybrid signs that contain syllabic elements, most of them do not require a secondary operation—and a tertiary one if we include the fact that the "sound memory" is hypothetical and must be imagined—as is the case with the Greek system. The alphabet operates in a synesthetic register. Unlike Chinese, it demands the ability to negotiate visual recognition *and* audial correlation, whereas Chinese only requires the former. It would appear to be the process of correlating visible shapes to pre-sound triggers that presents such difficulty, since one or the other activity on its own does not engender such problems. All humans, barring disabilities, *will speak* simply by dint of being born into a language-using community. No child anywhere in the world requires formalized training to produce speech sounds, but she requires highly specialized instruction to be able to write. In the absence of schooling, no such proficiency can ensue. Literacy can only be the result of sustained, intensive, systematized, highly repetitive instruction, a matter to which we return in the next chapter.

A system requiring several concurrent, complex operations can theoretically work, but only in the case that the number of signs is drastically limited. The costs associated with so severe a reduction are high. Even with the addition of vowels, the Greek system cannot avoid the residual ambiguities of the restricted cache of twenty-four letters, nor can the reformed and extended Roman version of twenty-six we use today. Because there can never be a one-to-one correspondence between phoneme and letter—since if there were, we could never remember them all—it is as if we have tacitly agreed to sacrifice whole vistas of meaning in order to conform to the stringent dictates of the code. The submission to alphabetics entails what Havelock describes as a multitude of unconscious limitations:

If you want your reader to recognize what you intend to say, then you cannot say anything and everything that you might want to. You must fit your intended meanings to meanings that he [sic] will be prepared to accept. The specific effects of this will register themselves in an unconscious limitation imposed upon vocabulary and upon syntactical arrangement of vocabulary and upon the subjects treated in the vocabulary.[29]

The incursions of alphabetics involve not only a reduction in the life-world, but also, and perhaps even more critically, a profound ambiguity that surrounds what remains. Chronic ambiguity propels the incessant drive to conduct elaborate processes of interpretation, all of which enact the ultimately futile effort to resolve, or at least manage, the inherent uncertainty of any inscription. Part of this ambiguity also results from the fact that, as discussed in the previous chapter, sound is only a fraction of language. Alphabetics distills language into the voice alone. And again, because of this radical de-contextualization, the only "context" one can use for clarification is that provided from within the text itself, and thus the only available means of interpretation is itself up for interpretation, *ad infinitum*. This is why more writing begets not more clarity but only more writing. In the mouth of Socrates, Plato notes as much: "He who receives it in the belief that anything in writing will be clear and certain, would be an utterly simple person."[30]

AMBIGUOUSNESS IS NEXT TO GODLINESS

Pronouncements from the Pythia were ambiguous. For the Greeks, ambiguity was a sure sign of godly origin. Indeed, there was a proportional relationship between the obscurity of the message and the certainty of its divinity. If it was not ambiguous, it did not come from the gods. Ambiguity signified authority, which—as the root of the word suggests—is, of course, another alphabetic phenomenon.

To some extent, the *Oedipus* dramatizes the problem of written texts and their absent scriptors and hence the ensuing problems of ambiguity. Much of the perplexity and distress comes from the fact that the scriptor—whether god or author—is not there but has replaced itself with an ambiguous proxy that speaks in its place. No number of interpreters or exegetes, however insightful and thorough, can defuse or correct this quandary, because it issues directly from the combination of decontextualization and the meager store of twenty-some letters.

Oedipus demonstrates an increasingly common predicament in the ancient world with its burgeoning dependence on literacy. Unable to face (or comprehend) what is written, he is equally helpless to negotiate or alter it. By the time the Christian era arrives, "so it is written" is already firmly connected to a celestial "text," inscribed by the god(s) and therefore synonymous with fate. The Pythia as a stopgap—and proto-alphabetic text—is compelling, for what is a god (or indeed an author) if not an assemblage of disembodied messages? The alphabet enshrines ambiguity, and literate cultures attempt to make of this a virtue. In subscribing to the idea of ambiguity as the mark of divinity, the Greeks absorb and ultimately celebrate the disorientations of literacy. If a prophecy were transparent, the Greeks would have rejected it as too human.

The ambiguous nature of decontextualized words is compounded by the fact that it is only to other words that one can turn for clarification, as opposed to material correlates of some kind. For Oedipus, "father" (Laius) does not equal "father" (Polybus) and "mother" (Jocasta) does not equal "mother" (Merope). The signs "father" and "mother" are no more site-specific in an alphabetized culture than are "man," "progenitor," "patriarch," "matriarch," "parent," "woman," "wife," and so on. These are not contextual—for what need would they have had to arise as discrete, abstract designators in an oral culture—but rather composite signs that are interchangeable from one situation to another. They are, to use Plato's phrase, available to be "bandied about." Because they contain within themselves no context, they can be imperfectly attached to any (all) of them. The sign "father" in its free circulation is substituted and transposed repeatedly in relation to Oedipus, such that it has the paranoiac potential to become any masculine form he encounters. Indeed, "father" is intercepted by the sign "vagabond" at the crossroads, and likewise for Laius, to whom Oedipus appears not as "son" but as "bandit." Signs must not only be detachable from their nominal referents; they must also be duplicable. As we know, "mother" performs multiply and notoriously in the play; its career within it is complex. "Mother" is the kindly woman at home as well as the queen to whom Oedipus is joined in wedlock. The problem of course is that *he cannot tell the difference.* It would seem to be inarguable that one's "wife" should not be overlain with or substituted by one's "mother." But neither can the signs "wife" and "mother" separate and reattach to their "proper" referents, as they never had any. The questions—which is "substitute" and which is "real" in terms of "mother," "father," "killer," "despoiler," and so on—are not so much answerable, as the play itself implies, as they are indications of an alphabetic encirclement that has already been accomplished.

The code does not (cannot) provide "clues" outside of itself. Oedipus visits the Pythia in person in the hope that he might notice something new, something missed by his parents, something extra-alphabetic that will provide a key. Yet nothing extra-alphabetic can pertain, not least because it must be deliberately shorn away. Regularity and predictability enhance transmission, which is why orthography—from "correct writing"—becomes increasingly important. The enframing structure of any text will ideally be the same each time. Everyone must spell identically; everyone must use the same direction of reading (first boustrophedon; later left to right); everyone must know she is looking at a text the purpose of which is to be decoded, etc., if literacy is to become firmly established in a non-literate Greece. The message may be novel, but the formatting never should be. The Pythia at Delphi offers an analogous framing device to encourage (vatic) communication, in a manner that anticipates the standardizations of typography centuries later. The ritualized nature of her pronouncements and the non-originality of the delivery allows the focus to be on the content. It is parallel to the uniformity of white margins; inked letters; punctuation and spacing; rectangular pages; standardized spellings; and so on, that will function as the readerly signposts for literate sense-making, and so allow decoding to become a pre-facilitated task. The same is the case for the female Delphian. The suppliant knows what is to be expected; it will be roughly identical each time. A female ventriloquizing a god; perimenopausal yet clad in a virgin's gown; the shaking of the laurel branches; the breathing in of smoke; the metallic odors of animal blood all around her; and the presence of the mysterious *pneuma* that permits her speech.

But because the words "ritual" and "format" both imply repetition of the same, there will be no extraneous clues, as Oedipus must acknowledge. So must he reckon with the strange fixity of the alphabetic text that the Pythia embodies: "I went to Delphi, but Apollo did not say what I had gone to hear. Instead, he answered questions I had not asked and told of horror and misery beyond belief [. . .] I trembled at those words and fled [. . .]."[31]

Inherently alphabetic, the oracle responds to queries one never asked and does "not say what one wants to hear," but only what is written. The anguish of Oedipus is that he has no choice but to submit to the unresponsive text, to yield to the non-negotiability that constitutes it. Plato considers it a weakness of the alphabetic text that it cannot be argued with, yet therein, I would suggest, lies the greater measure of its power. The Pythia repeats, as alphabetic texts will do, the same message she gave the previous generation. Abhorring the message, and checking it again for phantom clues, does nothing to affect its permanence. As Plato reminds us, every instance of writing "always says only one and the same thing."[32] Arguably, the notion of what is True for all times is something that arises alongside the alphabet. A shift occurs that changes *the text* "always says only one and the same thing," to "the Truth always says only one and the same thing." If the Truth is fixed, one can only blame her own personal failure to reconcile with it if things do not go her way. Still, we can detect a certain incredulity when it comes to the eternality of words, especially since the Greeks had been so recently in a state of complete non-literacy. Oedipus's anxiety is transformed into a noble quest for the Truth. He goes to the Pythia to "hear it for himself" under the assumption that the text will be less ambiguous this time, and that he might establish, *once and for all*, definitive meaning—which is to say, the Truth. What Oedipus misunderstands is that the Pythian and alphabetic texts cannot be made less uncertain this time than they were the first time, since ambiguity is structured into the mechanism of phonemes and arbitrary letters themselves, that is, the entirety of the alphabetic system. It is the alphabet itself that induces this search for "the answer," this yearning for the "Truth," and this desire to know. In the cultural imagination of the European west, moreover, this quest is considered not only morally upright, but positively heroic. We exalt the idea that Oedipus had been "willing to stake everything, his very rights as a human being, on the effort to know."[33] The propensity is to be celebrated even as (and perhaps *because*) it leads to self-mutilation. The quest as valiant is an extension of ambiguity as godly.

OEDIPUS AND THE TRAGEDY OF LITERACY

Lorenzo Veracini has convincingly likened colonization to a viral infection.[34] Writing is inextricable from colonization, such that the former may be said to instigate the spread of the latter. Spreading is, in many respects, the operative verb in the first stages of the colonizing process and is the means by which viral forms expand their "host range" and replicate.[35] The play opens upon Oedipus's arrival at a place seething with contagion. First performed in 429 BCE, *Oedipus Tyrannus* echoes the literal Plague of Athens, which had, until very recently, ravaged Sophocles's city. His choice to set the play in Thebes rather than Athens is also noteworthy in that the myth of Cadmus, who founded the city of Thebes, involves his legendary invention of the alphabet. In the first line of the play, Oedipus refers to the suppliants gathered there as the "sons of the ancient house of Cadmus."[36] Cadmus was said to have created the alphabet by slaying a dragon, extracting its teeth—one for every letter—and planting them into the ground. Having thus "sowed the dragon's teeth, they sprang up armed men."[37] Marshall McLuhan argues that the militarism inherent in this myth alludes to the ability of the alphabet combined with papyrus to organize imperial structures from great distances (thus exponentially expanding the "host range").[38] The plague in one city (Athens) and the alphabet in another (Thebes) may function as parallel and complementary events.

As the play begins, a priest beseeches Oedipus to help deliver the city from plague. The mention of the Sphinx in the first section recalls his triumph in solving her riddle, but it also suggests that signs are associated with a degree of menace. A person who can solve the Sphinx's puzzle will be feted, but no one before Oedipus had ever done so. The Sphinx "dashed to bits the body of each poor soul who tried and failed."[39] When Oedipus answers the riddle correctly, she dashes herself to bits.[40] Because Oedipus solves the Sphinx's riddle, he (mistakenly) believes he can overcome them all. Though he appears to master the signs in this instance, the same cannot be said for the signs of Apollo issued from the oracle at Delphi.

CONTEXT

Oedipus is eventually cast out of Theban society, but as it maintained elements of residual orality, he had already rejected it. In the scene where he confronts Teiresias, and again in resistance to Jocasta, he finds the oral order wanting, if not inferior or "backward," providing a precursory glimpse of colonial ideologies to come. He responds to Teiresias as though his old ways are deficient. If Teiresias's methods had been skillful, Oedipus claims, then when the Sphinx was terrorizing the city, he could have put down "the rhapsode bitch" himself.[41] Instead the Thebans required an adept at the new methods to step in and master the signs. As inductive divination had given way to inspired prophecy, Teiresias was mired in the former, compared to the autonomy and intellectualism of alphabetic man:

Her riddle would stagger the simple mind; it demanded the mind of a seer. Yet, put to the test, all your birds and god-craft proved useless; you had no answer. Then *I* came—ignorant Oedipus—*I* came and smothered her, using only my wit. There were no birds to tell me what to do.⁴²

The emphasis on "I" reinforces our hero as a self-contained unit. Oedipus who "came" from outside the situation should have proved "ignorant"—as well as the fact that he had not been a recognized diviner—yet he had no need of orientational cues, of context, nor of external help from augurs. He managed by his individual wit alone. Teiresias responds that because Oedipus has no context, in effect, he has usurped another and substituted himself there—all without his own awareness. Teiresias tries to apprise him of this fact, since up until this point, Oedipus thought he had outwitted the Delphian prophecy: "You, Oedipus, are the desecrator, the polluter of this land! . . . I say that you, Oedipus Tyrannus, are the murderer you seek. . . . I say you live in shame with the woman you love, blind to your own calamity."⁴³ But because he has repugned inductive signs, he pays them (and the messenger Teiresias) no heed. "Wit" alone is what one requires in a literate, self-reliant, "interiorizing" new world. When Teiresias challenges the false confidence with which Oedipus boasts of his own depth of knowledge, he answers, "You mock the very skill that proves me great."⁴⁴ Alphabetics, despite its harms, is worth everything, Oedipus believes, because it is the skill through which one is made great.

Not only is Oedipus decontextualized, but so is everyone else becoming so. They can "read" Oedipus no better than he can read himself. The Thebans mistake him for a "savior" of the city, an "allayer of sickness," and purveyor of answers. Because he does not know who his true father is, neither does Oedipus know where he is from. He believes himself to be a stranger to the city but will be revealed a "native Theban"; the chorus, too, assumes the murderer of Laius is a wanderer. Consider that for Plato, an alphabetic text is likewise "bandied about." It is not tied to the father—suggesting both indeterminacy as well as parricide. The father is either absent or possibly dead. As Oedipus is horrified to find that he is the killer, so surely will the Thebans be. The chorus also rejects Teiresias's prophecy when he intones:

The man you seek—the man whose death or banishment you ordered, the man who murdered Laius—that man is here, passing as an alien, living in our midst . . . . Both brother and father to the children that he loves. Both son and husband to the woman who bore him. Both heir and spoiler of his father's bed and the one who took his life. Go, think on this.[45]

No one is able recognize anyone apart from the signs they have mistakenly attached to this or that personage. Remaining perplexed, they cling to their own mis-readings and insist that the man who once solved the Sphinx's riddle and delivered the city from harm cannot also be the source of its blight. ("No! I can *never* condemn the king!")[46] In bewilderment, they narrate the "stranger's" attempts at escape, acknowledging that the letter of the prophecy (i.e., the Law) will find him, though he may "lurk in the forests and caves / like an animal roaming the desolate hills."[47] Enclosure by signs can neither be outrun nor their ambiguity lessened. The chorus notes how the stranger is slowed down by the crookedness of his carriage—his physical and perceptual "dis-ability"—though they have not connected the name Oedipus (which means clubbed foot) to the murderer in flight. The Thebans as well as Oedipus himself have become unmoored: "For I cannot affirm, yet I cannot refute / what he spoke. And I'm lost, I am lost—."[48] They ask questions addressed to no one in particular, such as "What am I to believe?"[49] In this way, the chorus reflects the anxieties of an order split apart by the alphabet, denied any semblance of a guiding precedent: "Can I test? Can I prove / [. . .] Who is right? Who can judge? / [. . .] Does the seer know? Do I?"[50]

ON THE DESTRUCTION OF NON-ALPHABETIC CULTURE

We may consider Jocasta as a "hold-out" and a figure of fidelity to the Greek oral-cultural inheritance, that is, its non-alphabetic remainder. Jocasta intuits that it is only upon (her) entry into the alphabetic regime that she will become "mother" to Oedipus and that this *designation* is the source of her participation in hideous crimes, not its anterior truth value. Indeed, in a culture without an alphabet (and thus detachable, circulating signs), to what extent would it be possible to lose track of one's mother; re-encounter her as an adult; mistake her for a matrimonial candidate; and produce four descendants with her? Or bludgeon one's father to death and not know it? Jocasta responds to Oedipus's frenzy by *resisting* the encroachment of signs—not, as he does, by attempting to outwit them. She aims to protect that (oral, non-alphabetic) state of affairs in which she might still maintain a certain relational integrity, situational coherence, and non-mutilation, in regard to her husband and children. The only way to avoid catastrophe is to ignore the prophecy. In nearly every scene in which she appears, she utters some form of admonition against the invasion of alphabetics. It is always on behalf of a situation, an "actual," embodied *context* and not a decontextualized norm, that Jocasta continually acts. She exhibits a prescient awareness of the generalized (alphabetic) maiming to come, of which her husband-son is the ultimate portent.

Jocasta encapsulates loyalty to the context in which, if Oedipus had never heeded the signs, she would not be his mother. It is this relentless desire to "know" that *makes her* his mother. "Mother" is a substitutable and indeterminate sign like any other. Jocasta may well have carried the fetus who would be Oedipus to term, but this is the full extent of the itinerary of the signifier, "Mother," or "Mother of Oedipus," where she is concerned. She did not even give him his name. If Oedipus had never been made aware of the oracle's prophecy, then Jocasta would never, in any important or necessary sense, have been his mother. The sign "wife" had been far more operative in his adult life. Martha C. Nussbaum argues a related point when she suggests that even if Jocasta is his mother, she is also not his mother. Invoking the incest taboo, she argues that it has not been violated if neither party is cognizant of the common lineage:

> Oedipus is not experiencing desire toward the person whom he takes to be his mother, toward the woman who raised him as a mother, nor, indeed, for any woman who nursed, held, or cared for him at any time. So far as the intentional context of his desire is concerned, Jocasta is simply a well-placed eligible stranger.[51]

In this reading, Oedipus should have desired Merope, and he should have slain Polybus. In fact, there is an instant in which, hearing word that Polybus has died of natural causes (and knowing that he did not marry Merope), he rejoices in the belief that the prophecy was wrong. Frederick Ahl suggests there is no proof that Jocasta is in fact his mother. He attributes her suicide to the fact that she despairs of ever convincing Oedipus of this.[52] Another thesis is that while she bore him long ago, she is fully prepared *to exit the regime of signs* in which this reality would prevail. It is a choice (within the diegesis of the play) that Oedipus too could have made. He might likewise have ignored or dismissed the prophecy and lived his life as he had been doing all along. In the act of being written, the alphabet makes one version of events "True"—perhaps given the false gravity of permanence—and so must likewise render all others "untrue." Yet this makes the chosen version arbitrary, as arbitrary as the visual shapes that comprise it. It is the one that just so happened to have been written down. Indeed, why choose *this* version of events to enshrine and anoint as True?

In one version—the (oral) one—Oedipus is kingly, wise, and contented. In the other, (literate) version, he is made hideous and wretched enough to stab himself in the eyes. "Apollo said so" is arbitrary; so then is the Law. Though Law would have been arbitrary prior to the alphabet as well, its non-fixity would have ensured a responsiveness to social flux, an adaptiveness to collective drift, coupled with various means of periodic recalibrating—all of which the alphabet prohibits by freezing what it has recorded and thus asserting itself as True *for all time*. In this way, only the alphabetic is true. In order to function as Law, it must exclude all other possibilities and all other iterations. *True in all contexts* is another way of saying without context.

Though he informs Teiresias that he needs no context, the rest of the play is an extended attempt by Oedipus to "re-situate" himself and thus reconstitute an already dispersed context. The things that Oedipus seeks to learn in an effort to clarify meaning are among the very orienting cues that the alphabet removes: the physical description of his father; the name of the area where he met his demise; the environmental landmarks of the site; the points in time when events transpired; the size of his entourage; the mode of transportation; the reliability of the information; the source of the reportage; and so on. None of the seeking, in other words, is philosophical or metaphysical, despite the exalted status such quests are normally assigned. Rather the "wisdom" Oedipus covets is exceedingly banal; again, it is no more than that which is lost through the dislocations of writing. Either he is asking for straightforward information, or else his questions could have been answered without "inspiration," that is, largely by the old inductive systems: Is it true, or isn't it? "Yes" or "no"?

At the same time, all his efforts to reconstruct a context are (always already) *too late*, just as Jocasta's remonstrance against the signs likewise bears this quality of being "too late." By summoning several people to appear "in person," by contriving situations of a "face-to-face" nature, in which all the participants in, and witnesses to, his abandonment as an infant, can finally speak as in an oral context, he hopes that this will somehow negate or at least modify the prophecy.

Derrida would condemn these Oedipal moves as the lust for "self-presence, transparent proximity in the face-to-face of countenances and the immediate range of the voice."[53] Insofar as such makeshift oral "contexts" can never yield results after the fact, Derrida is quite correct. That is, Ong's notion of "secondary orality"—of the attempt to invoke, or rediscover, a non-alphabetic state within a literate order—is similarly ill-fated. The Oedipal groping for a secondary orality that cannot be reconstituted (often called "nostalgia for lost origins" in postcolonial studies) is in fact due to a convergence of historical factors; it cannot be compared to a universal "metaphysics of presence." The so-called desire for "presence" is nothing more than the attempt to collect a set of orientational cues that a decontextualized (and thus ambiguous) regime of signs has revoked. The impetus is entirely pragmatic. Oedipus continues to ask after matters that are not concerned with "pure presence," but rather with *positional indicators*:

> Were you in the service of Laius? [. . .] What occupation? What way of life? [. . .] And where did you tend those flocks? [. . .] Have you ever seen this man before? [. . .] Have you ever met him before? [. . .] Did you, or did you not, give him that child? [. . .] Where did you get it? Your house? Someone else's? Where? and so on.[54]

What answers he gleans have no power to alter the alphabetic organization of society—and certainly no ability to provide "ontotheological" reassurance, which contra Derrida, had never been the objective anyhow. While his inquiries amount to an exercise doomed to failure, the motivation behind them is entirely material, not metaphysical.

Oedipus finally consents to the new order, and in so doing, foreshadows the fate of alphabetic man: maimed but still living, de-formed but somehow carrying on. Jocasta's resistance amounts to the idea that they might as yet escape. According to her logic, they must stop checking and rechecking the oracles and disengage from the written world altogether. As writing is what has dismembered them, they cannot expect it to provide them with reprieve. ("The consolation is always too late.")[55] Still, Jocasta senses that it is the alphabetic code that has and will prove the far greater source of damage and "deformity" than the incestuous genetic code ever could.

Jocasta realizes—or at least suspects—what she "is" some time before Oedipus does, and her response is to try to keep the information from him. She attempts to stall his plans to interrogate possible witnesses, saying, "Why? What difference does it make? Don't think about it. Pay no attention to what [was] said. It makes no difference."[56] Despite her increasing desperation, he nevertheless spurns her entreaties. When she exclaims, "Oedipus! I beg you—don't do this!," he answers, "I can't grant you that. I cannot leave the truth unknown."[57] Though not a Pythia, Jocasta can still predict the outcome of this pursuit far in advance of its occurrence. Without knowing the details, she can foresee his demise, her own, and the dissolution of the family. Yet her power to command his attention—insofar as she embodies oral tradition—is quickly waning. She cannot convince him to ignore the signs, nor to permit their extrication from the literate order. This is precisely what she urges, however, when she cries out, "God help you! May you never know what you are!"[58]

Perversely, it would seem, Oedipus is seduced by, even welcomes— perhaps encourages—the lacerations to come. When Jocasta exits, the chorus asks of him, "Why has the queen left like this—grief-stricken and tortured with pain? My Lord, I fear—I fear that from her silence some horror will burst forth." To which he replies, "Let it explode! I will still want to uncover the secret of my birth—no matter how horrible."[59] Non-alphabetic culture, it would seem, cannot sustain such levels of awed fascination for him. The oral cultural inheritance self-murders in the form of Jocasta; with her dies the opposition to writing. Even if Jocasta had not committed suicide, Oedipus was going to kill her anyway. As one witness to the scene reports, "He sprang at each of us and begged to have a sword. He begged to know where he could find the wife that was no wife to him, the woman who had been mother to him and to his children."[60] The defeat of Jocasta's point of view is the defeat of orality. For while some have argued orality and literacy persist with one another, and this is certainly the case in ancient Greece, the structures of oral culture are immediately undermined with the earliest incursions of alphabetic writing. This process is more dramatic in the colonies where the pace is greatly accelerated. Jocasta recedes the more Oedipus is impelled by the *jouissance* of his own desire to master the signs—to manipulate their inherent ambiguity and so to beat them at their own game.

More than this, however, Oedipus *believes*. He believes in (the) prophecy, enough to try all his adult life to subvert it. Enough that when his wife begs him to do otherwise, shrieking in anguish, "In the name of God, if you care at all for your own life, you must not go on with this. I cannot bear it any longer," he ignores her.[61] Belief, like submission to the Law, does not insist upon reason. Žižek suggests it requires the opposite when he defines "belief" as "an affair of obedience to the dead, uncomprehended letter."[62]

Why else does Oedipus insist on obeying the dead letter even as it brutalizes him and all he holds dear? In effect, this is what Jocasta demanded to know, but he can offer no response. In place of a reply, there is only a blind compulsion toward a "Truth," that provides no respite, and certainly no salvation, for its having been revealed. According to some, it is this scenario that makes Oedipus "great": "Oedipus is great because he accepts the responsibility for *all* his acts, including those which are objectively most horrible, though subjectively innocent."[63] These are *the same* acts, of course (horrible and innocent), and it is the *existence* of the codified Law that turns them into both. His greatness comes from his "inner strength: strength to pursue the truth at whatever personal cost, and strength to accept and endure it when found."[64] Yet is it not Jocasta who bears more "strength" in this regard, in that she identifies the object-source of their downfall—the proto-alphabetic oracle—and attempts to evade and destroy it by withholding consent, rather than suffer it as "inevitable"? Oedipus's panicked convulsions are never a rejection of the imposition of the code. It is only the content of the code that he abhors and not the code itself. It never occurs to him, as it does to Jocasta, that they might retreat, with their lives still intact, despite leaving their power and prestige behind them. The Oedipal thrashings that comprise most of the play simply represent the process of accustoming oneself, however violently, to the rule of the written law—that is, of gathering "proof" in order to cement and confirm, in an almost tautological manner, that indeed the Law *is* the Law. With Oedipus as Western civilizational exemplar, we yield to the Law, not because we are convinced of its reasoned definitions of justice, but as Žižek argues, because of its "traumatic irrationality and senselessness."[65] Incomprehensibility does not weaken the gravity of the Law. It is its very condition. Hence, "Far from hindering the full submission of the subject to the ideological command," he writes, "it is precisely this . . . senseless traumatism which confers on the Law its unconditional authority."[66]

It is Jocasta who represents the scofflaw or the "outlaw," (rather than Oedipus), in that she seeks to elude the Law and operate outside of it. For Jocasta, such mangled lives are not worth living. She pleads with him to sever their connection to prophecy: "It is better to live as you will, live as you can."[67] This is sometimes translated as, it is better to live *at random*, which is to say, without the superimposition of alphabetics, but as persons in a non-colonized culture for however long this is possible. That Oedipus has already "converted" to the alphabetic regime becomes increasingly evident. The new genre of tragedy is full of the "senseless traumatism" incurred by the transition to literacy, and grotesquery is its hallmark. When Oedipus finds Jocasta hanging from the noose, he plunges her golden pins into his eyes "again and again and again." He utters words about seeing but failing to recognize.[68] The witness to the scene explains: "And as he cried out in such desperate misery, he struck his eyes over and over—until a shower of blood and tears splattered down his beard, like a torrent of crimson rain and hail."[69] In a belated and momentary affinity with Jocasta, perhaps, he blinds himself so as never to "read" again. Yet this is temporary. Oedipus loves the Letter and the Law. He cannot fail to bear its incisions. His calm at the end of the play, his resignation to the literate order, provides a model behavior for which members of an alphabetic culture should strive (while expressing the futility of opposition). Creon steps in to fill the void left by Oedipus's exile, and the combination of this peaceful transfer of power, along with the relative serenity in which Oedipus removes himself, is crucial to the functioning of the play. Without this tone of acceptance, one might conclude that alphabetics had proved too costly and too catastrophic; that they were simply not worth it. Instead, Oedipus voluntarily receives what Deleuze and Guattari deem a new kind of punishment, one they consider worse than death or ordinary exile, in that "he wanders and survives . . . . The outcome is no longer murder or sudden death but survival under reprieve, *unlimited postponement*."[70] In this way the anxiety of permanent irresolution and nonclarity is dramatized. The source of tragedy in *Oedipus Tyrannus* is that he is surrounded by signs, none of which he can grasp and all of which he mistakes. By the end of the play, nothing has changed in regard to the prophecy, but Oedipus has regained his composure, and Jocasta is dead.

No one is delivered from the plague. Oedipus's ostracism is meant to serve as a decontaminant. Yet one could also argue that the pathogen (in the form of Oedipus) has not been cast out. It has simply become so widespread, it no longer calls attention to itself.

3 The Alphabet and Reproduction

The behavior of children at school, which is so often mysterious to the teacher, ought surely to be considered in relation with their germinating sexuality.
—SIGMUND FREUD[1]

For Fritz the 'Excellent' written by the schoolmistress on a good piece of work was a costly possession.
—MELANIE KLEIN[2]

Literate societies require the ability to read with a high level of automaticity. Arguably, it is not so much the invention of the alphabet itself, as it is the era of mass schooling that produces the most profound social changes. Over several centuries, the Greeks and Romans would arrive at the conclusion that it is only possible to achieve a level of literacy that has become an "unconscious reflex,"[3] as opposed to a laborious ordeal, if one begins with the very young. So, whereas the compulsory schooling we know today is many centuries into the future and will require such innovations as the printing press (and the Protestant Reformation) before becoming fully established, it nonetheless became a priority to alphabetize the youth of a certain class. Because the Greeks had no literate mentors, how exactly this was to be done had not been entirely clear. Nor is the answer to Kittler's monumental question much clearer today: how is it possible to make "the coercive act of alphabetizing"[4] seem pleasurable to the child? By current standards, the Greek systems of punishment and rewards appear extreme.

Our approaches now are muted by contrast, though arguably the methods contain a similar logic.

Consider the overtly painful and sexual scenarios practiced in Greece when the alphabet was in its infancy, as opposed to more modern methods, in which such approaches are unnecessary. There is far less physical violence in use today, and sex with minors is illegal. Bodily punishment is less useful, because the contemporary schoolroom tends to anesthetize the body rather than to shock it into complacency. The body under the alphabetic schooling regime is neither in pain nor free from pain but is ignored, numbed, or forgotten through disuse. Moreover, sensuality is more in keeping with Freud's recognition of infantile sexuality as "polymorphous" and not yet localized in the erogenous zones as with adolescent and adult sexuality. Sensuality, then, is more appropriate to the school years. Sensuality and anesthesia would appear to be at odds, though sensuality in the classroom both piques and diffuses such energies. It is used instrumentally to stimulate an interest in and promote attention to an emergent literacy practice, rather than provide pleasure in and of itself—even when it serves as a reward.

While it is a formidable task to alphabetize a single child, that child must exist in a "community" of other alphabetized children if "literacy" is to become a fully operational social state. While this might seem obvious, it contains a noteworthy dimension (if not a contradiction) of alphabetic cultures, wherein literacy creates a version of solipsism, but so must it create an aggregation or collectivity of solipsists, if it is to function as intended. Havelock writes,

> Whereas we can apply the term 'literate' to an individual, its operative meaning derives from the fact that his [sic] literacy is shared by a given number of people, all of whom are readers; not only do he and his fellows exercise a common skill employed upon a common material, but in exercising it they place themselves in automatic communication with each other. First, he is literate in so far as he reads documents and also does so as a matter of habit, not painfully deciphering them, but fluently and rapidly recognizing what has been written. Second, this body of writing would not exist for him to be read if it had not been composed for others to read as well. A Robinson Crusoe could theoretically step onto his island equipped with a small library to refresh his solitude, but this artifact could never have come into existence for him alone. Its 'authors' had created it solely in the expectation of its use by a reading public.[5]

The "automatic communication" shared by literates is rarely concretized. Arguably, it amounts to little more than an inchoate awareness that others are reading the same material that I am reading, and that this material is thus impersonal (i.e., not addressed to me), yet designed in such a way as to pretend that it is addressed to me (i.e., "Dear Reader"). Walter Ong provides a memorable image in illustration of this feature of alphabetics, when he describes a modern schoolroom:

> Writing and reading are solitary activities that throw the psyche back on itself. A teacher speaking to a class which he [sic] feels and which feels itself as a close-knit group, finds that if the class is asked to pick up its textbooks and read a given passage, the unity of the group vanishes as each person enters into his or her private lifeworld.[6]

THE FOURTH CRITERION

In explaining the difference between a syllabary system and the deviation of the alphabet, Havelock outlines four criteria, the first three of which we considered earlier. The departure from previous scripts requires 1) a range of shapes that cover (ideally) every potential sound in the language; 2) few enough of these shapes to avoid overwhelming the memory capacity of the reader; and 3) the shapes must be arbitrary so as not to interfere with the meaning transmitted in the content.[7] As we have seen, criteria 1 and 2 remain in a perpetual state of uneasy compromise. To add additional shapes would conceivably reduce ambiguity by making it possible to cover a wider array of noises in a language, but every additional shape impedes automatic decoding. While a clerical elite can function perfectly well with a system of mnemonic cues that prompt familiar sound assemblages, an alphabetic system, especially one that radically transforms the society in which it is practiced, must satisfy a fourth criterion—one in which "a system of instruction is devised to impose the habit of recognition upon the brain before it has fully concluded its growth."[8] Writing in the 1970s, Havelock mentions prepubescence, but contemporary theory suggests the need to begin much earlier. The goal is to access the window of greatest malleability, "when mental resources are still in a plastic condition . . . so that the act of reading is converted into an unconscious reflex."[9] The fourth criterion is basically the invention of "school" and with it, the child.

Longer, as opposed to *sooner*, had been the order of the day in medieval Europe. In Philippe Ariès's foundational work on the "discovery of the child," one gets the impression that the category of childhood is invented for this purpose (that is, to be schooled). He dates the emergence of childhood as a discrete category to the early modern period in Western Europe. This "discovery" roughly coincides with the establishment of schooling as a long-term process. Prior to that, European notions of "childhood" scarcely existed. There was infancy, and then, sometime between the ages of five and seven, "the child was immediately absorbed into the world of adults."[10] An intervening period between infancy and seven-year-old "adulthood" had no special designation at the time and was not recognized as marking any "stage." The notion of a childhood—as that which separated infancy from a now dramatically postponed adulthood, indeed, an *extended* or "long childhood" was, according to Ariès, the result of the political influence of certain "pedagogues and moralists." These were, he writes, precisely the "same men" who were responsible for erecting and controlling the schools.[11] The interests of extended schooling would produce the category not only of "childhood" but of "long childhood," and both "childhood" and "school" mutually constitute one another from their inception.[12]

One of the features characterizing this system is sequestration from adults. When Jacqueline Rose writes of the burgeoning desire for the child, she specifies that it is not in the sense of "an act which is sought after." Rather, she states,

> I am using desire to refer to a form of investment by the adult in the child, and to the demand made by the adult on the child as the effect of that investment, a demand which fixes the child and then holds it in place. A turning to the child, or a circulating around the child . . . .[13]

It is to want the child in the sense of wanting something *from* the child, something that, it might be added, she has no choice but to deliver. She would not have been "discovered" at all perhaps, in Ariès's sense, if we did not want (something from) her.

MASS SCHOOLING

In his *Technics and Civilization*, Lewis Mumford wryly discusses literacy measures for the non-elite, writing, "With the large scale organization of the factory it became necessary that the operatives should at least be able to read notices, and from 1832 onwards measures for providing education for the child laborers were introduced in England."[14] Much like Foucault, he describes the school as containing all "the happy attributes of jail and factory combined."[15] The reigning school environment consisted of "silence, absence of motion, complete passivity, response only upon the application of an outer stimulus, rote learning, verbal parroting, [and] piece-work acquisition of knowledge."[16] Though he and Foucault underscore the bleakness of the school setting, we might also emphasize its aspects of pleasure. For Susan Willis, this entails literal sweetening. Her research highlights the role of sugar in the industrial revolution in which "the forces of capitalism brought about the dependency of the working class on cheap stimulants, the maintenance of working-class energy balanced against the erosion of general health and longevity, and an immensely profitable system of production and consumption."[17] In nineteenth-century Britain, "working class children could expect bread and jam for two meals out of three." This was due to the need for "efficient, high-energy foods"—that is to say, "[nutritionally] impoverished quick-energy non-foods"[18]—with which to meet the caloric needs of an industrial workforce and its dependents cheaply. Such a diet included simple carbohydrates, caffeine, and ample sugar. It was, in effect, a staple regimen of "bread and jam, tea and sugar."[19] Even today, sugar may provide the only commodity that capitalism makes accessible to all.[20] Its uses, especially in children's lives, are considerable. Willis argues that sugar and capitalism are inherently connected (not least, I would add, by way of colonialism and the slave trade), and that candy may offer a sense of "appeasement" and "payoff" for an otherwise "unfulfilled desire for social relationships where neither domination nor the commodity would prevail."[21] Like industrial Britain in the 19th century, the contemporary long-term health ramifications of diets based on "quick-energy non-foods" cannot compete with the greater significance of—and overall investment in—successful, or at least adequate, alphabetization.

EXTREME TECHNICITY

It is difficult to fathom, from the vantage point of already knowing how to read, just how complex an undertaking literacy is. The alphabetically dependent society must ensure the ability of each person to decode at three stages of remove (the signs of signs of signs). The demands upon small children to become "automatic" at mastering multiple levels of abstraction might be considered preposterous if it were not already customary—that is, required by law. Alphabetic literacy is the most involved, difficult, prolonged training any of us will ever undergo. If we could not already read and write, indeed, if we had not spent most of our waking lives practicing some version of one or the other, we would be quite unprepared to take it up now. Once we outgrow the extreme plasticity of the infant brain, literacy would be nearly impossible for most of us to master with anything approaching automaticity, or "unconscious reflex." This is why adult learners struggle more intensely than small children and why the pursuit later in life is commonly abandoned.[22] Schooling in the industrialized world, meanwhile, arguably comprises the most extensive and highly systematized project of technological and social engineering the world has ever known. I have not encountered the work of a literacy specialist who does not express concern that the standard of thirteen years (age five to age eighteen) is too brief to undergo this process and that it must begin much sooner. Current educational theory demands an even longer childhood than Ariès's "pedagogues and moralists" ever did. Much of it based in cognitive neuroscience, it would conscript toddlerhood, infancy, and even the period in utero in the service of alphabetization. "Longer" still remains operative even if "sooner" has begun to take priority. The fact that alphabetization ideally begins in the womb does not mean that the initiation will be "finished" by age twelve instead of eighteen. The continually expanding duration set aside for alphabetization speaks not only to its extreme technicity but to a pressure to intervene in cognitive development, before brain structures can solidify in the wrong (i.e., non-alphabetic) directions.

While some theories suggest that an infant's brain is already fully intact, and that it is essentially a small adult brain, for which the more complex capacities, already existing in germ, will become "activated" with the passage of time, the more convincing theory is that the newborn brain is essentially formless. The human cerebral cortex contains more than 100,000 trillion synapses separated by intervening gaps. During infant development, the axonal and dendritic trees proliferate and, as the early neuroscientist, Jean-Pierre Changeux, puts it, "branch and spread exuberantly."[23] "At this critical stage, there is redundancy," he writes, "but also maximal diversity in the connections of the network."[24] Such diversity means that any number of different circuits is possible, and that those paths which ultimately cohere to form networks do so as the result of repeated manipulations of a highly specific kind, a process known as selective stabilization. Alphabetic cultures preselect which networks it will stabilize, of course, and these are the "emergent literacy" pathways. It should be noted that such types of input are only one alternative among many. Other sorts of influence—different kinds of cues, signals, and stimuli—produce "dramatic differences in cerebral circuitry."[25] Once the child's brain is ordered and reordered for expectant literacy—once it is deliberately and repeatedly "guided into position" in this manner—it simultaneously discards (quite literally at the cellular level) other, non-alphabetic pathways of knowing, organizing, or experiencing the world. In his *Language at the Speed of Sight*, Mark Seidenberg writes that alphabetization has a universalizing effect, as there are "things that all readers do the same way because their brains are essentially alike."[26] The entire brain is given over to the process of reading, rather than, for instance, a limited region devoted to a singular skill. This goes some way toward explaining why non-alphabetic ways of knowing are unimaginable, if not anathema, to the literate brain. They are objectively outside the scope of its structure. Walter Ong suggests that trying to conceive of what oral culture was like to a literate person is akin to describing a horse to someone who has never seen one before as a "wheelless automobile."[27] That is, as something distorted, strange, non-functional—and nothing like a horse.

Consciously or no, alphabetized adults already code the world through literate dispositions. In so doing, they surround the developing child in an atmosphere saturated with such things as "phonemic awareness"—understanding language as a strictly vocal phenomenon that can be dissected into isolable, segmented units; "print awareness"—knowing how to negotiate, handle, and manipulate alphabetic messages (and the various material media that disseminate them); "letter awareness"—taking the twenty-six shapes (falsely as we have seen) to be the symbols of sounds; "print motivation"—accepting that text has value by showing interest in it; and so on. We may think of parents, caregivers, educators, and policymakers, as collectively desiring, apropos Jacqueline Rose, as well as carving children's brains:

> Just like a sculptor who creates a statue with a block of stone and a chisel to remove the unwanted pieces, the brain has a parallel system in which unneeded cells and connections are removed by cell death and synaptic pruning.[28]

The "exuberance of synapses" is a temporary state, and critical periods of exceptional plasticity do not wind down or taper off but abruptly end, as the "brain slams on plasticity brakes."[29] It does so as a "way to protect the newly optimized brain circuits from disruption by further input."[30] Once the circuits strengthen and prune, they become permanent. "Braking" is necessary to preserve these networks; for if the brain were always exceptionally plastic, it would cease to function. Though experiments are underway in which drugs may be used to help reopen the critical windows in adulthood, the potential for widespread brain damage as a result makes these processes prohibitive, to put it mildly. So, while neuroplasticity is indeed possible throughout the lifespan, it appears that these changes are "functional" rather than "structural." While an adult might form new neural circuits by learning a musical instrument, for example, her alphabetization by contrast is permanent.[31] Outside of the critical periods, it may be possible to *add* circuits, yet in infancy the far greater number of existing (but insufficiently trophic) circuits and the multiplicity of what are known as "expectant circuits" will disappear. With enough directed intervention upon the "experience expectant circuits," these will take on form at the same time that they foreclose the unused (atrophic) options. As Changeux explains, to learn is not to add new growth—rather, "*To learn is to eliminate.*"[32] The large-scale neural circuits take form according to "particular task oriented demands," such as those consistent with emergent literacy and with eventually recognizing, decoding, and producing alphabetic messages. Other potential pathways—those which have not been sufficiently utilized or reinforced—undergo a self-terminating process. In this way, the brain is coded through repetition, but it is also the case that non-alphabetic ways of knowing become effectively removed.

Between four and twelve months, the infant brain contains 150% of the number of synapses found in an adult. The peak period of synaptic density is between seven and twelve months. In a one-year-old child, this massive profusion of synapses in the cerebral cortex "appear to be as yet unspecified for function."[33] Unspecified for function belongs to the realm of Catherine Malabou's research, in which she describes early cognitive plasticity wherein "the synaptic openings are definitely gaps, but *gaps that are susceptible to taking on form.*"[34]

A MONUMENTAL TASK

The association of sweetness and literacy is at least as old as Horace, who wrote of "giving little cakes to boys, to coax them into wanting to learn their alphabet."[35] In the 5th century, St. Jerome mentions putting "little honey cakes" in front of the pupils in order to entice them to learning, along with "sweets, flowers, gems, and dolls."[36] The excavation of a series of unusually well-preserved Roman mosaic panels offers access to a scene of pedagogical norms in Italian antiquity, the commonalities of which are confirmed in similar sources such as a depiction of schooling found in Pompeii.[37] The panels form a narrative sequence in which an unknown boy called Kimbros progresses through each step of his education. The first panel features both actual and personified figures alongside the young student. Of the latter, Glukera is prominent. Glukera is the personification of pleasure. Her name was associated with sweet things as well as persons and objects that brought gratification or were otherwise "perceived to be enjoyable."[38] The Greek version of her name (from the roots *deliciae, delicia*) indicated anything that "brought delight."[39] The tone changes abruptly in the following panel, where the boy Kimbros is undergoing corporal punishment. The practice of flogging and beating pupils is well documented, though this scene is unusually explicit. It shows Kimbros on a rack, naked from the waist down, lying on his stomach with buttocks exposed, arms outstretched as if seeking deliverance, registering pain, or both.[40] The Pompeii panel was found on the wall of a schoolroom, presumably as a deterrent to mischief, in which two adults participate in the scene: one to hold the child aloft on his shoulders, the other to lash his bare behind. The violence of the school setting is extended onto the following panel, where it appears in the form of a threat ready to break out rather than an act in the midst of occurring; hence Kimbros's tutor raises the stick against him but has not yet wielded it.

The threat in the third panel indicates less overt forms of violence used in educational practice, including the muted but eternal *prospect* of violence, rather than specific instances of its use. Althusser argues that the repressive state apparatus (the RSA) is never far from the ideological state apparatus (the ISA), because they must be understood not as replacements for one another, but as operating on a spectrum.[41] We may also regard the threatened, but as yet unactualized, violence of the third panel as the internalization of power by the individual, as Foucault would argue, and thus the elimination of the need, except on rare occasions, for outright force, as depicted in the flogging scenes of the Roman mosaics. The raised arm may be all that is required to engender compliance. The adoption of self-policing, even as early as preschool age, is among the necessary conditions for the child to become literate. Much of the efforts toward self-regulation in small children today have to do with sitting still or being quiet, neither of which they will do if left to their own devices. So begins a training in which persons in an alphabetized society become accustomed to repressing and ignoring their bodies. An exception is toilet training when knowledge of and quick response to bodily needs is encouraged. Children must usually be toilet-trained before they can be admitted to a school. Indeed, assessments of preschool "self-regulation" measure the "regulatory strategies that children use to exert control over involuntary, reactivity-based responses."[42] In order to attain academic success, small children must control the uncontrollable (i.e., the involuntary) within their own bodies. To exert voluntarism over the involuntary, a major part of executive function or self-regulation, is a strong indicator of progress in school, according to the research. Moreover, the ability "to shift and sustain" *visual attention* also predicts favorable outcomes. The authors argue that sustained visual attention provides a means to cope with stressors so that the child can "divert or focus in order to better handle conflicting stimuli, retain information, and plan their next actions."[43] Many scholars have noted the unique and overarching stress on visuality in an alphabetic context, especially since letters supposedly capture sound. This synesthetic shift to so-called "visible speech" is another artificial hardship for toddlers, such that they must regard their prior babbling, chattering, vocalizing, and singing as made up of imaginary segments that it is now their job to identify—added to the fact that these are things one *sees*.

Little is less intuitive than the notion of phonemes, which are the ostensible results of the process of "cutting" or "cutting down" what is otherwise a continuous stream of sound. Preliterate children must be made *aware* of something that does not exist. "Phonemic awareness" is often cited as the single greatest predictor of future fluency in literacy, and therefore, life outcomes. The need to invent phonemes suggests that words, too, are not "discriminable constituents" until the "spaces" between them are constructed by (relatively recent) typographic conventions. One need only attempt to understand a foreign language that she has learned through books to realize that there are no such helpful "cuts" or "segments" in the stream of spoken French, for example. But because one has learned to speak and listen "literately," she will still try to identify these cuts and to envision the "white spaces" in between the "words" in a continuous flow of the French language. Again, it reflects the synesthetic confusions of the early childhood classroom because one is attempting to visualize something she experiences acoustically. There are the cuts comprising each letter, the minimal space between each printed letter, which represents the ostensible discreteness of each phoneme, and then there are the larger spaces between printed words which also discriminate one from another. Phonemes (and additional alphabetic components in the form of cuts, segments, isolable units, and spaces) "are *not* identifiable elements of the acoustic stream."[44] That is, "It is simply not possible to identify segments within a spectrographic representation of continuous speech," because it is "an indissoluble continuum, with no natural boundaries within it."[45] This is why phonemes are unknown outside of alphabetic cultures.

Even with concerted efforts to avoid outright corporal punishment, children nevertheless experience the violence, however displaced and sublimated, of the school setting. Phonemic awareness and the serially segmented nature of "language" must surely prove bewildering to children, and this alone is likely to cause frustration. Melanie Klein suggests as much in her strange and fascinating essay, "The Rôle of the School in the Libidinal Development of the Child," where fantasies and fears about cutting appear throughout. Mutilation, often of a sexual nature, crops up in many of her analyses of children in relation to their schooling. Young Grete insists on the parallel between diagramming sentences and butchering animals. The basis of the violent and sexualized scenarios elaborated by schoolchildren, Klein theorizes, is the desire for the cutting up of the mother. When they are packed off to school, children encounter a "new reality," one which "is often apprehended as very stern."[46] In this sense, Mother's abandonment, a surrogate installed in her place, might inspire a child's imaginary version of revenge. Klein argues that the major source of conflict in regard to schooling, however, is the repression of the libido and hence the forceable transfer of things sexual onto things cerebral. As expressed in Plato, the discharge of libidinal energy must not be spent for the sake of its own enjoyment,[47] but rather harnessed and redirected through signs. Grammar, as taught to children, involves ordering, spelling, arranging, and "dissecting" the ostensible segments of language, and thus it imprints the belief that language is itself already comprised of a series of segments of varying "length," from phoneme to word to sentence. On the "libidinal significance of *grammar*," Klein observes:

> In reference to the analysis of sentences Grete spoke of an actual dismembering and dissection of a roast rabbit. Roast rabbit, which she had enjoyed eating until disgust at it supervened, represented the mother's breasts and genitals.[48]

The other cluster of associations Grete has with schooling relates to an occasion in which a cart filled with "sweetmeats" appeared in the schoolyard. Before she could buy them, however, her schoolmistress appeared. Grete became preoccupied by the sweetmeats (candies, confections) and the depths of sugar-wadding (spun sugar, cotton candy) in which they were enveloped. Though these items "interested her extremely"[49] she did not venture to obtain them, presumably because of the presence of the schoolmistress. She held the first chair in singing in the school choir. According to Grete, the schoolmistress had come close to her during a rehearsal and looked directly into her open mouth: "At this Grete felt an irresistible need to kiss and hug the teacher"[50]—a need she presumably repressed. Though these scenarios are dated, they nonetheless speak to the current school dynamics in which both a provoking and a denying of sensuous pleasure structures the learning experience. The consolation of sweets and the desire to be wrapped in affection are occasions that constantly present themselves *as possibilities* in the schoolroom but are, at the same time, also rejected as possibilities. (She does not kiss and hug the teacher and she does not gorge on sweets, as disapproval at both has already been anticipated.) This is all overlain, of course, with a sense of restriction and regimentation, for which the potential for affection may appear as a reprieve, but often a thwarted one. As per Willis's description, Grete seeks "appeasement" and "payoff" for an otherwise "unfulfilled desire for social relationships where neither domination nor the commodity would prevail."

In rebellion, perhaps, against an environment in which "cutting" is foregrounded and solace is pretended to but always interrupted, young Fritz expresses a longing to both cut and eat his mother, as he believes all children do. Klein writes, "Really every child wants a bit of his mother."[51] A desire to be reintegrated with mother is likely not unusual, though Klein suggests its violent character results from the traumatic nature of schooling. As Grete resisted diagramming as rabbit-cutting, Fritz likewise rejects dividing. Klein attempts to discuss Fritz's "marked resistance to doing division sums"[52] with him, for even though he understood them well, he nonetheless delivered the wrong answers. He responds to her questions with a story about a circus lady, who having been cut into many pieces, miraculously reassembles herself and lives on. Doing division, Fritz decides, is like mother standing on a ledge (presumably the division sign) and watching as someone comes along and tears out one of her arms.[53]

Fritz had demonstrated great joy in learning before school, but now that he had entered it, he began to resist all the "difficult tasks" he was asked to perform. In a naïve anticipation of Foucault, Fritz likens himself to being in a penitentiary, having to do all manner of difficult tasks, one in particular being the demand to build a house by himself in eight days. Klein writes, "In one phantasy, I too was put in prison and compelled to perform difficult tasks, and, indeed, to build a house in a few days and to fill a book with writing in a few hours."[54] Another child, Felix, by contrast, seems to suffer the school tasks in silence: "At first one is very frightened, and then one starts and it goes somehow, and afterwards one has a bad sort of feeling."[55]

THE USES OF PLEASURE

The promise of a mother (or her surrogate) who dispenses treats and pleasures also contains the inverse: that she could withhold or take them away. The use of this tension to teach children the alphabet is apparent in the discourse networks of 19th century Germany, which advises "that *Mothers* would perhaps make the best teachers."[56] When Mother offers sweets two sources of pleasure are combined into one. The first is proximity to the Mother's mouth, purveyor of the mother tongue; the second is the prospect of mother baking delicious "edible letters."[57] These would serve as both instructive in "letter-games" and as rewards for good performance. Letter-shaped foodstuffs persist today, as with "biscuits decorated with iced letters" and alphabet soup.[58] Children's birthday cakes often feature their names and other script. Within this discourse network, Mother has been instructed to practice her flawless high German for perfect pronunciation, and to segment language (here syllables) as a prelude to, and as a test of worthiness for, devouring the selfsame items: "*pud-ding—cook-ies—rai-sins—straw-ber-ries.*"[59] Kittler refers to these as "pleasure-promising" words.[60] Mother combines sensuous pleasure with alphabetization, and anticipation with language segmentation. Another advice manual counsels a similar practice, but with the added pedagogical tactic of a threat:

> As soon as the child's awareness has developed sufficiently, sometime in its second year, it will hear its mother speak each time she gives it something: 'Look what Mother has for you.' Later, or as soon as it has a better understanding of language: 'You're hungry, you want to eat; it wouldn't feel good to go a few more hours without food, or if no one were here when you're

hungry, if no one loved you and wanted to help you. Don't worry my child! Your mother is here!"[61]

Mother obliquely threatens abandonment—invoking a scene in which she not only delays sustenance but withholds it altogether (as she is not "here"), having taken "love" and "help" with her. In the next instant, she removes the threat and announces as much ("Don't worry my child!"). Yet the sudden invocation of a nightmare scenario (starvation, helplessness) is scarcely assuaged by its equally sudden retraction. The child should now feel relief, according to Mother, who restores nurturance jubilantly—the appropriate demeanor with which she should perform these tasks is demonstrated by the exclamation points. But from the child's perspective, the return of harmony only makes its prior existence feel dubious. Indeed, a sense of dread is likely to linger. Violence implied is not, of course, violence enacted but it has entered the scene nonetheless; it is endured in the form of postponement. The pedagogical theory in this "discourse network" is not entirely dissimilar to our own, nor that of the Greeks. Corporal punishment is in disfavor, though other forms of discipline are not. Intergenerational sex constitutes a criminal act, not as in Greece, when it performed a central role, as one classicist describes in no uncertain terms: "Acceptance of the teacher's thrusting penis between his thighs or in the anus is the fee which the pupil pays for good teaching."[62] This may or may not be preferable to striking a blow, which the Greeks also found indispensable. Pain teaches.[63] Though Ernst recalls a headmaster who struck a classmate, there is little mention of corporal punishment in Klein's article. Nevertheless, a marked sense of (sexualized) violence seems to inform the children's outlook, a change in them that takes place upon entering the school setting. Klein also postulates that writing and reading constitute the height of sexual-symbolism and that her colleagues likewise found this to be "*typical*."[64]

Less overt, however, does not mean removed. The convergence of sexuality, cruelty, and violence certainly make an impression, but today we understand that such methods are neither necessary nor productive. Instead, the dominant model cultivates a certain suppression of the body, as opposed to frequent reminders of its sensitivities. This model does not exactly promote disembodiment but rather, as Foucault was one of the first to document, a profound micromanagement of the body. In the school-prison-factory, we confront a "policy of coercions that act upon the body, a calculated manipulation of its elements, its gestures, its behaviors."[65] Not expressly violent, such discipline nevertheless "produces subjected and practiced bodies, 'docile bodies.'"[66] He continues, "Good handwriting, for example, presupposes a gymnastics—a whole routine whose rigorous code invests the body in its entirety."[67] The "gymnastics" of handwriting alone is noteworthy: it includes crabbed fingers positioned at precise locations on the writing implement; posture that is largely immobile except for the dominant hand; a certain hunched attitude for better ease of viewing; restrictive furniture (i.e., a chair attached to a desk) that is often welded into the shape the child's body must take, and so on. The design of this chair-desk discourages spontaneous movement, making it difficult to get in and out of. In a sociological study of children's bodies at home and primary school, Berry Mayall considers the "many occasions demanding strict physical conformity"[68] apart from the activities concerned with literacy and its variations. She writes of

> The demand made by the school regime for control over the body and legs, folded arms, no touching of other children, eyes front (towards the teacher). Lining up was also a strictly defined social event: movement was to take place only on the word Go! Requisite behaviours included due but not undue speed towards the line, lining up in single file, not jostling or pushing in, keeping your arms to yourself, not shouting. Infringements were quickly identified and reprimanded. A boy's enthusiasm to get to the playground and a girl's slow movement both called up comment.[69]

By the age of nine, when the children had internalized school norms through the intervening four years, they "did not complain about sitting on the carpet, lining up, getting a drink, going to the lavatory. They had grown accustomed to the regime."[70] As young Felix said resignedly, "it goes somehow."

THE PERMANENCE OF ALPHABETIZATION

Lidia Stanton shares the joke amongst her colleagues in the fields of neuroscience and cognitive psychology that reading "is a form of brainwashing."[71] This is because, she explains, it makes one "defenseless against an army of 26 letters in the alphabet."[72] To prove her point, Stanton shows the following block of text, and asks us not to read it, but only to consider the "visual look of the words."[73]

**Lucy is going to
the park and
she is taking the
dog for a walk.**

Your brain will automatically decode the writing, Stanton says, "before you decide whether to read or not." Childhood alphabetization is irreversible. Its particular organization of biomatter cannot be undone. As one clinical neuroscientist argues, it is a romantic fantasy that critical, or "sensitive" periods (of neuroplasticity) as they are sometimes called, can be prised open again in later years: "Some things just don't unhappen."[74]

Historically speaking, such a state is unprecedented. Other apprenticeships in social technologies did not include a process whereby the tool and the body of the user cannot be separated—indeed, in which they *grow together*. When the thusly coded brain encounters material sources of activation—that is, text—it cannot help but "run," as this is what it has been lengthily programmed to do. Stanton's use of the word brainwashing is too mild at some level because it suggests a temporary state that will wear off with sufficient time, the removal of the victim from the site of its occurrence, and so on. However, children do not "recover" from alphabetization. No literate adult "forgets" how to read. As with Stanton's army of 26 letters, one cannot stop herself from reading if words enter her field of vision. This is also unprecedented in terms of ideological saturation, if not closure. Under no other ideological regimen is it *impossible to ignore or resist* the interpellation. As Althusser reminds us, "no other ideological State apparatus has the obligatory (and not least, free) audience of the totality of the children in the capitalist social formation, eight hours a day for five or six days out of seven."[75] Though he did not identify alphabetics as the specific mechanism, he nonetheless emphasized the school: "It takes children from every class at infant-school age, and then for years, the years in which the child is most 'vulnerable' [. . .] it drums into them, whether it uses new or old methods, a certain amount of 'know-how' wrapped in the ruling ideology."[76] This alphabetization—this long, treacherous, sometimes pleasurable, but always outsized task—this work of inscription, we might say, has become childhood itself.

4

Plato and the Forms of Alphabetic Writing

The literature on soul and immortality originates with Plato. The only possible way one could work out a systematic, *fixed* idea about soul was in writing.

—JASPER NEEL[1]

Though his book is entitled *Speaking*, much of what Maurice Merleau-Ponty's student and contemporary, Georges Gusdorf, examines is directly or indirectly concerned with writing. For Gusdorf, writing does no less than "transform the face of the world."[2] The invention of the alphabet instantiates an "overthrow" of the "first human world" by enacting changes that alter the construction of time and space itself. In a non-alphabetic world "scope and duration" are limited, whereas

> Writing permits the separation of the voice from the present reality and thereby expands its range. Writings remain, and by that means they have the power to fix the world, to stabilize it in duration. Likewise they crystallize and give form to a personality which then becomes capable of signing his [sic] name and of making himself [sic] felt beyond his bodily limits. Writing consolidates speech. It creates a deposit that can wait indefinitely for its reactivation in some consciousness to come. The historic personality poses before future generations. He [sic] inscribes on basalt, granite, or marble the chronicle of his deeds.[3]

Writing includes a deposit of itself that is fixed, unchanging, and identical, irrespective of the amount of time passed or space traversed. It creates the impression of an author who is likewise fixed, unchanging, and identical. Both text and author contain and carry their "context" within themselves. The crystallization of one presupposes the crystallization of the other. Gusdorf's "voice," "name," "self beyond bodily limits," and "personality" are all contingent upon the "power to fix" and "to stabilize" occasioned by alphabetic writing. We have seen that "voice" and the effects of "throwing" it onto unlikely surfaces far removed from bodily constraints are novel and specific to the Greek invention. The others—"name," "self," and "personality"—also require comment as these, too, are alphabetic effects.

WORKING MEMORY

As previously noted, "working memory" primarily involves one's capacity to retain a limited amount of information long enough to carry out a certain goal. We are all familiar with the fact that this capacity is highly subject to time-decay and various other types of interference. We experience this issue every time we walk from one room to another and forget what it was that took us there. More precisely, working memory refers to the "relatively small amount of information that one can hold in mind, attend to, or, technically speaking, maintain in a rapidly accessible state, at one time."[4] Working memory capacity (which actually seems to vary little among individuals) is such that a person can only maintain one goal at a time. This is why "multi-tasking" is ultimately inefficient: it is simply the act of alternating quickly between one primary goal and another. The problem with talking on the phone while driving, for example, has less to do with occupying one's hands than it does with momentarily relinquishing the primary goal of driving safely in favor of the competing goal of producing meaning through language, that is, carrying on a conversation or reading a text. Driving safely can easily become a background goal to the now primary goal of formulating speech acts or composing messages. Within the working memory constraints of a human brain, only one activity can be the primary goal at a time. Gusdorf states that "mental" projects prior to the advent of writing "can attain in scope and duration only an horizon limited to the fleeting boundaries of consciousness."[5] This recalls the language of early philosophers of memory who spoke of "the trailing edge of the conscious present."[6]

Hence the difficulty, even among classicists, of accepting that Homer had not been literate, nor had he been, as was intimated above, a single personality. Yet it stood to reason that the sheer length of the epic poems, never mind their complexity, could not have been composed without an alphabet. It was only with the diffusion and recognition of Milman Parry's extraordinary work that it became possible to understand the Homeric age as completely oral. We will come to Parry again shortly. The issue with elaborated thought-processes prior to alphabetics has to do with the cognitive impossibility of maintaining multiple goals simultaneously. Let us consider carrying out an operation such as philosophical logic without any means of writing. A human brain cannot hold a premise (primary goal) in the "workspace," then formulate a proposition (secondary goal), and then include additional propositions (tertiary and quaternary goals). Not only does the logician need to maintain the premise, she must also remember and integrate P2, P3, and P4 in accordance with the principle of non-contradiction while arriving at a valid (i.e., internally consistent) conclusion. One could possibly alternate between two or three goals at the most, but this would quickly meet with diminishing returns. Whatever conclusion one might be able to draw with an exceptionally capacious "workspace" would nonetheless be forgotten, or at least thoroughly eroded, by the end of the day. Even if she were able to engage in some form of "phonological looping"—that is, repeating it to herself over and over again—until the point at which she could relay it all to another person, that person would then encounter the same problems. Without the technology of writing as a medium encouraging accumulation by means of recursion, it is difficult to imagine such operations ever taking place. With an alphabet, however, one can arrest the issues of working memory and time decay. In this regard, one can effectively stop time.

OF WORDS

One of the more significant consequences of the shift from oral culture to literacy in the West, as we have seen, is the enormous proliferation of words and the increasing importance of words to the detriment of most all other cues. As Ong points out, prior to the advent of writing, an utterance is "always part of a context that is predominantly non-verbal."[7] The signal or the utterance itself does not require heightened precision; it is only one in a constellation of factors between communicants. Neither do utterances require (or offer) a means of repeating and scrutinizing them. Utterances in an oral culture work upon a social field and modify that field. They are not set apart from it. The field of relationships, moreover, "always includes much more than words, so that less of the total, precise meaning conveyed by words need rest in the words themselves."[8]

Words only need to be pushed to greater levels of exactitude when there are no other cues by which to produce or gather meaning. In this respect, according to Ong, it is the non-verbal, *total environment* that bestows coherence on the message in a non-alphabetic culture. With writing, by contrast, every "utterance" is removed from the "plenum of experience," so that this fuller, situational meaning must be synthetically erected by way of other words. The shift away from their previous place of relative inconsequence to a disproportionate emphasis on words in and of themselves is unprecedented and causes each word to bear inordinate significance. Ong describes the difference between an oral-cultural plenum and a piece of alphabetic writing thus:

> In a text, the entire immediate context of every word is only other words, and words alone must help other words convey whatever meaning is called for. Hence texts force words to bear more weight, to develop more and more precisely 'defined'—that is, 'bordered' or contrastive meanings. Eventually, words used in texts come to be defined in dictionaries, which present the meaning of words in terms of other words.[9]

Though concerned with questions of ontology, W.V.O. Quine's description of this phenomenon is pertinent when he writes, "A question of the form 'What is an *F*?' can be answered only by recourse to a further term: 'An *F* is a *G*.' The answer makes only relative sense: sense relative to an uncritical acceptance of '*G*'."[10] When I accept "*G*" (uncritically), I have made sense of "F" for myself, though this state of seeming clarity is little more than a momentary reduction in the anxiety of ambiguity. Consulting the dictionary—that is, seeking definitions—briefly postpones the inevitable experience of more ambiguity and more anxiety. In so doing, it also establishes the "authority" of orthographic, typographic references, and it returns me to the circularity of words embedded with other words to begin the cycle anew. The heightened importance of words is what leads to their proliferation in an effort to achieve a "Truth" that continually eludes us. It should not be surprising, perhaps, that the formalization of this pursuit evolves in Greece as the activity of "philosophy" wherein the Truth is revealed by way of ever greater lexical precision. The philosophical endeavor as practiced in the Socratic tradition reinforces our increasingly firm commitment to the notion that "meaning" exists apart from, and in many respects in direct contradistinction to, the plenum of experience. It may even encourage a certain disdain for this plenum or a distaste for all that is bodily or subject to decomposition.

PLATO'S FORMS

Scriptural and linguistic precision are the foundations of the Platonic project insofar as his search for Truth is foremost a search for definitions. What Plato is working against is situated thinking or operational knowledge, that is, oral-cultural tradition. One encounters an apple that is a particular shade of reddish green; it is imbued with this collection of bumps and contours, that level of waxy coating or sweetness. The next day one comes by a different apple. This one is more green than red. It is wetter, faintly sour, and less uniformly round. Another apple on another day has a large bruise in the center and upon biting it, a profusion of juice, and so on. These apples are not the same, yet each one partakes of some quality that causes it to deserve the appellation, "apple." Just what is this quality that makes an apple an apple, that is, an apple *in itself*? Of what would the perfect apple consist, such that (all) others would be flawed by comparison? What would an apple be without distinguishing characteristics (red, round, bruised, rotten)? What is an apple without qualities? For good or ill, this kind of inquiry is somewhat familiar and intuitive to the schooled literate. But one may wonder what benefit could be gained by such exercises in an oral culture, which requires an alphabet to indulge them in any event. Because each individual apple is different—that is, made up of *particulars*—and because even a single apple changes over time, these cannot be a means to truth, according to Plato.

In arguing that an apple "itself by itself" is meaningful in a way that its various incarnations are not, one must conceive of an *illusory* world—invisible from the perspective of this world, but knowable through the shadows of its particulars—in which there are no mortal bodies, no context to speak of, and no change. We spoke earlier in terms of a hypothetical plane and an actual plane. What Plato advocates in the Two-Worlds Theory can be construed as a world of context in which apples necessarily always appear to us through various kinds of sense data (color, position, light, texture, shape, etc.), and the superior world with no context—in which the "idea" of an apple, an apple shorn of all context whatsoever, an apple without qualities—reigns supreme. Here Plato contrives abstraction. Abstraction is another way to say universal since what is universal is (definitionally) not particular. Abstraction is the only modality for which its context is that it has no context, and the precedent for this can only be alphabetic writing.

We encountered the ventriloquism of proto-literate forms in the oracle at Delphi and the early conceptions of a "thrown voice" that her presence negotiated. The voice becomes a synecdoche for the entire person, such that the human body becomes secondary, if not a thing that can be largely dispensed with. (And is this not the dream of the "uploaded mind," in which one's consciousness enters the cloud and lives on forever, quite apart from her mortal body?)[11] And is not that dream a high-tech version of another: that of a "soul" that ascends to a realm without pain and without death? Though notions of the singularity, the uploaded mind, and other futurist projections feel quite recent, such ideas had already begun to stir in the Platonic era. The "voice" that is metonymic of the body can also depart from the body. Not only does Apollo ventriloquize the Pythia but at another point in time, the Pythia might have thrown her own voice onto papyrus—which is precisely what Plutarch does when he describes her in his writings. We take for granted that a voice has become an *entity*; one that exists quite independently of the body in other forms (as fragments that have split off and grown anew elsewhere; is this not at some level what a colony is?). In a self-corroborating move that only writing can permit, the voice gains a discrete existence that is no longer dependent on working memory capacity or even a body, after a fashion. Indeed, the body by contrast is bound to time and space and appears to be lesser for this fact. It is made up of particulars and has, for the new realm of philosophy, already assumed an air of ill-repute—a source of suspicion, capriciousness, and change that cannot be trusted.

According to Julian Jaynes, it may have been Pythagoras—whose travels in Egypt could have lead him to encounter talk which he would go on to interpret (very liberally) as the transmigration of souls—who first offered the idea of "a 'life' which could be transferred from one material body to another," into the Greek lexicon.[12] Jaynes argues this Pythagorean imposition was a misunderstanding of two Egyptian notions—a "hallucinated voice" emanating from the dead (*ka*) and the physical guise this voice took, often in the form of a bird (*ba*). He argues that Pythagoras pressed the ill-suited Greek term, *psyche*, into the service of his notion of a "clearly separable soul that can migrate from one body to another as could an hallucinated voice in Egypt."[13] The mystical sect Pythagoras founded in Crotona, Italy, upon his return, made much of this new understanding of *psyche*. Curiously, too, the "secret society" promoted a strict practice of illiteracy, as the belief was strong that to "write things down was in error."[14] In fact, we only know of his doctrine of the transmigration of souls from much later, third-hand writers,[15] though one may wonder if the use of writing seemed to Pythagoras to be an impious and pale imitation of the "hallucinated voice." To throw one's voice—to inscribe it in papyrus—would be a version (perhaps to his mind a counterfeit one) of a transmigrated soul, which Pythagoras believed was something akin to the modern doctrine of reincarnation: "After death, a man's soul enters the body of a newborn infant or animal and so lives another life."[16] Alphabetic writing similarly splits off from the body that writes it and lives another life. It would appear to be somehow of this body and yet it does not depend upon its continued integrity (or even continued existence) in any way. The text maintains itself separately from the physical incarnation of the writer because it has its own physicality. Indeed, it can "transmigrate" thousands of miles away from its source and yet retain the identical authorial "voice," travelling without loss and without distortion, and it can do so until the end of time, for even though the materials in which it appears might decompose, the words can be recopied exactly as they first appeared. The scratches, impressed upon the surface, appear to be themselves living (they speak, after all). They even seem to breathe, since one "hears" them in the form of a voice as she reads.

By producing "living" words that endure I can, in a sense, overcome my own death; my inscriptions will far outlast the length of my lifespan, which will be modest by comparison. Neither are the inscriptions bound, in any nontrivial way, to the geographical space I happened to occupy as I produced them. (*Ka* endures after my death, but it is also separable from me when I am still alive and can operate quite apart from me. *Ba* is the animated capacity for movement across space. It does not wear my body, but it wears my head.)[17] When Pythagoras consolidates the two under the rubric of *psyche* as a new concept of "soul," it is because the Greek technology, the alphabetic text, supplies a kind of exemplar of the moveable, transposable voice. It has managed to outstrip the physical laws accorded to mortal flesh: decay, gravity, decline, inertia, and spatial boundedness.

The idea of "life" that could persist quite independently of the body would have struck the casual Greek listener as unintelligible. The "soul" was as inchoate and as easily dismissed a notion in Greece as it was in Egypt, where *ka* and *ba* could not be meaningfully translated in this way,[18] had it not been for alphabetic writing.

Writing spans vast distances; it even postpones its own interception, perhaps indefinitely. Rootedness in a site and a time, that is, a body, is replaced by a form of bilocation, in that one is simultaneously "in" one's body but also elsewhere, on a page. In this sense, writing induces a crude form of what was once called "astral projection." Without the protocols of writing already in place—without the normalization of transfers "from one material body to another"—the notion of a separate soul hidden within the body could not have taken hold. We see iterations of the notion after Pythagoras, but they are scarcely compelling and even Plato seems hesitant for a time. Where it is and what it is made of, its location within or outside of the body, is subject to debate: for Thales, water; for Anaximenes, blood and air; for Xenophanes, breath; and for Heraclitus, fire.[19] Socrates mentions, though quickly passes over, the possibility that there is no soul and that death brings "virtually nothingness, so that the dead have no consciousness of anything," though he is more sympathetic to the idea, still ill-received by his interlocutors, that death "is, as people say, a change and migration of the soul from this to another place . . . a change of habitation . . . ."[20] He concludes with, "If what we are told is true, the [dead] are immortal for all future time."[21]

Talk of the soul in the early dialogues is often qualified by phrases such as "some people say." Plato is influenced by the belief systems of a minor cult called the Orphics, for whom there is a soul which is imprisoned for unknown transgressions inside a mortal body, "as in a tomb."[22] The Orphic poets proceed "with the idea that the soul is undergoing punishment for something; they think it has the body as an enclosure to keep it safe, like a prison [. . .] until the penalty is paid."[23] Other, less appealing ideas persisted: one regarded the soul as a quantity of trapped air that was released at the moment of death in a puff; another viewed it as a "witless and feeble thing" that drank blood in order to regain consciousness for short periods of time.[24] Others located the soul somewhere near the midriff and claimed it perished with the body.[25]

Plato first invokes the "soul" in the *Phaedo*, at a time when it was still neither intuitive nor widely accepted. Imprisoned and condemned to death, Socrates attempts to console his visitors with the idea that he has a soul and that it will carry on after his death for eternity, but this is received as quite strange. His visitors are baffled, and one imminent classicist remarks, his use of "soul" likely came "as a shock to the Athenian of those days, and may even have seemed a little ridiculous."[26] If they can discern a referent for the notion, they clearly do not associate it with immortality. When Socrates had finished, Cebes answered and said:

> Socrates, I agree to the other things you say, but in regard to the soul men are very prone to disbelief. They fear that when the soul leaves the body it no longer exists anywhere, and that on the day when the man dies it is destroyed and perishes, and when it leaves the body and departs from it, straightway it flies away and is no longer anywhere, scattering like a breath or smoke.[27]

Cebes questions whether "soul" can exist "anywhere by itself as a unit."[28] After more discussion, Cebes's companion, Simmias, is still not convinced and states, "That it will still exist after we die does not seem even to me to have been proved, Socrates, but the common fear, which Cebes mentioned just now, that when a man dies the soul is dispersed and this is the end of his existence, still remains."[29] Cebes and Simmias are skeptical about the soul for a time but become convinced. As much of the dialogue demonstrates, however, the idea is scarcely plausible. From the earlier section of the *Phaedo,* in which Cebes and Simmias were at a loss as to what was meant by the soul, through to the end when the soul is posited as self-evident, we see an important shift, which Plato has, perhaps, purposely dramatized here. Julian Jaynes locates a profound alteration in the way *psyche* or soul comes to be used in this period: what had been associated simply with life or "livingness" was transformed into its opposite, that which survives in death. Thus "the word *soma* had meant corpse or deadness, the opposite of *psyche* as livingness. So now, as *psyche* becomes soul, so *soma* remains as its opposite, becoming body."[30]

Plato's work increasingly attests to the idea that there are Two Worlds—one which decays and changes and one which remains pure and immutable—and the soul forms an integral component of this view. The soul acts as a precursor to the Forms as itself a kind of [F]ormal fragment. What disunites the soul from the Forms, of course, is the material body. This line of thinking requires a sometimes subtle, but still relentless, attack from Plato on all that is bodily. In the following section of the dialogue, the soul is already a pre-sumed, discrete entity that somehow resides within the body that betrays it, and the senses are not a vehicle for knowledge but a diversion from it:

> Now we have also been saying for a long time, have we not, that, when the soul makes use of the body for any inquiry, either through seeing or hear-ing or any of the other senses—for inquiry through the body means inquiry through the senses,—then it is dragged by the body to things which never remain the same, and it wanders about and is confused and dizzy like a drunken man because it lays hold upon such things?[31]

The answer comes as "Certainly." What follows in the dialogue is a sugges-tion that one can escape the body entirely by circumventing its dangers and temptations and communing with the Forms "directly." Yet how should this be done?

Alphabetic writing becomes the enabling medium—and its products the many exemplars—through which the bounded soul is transformed from a mere cultic rumor into a solidified and separate entity that does not change and does not die. Writing provides conceptual examples of both "soul" and "Form," that is, *entities that exist outside the so-called chain of causality*, apart from the vicissitudes of change or circumstance. Unencumbered by time or space, texts show the way to the Forms. According to Plato, the soul gravi-tates to the realm of the Forms when it has "overcome" the shifting whims of its physical body and is intent on discovering knowledge. He has taken the alphabetic text and internalized its function in order to create a reflexive "inner space" he calls the soul.[32] The invention of the soul coincides with the discovery of the realm of disembodied "thought," and the interpolation of an internal "theater" in which to process such thought. As one who writes, I become accustomed to understanding myself as *not* (finally) my body—but rather as a portable consciousness that can be "transferred" to another sub-stance. The beginning of the subject who seeks to know, to commune with the gods, God, or the Forms (whose true nature is the soul), represents a significant turn in the history of European thought. Plato's avowal of a fully reified soul as the counterweight to the mortal body, and this opening up of the Two-Worlds, will have enormous consequences.[33]

Writing comes to be depicted as a "transfer" of some quantity from *within* me onto the receptive surface *outside me*. It is in this period, according to Julian Jaynes, that dualism, "the supposed separation of soul and body," begins to crystallize.[34] He notes, "It is now the conscious subjective mind-space and its self that is opposed to the material body. Cults spring up about this new wonder-provoking division between *psyche* and *soma*."[35] The most successful of these cults will be Christianity.

If all deception comes from the flesh, and knowledge arises from the soul engaged in (non-bodily, non-sensorial), that is, decontextualized thought, Plato's insistence on this split guarantees his and Socrates's roles as "honorary Christians" among the early Church apologists despite the uneasy fact of their paganism. Without Plato's use of the Greek technology, the grounds for the monotheistic religions could scarcely have arisen. Judaism is nothing if not a textual religion, but surely it is Christianity that bears the dubious distinction of the first fully alphabetic religion, of which we will have more to say in a later chapter. Augustine uses unmistakably Platonic conceits throughout the *Confessions*: "I could still see plainly and without doubt that the corruptible is inferior to the incorruptible, the inviolable obviously superior to its opposite, and the unchangeable better than the changeable."[36] Unlike Judaism, Christianity exercises another alphabetic logic, which is to spread—to exit its own context, ostensibly to "convert," to change what is not itself into itself. This becoming "context-free" is unique amongst writing scripts and unique amongst religions; the drive to "translate" all knowledge into alphabetics is one and the same drive to "convert" all human individuals into Christian souls. Before writing, no one could have taken leave of their context any more than they could take leave of their bodies. Without the Greek technology, we would have no basis on which to confer reality onto the notion of a soul and of course, no foundation on which to propagate religions of the Book. As Henri-Jean Martin notes, the alphabet "permitted religions of the Book to flourish, and in turn they favored teaching and the diffusion of reading. When the written word and the divine Word eventually joined forces they encouraged religions in which an invisible God was known by his Word alone." [37]

Though monotheism is invented by the Jews, it is not yet truly universal, since Jewish monotheism still maintains an inextricable connection to an ethnic group and a sacred site.[38] Though they invent monotheism, because they use a syllabary rather than an alphabet, neither the religion nor the texts on which it is based can effectively spread. The alphabet and Christianity will be the "adjustments" (to the syllabary and to Judaism) that encourage global dissemination:

It was the earliest Christians who severed the ethnic roots of God. Above all, Paul, who was born a Jew, declares again and again in his pastoral letters that since there is only one God, he must be the God of all peoples and all individuals, so there is no reason to make any distinction between Jews and non-Jews.[39]

Islam, too, though also a monotheistic religion of the Book will prove to be functionally non-universal, because it is tied to the Arabic language. The Qur'an, of course, is not supposed to be translated out of Arabic—rather one learns Arabic in order to study it properly. This in itself erects one of the barriers we encountered with syllabaries—though Allah may enfold all of creation, he surely does not imagine a time in which all people everywhere will speak Arabic and convert. Persons do of course convert to Islam, as they convert to Judaism, but proselytizing and the impetus to convert is not fore-most for Judaism and Islam as it is for much of Christianity, because again, the first two still contain certain circumstantial exclusions. It will require Christianity to propel monotheism, the notion of a single God for all peo-ples at all times in all places. It seeks to render *everyone, without exception*, to the target code, which is Christianity. Christianity presents a single deity, borne by a single man, contained in a single book, which can be translated into any language whatever. Catholic with both a capital and lower case "c" is—*means*—universal, which is co-incident with the alphabet as the first, indeed the invention of *the idea of universalism*. The combination of capital-ism and Christianity are the drivers of colonial expansion, though all three (capitalism, Christianity, and colonialism) are comprised of a similar con-versionary logic.

By the end of the *Phaedo*, Cebes and Simmias no longer balk when Soc-rates describes attributes of the soul, nor do they question its autonomy from the body. Yet for Plato, it will not be enough to posit the soul. This philosophical development entails much more besides. The distrust of the body is not simply that; it is also a concerted effort to disengage from the oral-cultural milieu in which he is still ensconced. His famous distrust of the poets is a direct expression of his hostility toward what of Greek culture remains appreciably *non-alphabetic*, of which Homeric (oral) discourse is most prominent and most tenacious. When Derrida argues that Plato priv-ileged oral speech over writing, he misrecognizes (as Plato himself did) the role of the alphabet in his thinking. Plato did not seek "presence" in the oral setting, and despite the occasional criticism of writing, he did not privilege speech over writing. Quite the contrary: only the soul contemplating itself could provide such fullness of "presence," and this is solely the terrain of a literate orientation. The bodily, meanwhile—which is unavoidable in a speech situation—always distracts from the Truth. It does not provide the means to unveil it.

THE "DISGRACE" OF FORMULAE

According to Plato, the Greeks were made dull and rendered unquestioning by the mesmeric rhythms of epic poetry; physical comportment as befitted a Homeric recitation was one in which the whole bodily sensory apparatus was engaged by way of dance and movement.[40] Such enthusiasts were ones entangled in "the thrill of song." Oral-poetic knowledge was not knowledge, according to Plato, but simply repetition and imitation. It was not even original.

It was commonplace before writing to use such devices as meter to serve as a mnemonic aid and to facilitate the bard's ability to draw upon a vast repertoire of metrically-fitted phrasings as suited his performance on any given occasion. The gifted classicist Milman Parry made this rather "scandalous" discovery in the 1930s, confirming the predominance of formulae throughout The Iliad and The Odyssey. Years of research, coupled with an ambitious program carried on by Alfred Lord after Parry's untimely death, demonstrated that Homer did not write anything down. Despite the appearance to our contemporary eyes of elaborate and novel invention, Homer and the other Greek bards had in fact hewn rather closely to a flexible but fixed cache of phrases, designed to fit those rhythmic patterns that best afforded memorability. Each recitation included improvisations by the individual poet, but even these were restricted to a considerable degree by the shape of the hexameter line.[41] The poetic choices made by Homer and other oral poets in general had to do, not with verbal inventiveness or expressive genius, as we are wont to believe, but with "metrical exigency."[42]

They drew upon a lengthy but roughly uniform narrative "encyclopedia" and likely adjusted the narratives to the mood and energies of the audience, for whom the events were much more participatory than the sort of passive spectating with which we are familiar today. All of these intangibles came into play on any given iteration of the saga and thus it was told slightly differently each time. None of this was a welcome revelation. In fact it all but destroyed the exalted Homeric myth, since genius was supposed to be unpredictable and indeed, inexplicable, whereas Parry had just explained it, and in devastating terms: "There was no use denying the now known fact that the Homeric poems valued and somehow made capital of what later readers had been trained in principle to disvalue, namely, the set phrase, the formula, the expected qualifier—to put it more bluntly, the cliché."[43] The Homer who stitched together prefabricated poetic pieces is so repugnant to the Western self-narrative, in which individual invention and novelty are paramount, that scholars such as George Steiner have taken to flatly denying it, writing that it "simply won't hold."[44] This attitude was already in place with Plato.

We understand poetry as pertaining to words and arrangement on the page. Yet again, in a non-alphabetic context, the exact phrasings would not have been the focal point. These were far less important than the occasion itself, in which to gather and take part in the production of common cultural knowledge (as opposed to restricted or rarefied knowledge). Oral poetic recitations were how collective "information" was stored and transmitted prior to alphabetic archives. Though the values would have been adjusted according to new developments and unforeseen situations, and reorganized in their multiple retellings, they would also have remained easily recognizable and entirely familiar. Everyone always already knew The Iliad and The Odyssey and in a very real sense helped to construct them anew with each performance, since they did not exist apart from the bodies of the Greek people themselves. Otherwise (without writing) they could not have been retained.[45] It is fair to say that in oral culture, "Communal inheritance hangs on the continuity of men [sic]. It cannot be preserved and profited from outside the circle of living."[46] Plato effectively removes knowledge from the "circle of living," and entrusts it to those who act through logos (reason) as opposed to the oral-poetic modes of knowing, which constitute mere doxa (opinion). Poetry is mimetic. Homeric discourse supported a kind of collective entrancement, according to Plato, which was not conducive to mental agility. (It did not count as knowledge; only thought as generated in and toward the soul constituted sophia.) Greek oral culture was too corporeal, too unreflective—it lacked dis-embodiment and reflexive self-regulation. It was also ephemeral, as all orally-based cultures must be, and therefore too tied to the scene of its own expression. It had no means to extricate itself from itself and make judgments, since it was gone as soon as it was said.

Homer was not a single person but an amalgamation of bards and oral traditions. When Plato disparages the poets with the term "imitators"[47] it is an apt choice, and not everyone would see this as an insult. Parry's remarkable discovery consists in identifying the precise mechanism whereby oral epic poetry is produced and preserved without an alphabet: it is the formula. As he explains,

> In a society where there is no reading and writing, the poet, as we know from the study of such peoples in our own time, always makes his verse out of formulas. He can do it no other way. Not having the device of pen and paper which, as he composed, would hold his partly formed thought in safe-keeping while his unhampered mind ranged where it would after other ideas and other words, he makes his verses by choosing from a vast number of fixed phrases which he has heard in the poems of other poets. Each one of these phrases does this: it expresses a given idea in words which fit into a given length of the verse.[48]

Formulas hewed closely to the requirements of the hexameter line. Parry exhaustively shows that the poems were comprised of tightly controlled metrical phrases—ones that had been borrowed, rearranged, modified, and shared, and that this had taken place over innumerable generations. In other words, there is no determinable point at which they could have been presented to the audience as novel material, as "new," since they had never *not been known*, but had always been woven into the fabric of collective existence. The memory of *The Iliad* and *The Odyssey* was distributed amongst, and preserved across, the Greek people. With each retelling, the content of the tales was recalled, refashioned, and recommitted to the bodies of poet and audience member. Parry (and Lord after him) are at pains to stress that the poet is no less artistically masterful for functioning solely in an oral register. The poet not only animates the crowd and revivifies the life of the tales, but in so doing, performs astonishing feats of memory. Because the poems could have had no independent existence apart from the performance of them, we can assume that a poet had heard and absorbed the stories from earliest years, internalizing a great store of phrasings while honing the craft alongside other bards. *The Iliad* and *The Odyssey*, in other words, do not have a beginning in the usual literary sense. They have no date of inscription, and therefore no point of origin or identifiable "source." A "Homer" may have been "responsible" for the *Iliad* and the *Odyssey* in some sense, *but he did not write them*. As Milman Parry is the first to confirm, no one wrote them. They came from no *one*.

Having thus displaced "the controlling hand of the individual artificer" from the work of art,[49] Parry was accused of effectively destroying both. One consequence of the Parry-Lord thesis is that the poet will not have made choices based on purely aesthetic considerations. On each occasion of the poem's retelling, pairings or adjectives were less about poetic insight or descriptive power, and more about what the meter demanded. One reviewer suggested that his role as a literary critic had been undermined by Parry, since he could no longer use his own skills of discernment to explicate the same in Homer. Another outspoken critic, S. E. Bassett, writes: "History [. . .] has shown us that every work of poetic art comparable in greatness to the *Iliad* and *Odyssey* bears the stamp of a single great creative mind."[50] The absence of a determinable agent provokes an extraordinary amount of discomfort. Instead of finding fault with Parry's methods, his critics do little more than reassert the ideology of "agency," or in this instance, the ideology of the "author-function."[51] Even if it could somehow be shown that Homer was indeed an individual, he would only have been the one who just so happened to consort with a scribe, meaning there were countless others who did not. The "individuality" of the author of the *Iliad* is itself highly attenuated by the fact that there would have been hundreds, if not thousands, of "Homers."

For his part, Parry seems to attach no value judgement whatever to either the mechanism of formulae or to the dissolution of the author as originating source. The fact of epic poetry's oral construction entails no cultural embarrassment for him. It did, after all, produce *The Iliad* and *The Odyssey*. Most problematically for others, however, is that his research establishes ancient Greece as an oral culture comparable to every other oral culture, with like poetic structures, mnemonic techniques, and methods of preservation. The Parry-Lord thesis supposes (and demonstrates precisely how) such poetic—and other, parallel aesthetic achievements—would have existed in all human communities.

A Western sensibility cannot abide formulas, borrowings from a common "store," the recycling of themes, or the dictates of meter. It rejects the notion that the poems were collectively constructed over great swathes of time. Homer as a non-author is objectionable enough, though Bassett argues that it is the second aspect of Parry's thesis that "is still less reasonable." He writes, "Parry assumed that Homer's poetry was only the result—except for its choice of phrase among those of tradition—of an infinitely long, exceedingly slow, and apparently entirely uniform, development."[52] To high literates such as ourselves, to describe a piece as "formulaic" (or, unaccountably, "uniform") ranks as the greatest possible insult. If a work has no origin, then it is by definition "unoriginal." Bassett connects the lack of origin to a failed individualization: "We must also grant to Homer some degree of originality in the use of poetic language . . . . Parry denied to Homer any individuality of style whatsoever."[53] An oral culture like any other cannot be reconciled, especially among the Hellenists, with the perceived grandeur of ancient Greece. Nor can the insight that it was not peopled with individuals or those who would have understood themselves that way. Parry's work inadvertently represented an assault on the exaggerated esteem in which much of the "West" had always held itself as the "cradle of civilization."[54] The use of formulae may have been applicable to lesser world poets, Wade-Gery argues, which is to say, "the narrative minstrels of other peoples,"[55] but to ascribe such banality to Greece is unacceptable.

Such criticisms of Parry are within the same universe of thought that permitted Plato to repugn the oral cultural tradition. The critics above can only accept that tradition themselves if it was *not what it was*—only if it can be rewritten as the birthplace of a single genius, whose agential autonomy preexisted the composition of "his" poetic texts (*The Iliad* and *The Odyssey*), who lived out his days by the name of "Homer." While we might attribute these sentiments to basic intellectual snobbery, there is also a colonial outlook here that strongly endorses the idea that oral cultures are *ipso facto* unworthy, and it begins with Plato—one of the first alphabetic thinkers.

The corporeal condemns men to the appetites and drives, and distances them from the Forms. More disturbing, however, is the suggestion that whatever constitutes oral culture—what is perceived by the senses and what surrounds and includes the body—is not only negligible and inferior, but also somehow not real. In the *Phaedo*, materiality serves as the basis of unreality. And how does one investigate matters without the help of the body?:

SOCRATES: Then when is it that the soul attains to truth? When it tries to investigate anything with the help of the body, it is obviously led astray.
SIMMIAS: Quite so.
SOCRATES: Is it not in the course of reflection, if at all, that the soul gets a clear view of facts?
SIMMIAS: Yes.
SOCRATES: Surely the soul can best reflect when it is free of all distractions such as hearing or sight or pain or pleasure of any kind—that

is, when it ignores the body and becomes as far as possible independent, avoiding all physical contacts and associations as much as it
can, in its search for reality.

SIMMIAS: That is so.

SOCRATES: Then here too—in despising the body and avoiding it, and
endeavoring to become independent—the philosopher's soul is
ahead of all the rest.

SIMMIAS: It seems so.[56]

If one wants to pursue "truth" and "reality," she must "ignore," "avoid,"
and "despise" the body. The more stringent the renunciation of the body,
the closer the soul—that strange, immaterial posit—gets to pure knowledge.
Plato was increasingly disdainful of the oral-cultural milieu that surrounded
him.[57] Ong describes this cultural discord as owing to the new literates and
their worldview, stating,

> it marked the point in human history when deeply interiorized alphabetic
> literacy first clashed head-on with orality . . . . The relationship between
> Homeric Greece and everything that philosophy after Plato stood for was,
> however superficially cordial and continuous, in fact *deeply antagonistic*, if
> often at the unconscious rather than the conscious level.[58]

Plato could not acknowledge the extent to which the soul and by extension the Forms were byproducts of his use of a contingent, local technology.
Otherwise, he would be unable to proceed. Plato very likely distrusted writing because of his nascent suspicion that a Form, the object of knowledge
"itself by itself"—*auto kath auto*—was not an aspect of the divine, but rather
the product of a man-made contrivance. Havelock argues that he was cau-
tious not to use the wieldier term, "concepts," but rather spoke of *eternal*
"Forms." Concepts are mere effects of the human mind whereas "Forms" are
beyond what is human and worldly, thus "invisible" and "immaterial." To
use human-derived categories would suggest Plato had devised the Forms
rather than come upon them through logic. His philosophical program was
designed to reveal what was always already there but obscured by embod-
iment. He did not acknowledge the role of writing, and on occasion criti-
cized it, because to recognize alphabetic writing—not as a neutral vehicle,
but as the condition of possibility of the Forms—would have been to deny
that they exist.

All other things being equal, Plato preferred face-to-face dialectics, which Derrida supposes is an expression of his privileging of speech over writing. Yet it is also apparent throughout the dialogues that the students and interlocutors figure as little more than reassuring affirmations of the philosopher and his words. In its way, this is not unlike writing something down. I understand my dictation as a reflection of my inner space: from me to the paper, back to me and forth to the paper, again and again, until the page is covered (or in the Platonic realm, consensus is reached), which I accept as tangible "proof" or verification of the success of the process. Whether Plato's dialogues are actual scenes or fabrications, they are always committed to paper solitarily—as writing is always a solitary act—containing only the most strained sense that an actual exchange between two parties is underway. Of course, dialogue was the basis of Socrates's methods and was undoubtedly important in Plato's Academy. For Plato's writings, however, the notional capture of a dialogue is a framing device, a conceit for the elaboration of ideas by an individual. Plato is less concerned with the conceit itself—contra Derrida, he does not fetishize speech—than he is with fully articulating his belief system and leaving it for posterity. The production of knowledge in Plato is not modeled on speech. It is a model diffuse with, derived from, given over to, and largely mirroring, *the act of writing*. In other words, Plato's dialogues are not that; they exhibit a single author (monologically) constructing the basis of philosophy—which is a very alphabetic thing to do.

His subsequent turning away from oral culture had to be as pitiless as it was thorough. In no other way could such a profound severance be enacted. He deems poetry "a crippling of the mind."[59] When Plato casts the poets out of the Republic, it is the whole oral tradition, of which the epic poets are the heart, that he is attacking. And the counterweight to orality is the consolidation of "interiority," the invention of the inner space, reinforcing the soul-as-subject. Havelock's description of the Platonic refusal of Homeric discourse and the setting of a very particular trajectory for Western civilization is worth quoting at length:

Men who have remained in the Greek sense 'musical' and have surrendered themselves to the spell of the tradition, cannot frame words to express the conviction that 'I' am one thing and the tradition is another; that 'I' can stand apart from the tradition and examine it; that 'I' can and should break the spell of its hypnotic force; and that 'I' should divert some at least of my mental powers away from memorization and direct them instead into chan-nels of critical inquiry and analysis .... This amounts to accepting the prem-ise that there is a 'me', a 'self', a 'soul', a consciousness which is self-governing and which discovers the reason for action in itself rather than in imitation of the poetic experience. *The doctrine of the autonomous psyche is the counterpart of the rejection of the oral culture.*[60]

What is an "I" without a culture? A signatory, as we discover in the next chapter, and likewise a debtor.

A simple utterance leaves no trace. Writing leaves itself behind, which is precisely what a vocalization in an oral environment can never do. By producing an artifact of itself, writing fabricates an object to which other fixities, other deposits (or to which other primary, secondary, tertiary, qua-ternary, etc., goals) can be attached. This new fixity provides opportunity for embellishment, embroidery, and elaboration. Writing contains within itself the possibility of not only reading but re-reading, not only consulting but re-consulting. It founds the action of *revision,* which literally means, *to look at again.* No one is capable of looking at a speech act, much less looking at it again, which is why Walter Ong is at pains to stress that prior to widespread literacy, a vocalization is *not a sign.*[61] Yet when a literate person is asked to think of a certain word for just a few seconds, she likely cannot do so with-out "visualizing its letters."[62] It is not unlike the fact that—as we saw in the previous chapter—one cannot refuse to read an alphabetic message when it enters her line of sight. In both instances, I am unavoidably experiencing my own alphabetization.

In a mass effort to improve literacy rates amongst rural inhabitants of Russia, during the early years of the Soviet revolution, the famous psychol-ogist A. R. Luria noticed something curious amongst persons with varying levels of literacy. Those with no alphabetic acquaintance at all had profound difficulty undertaking what he called "self-analysis." Without being alpha-betized, they lacked the illusion of an introjected inner space. The "I," he argues, does not appear as a fixed quantity but shifts continuously into "we." When asked to describe their personal traits, none of them produce pertinent answers: "In all these cases, questions probing for an analysis of personal qualities were either not grasped at all or were related to external material circumstances or everyday situations."[63] Of a second group, how-ever, who differed in that they all had some acquaintance with alphabetic writing, Luria noted substantial contrasts, including the "appearance of an attempt to evaluate their own traits in accordance with characteristics of an 'ideal me.'" The more familiar was the individual with alphabetic literacy the more, Luria found, was she able to "delineate [her] own character traits and consciously formulate [her] psychological peculiarities."[64] Luria concludes that the development of a self, the experience of an "interior space" as the extension of an ideated realm, fully separable from the material realm, can only be a byproduct of alphabetic literacy. Ultimately Luria must reject the theory that the "self" has always existed and argues against the idea that "self-awareness is a primary and irreducible property of mental life, with no history in and of itself."[65]

5
The Alphabet and Money

Money arose not long after a writing system that strove to be universal, and money was to become the spur and motive for everything in the West.

—HENRI-JEAN MARTIN[1]

Signing one's name originates in the contract. When Hobbes discusses the nature of contract in *Leviathan*, he speaks in terms of time. Words that inaugurate a contract are temporal: "And such words are either of the time *Present*, or *Past*; as, *I Give, I Grant, I have Given, I have Granted, I will that this be yours*: Or of the future; as, *I will Give, I will Grant*: which words of the future, are called PROMISE."[2] Nietzsche characterizes the human as the promising animal.[3]

The Covenant, or promise, itself creates a quantity of time—a temporal lag—from the point at which agreement is reached until the point in the future when the obligation is fulfilled. Thus Covenants, according to Hobbes, are always of the nature of "the time to Come, as, *To morrow I will Give*."[4] They orient action toward the future, even though at the time of their occurrence, they express only an "act of the will Present."[5] In a social order based upon the contract, the difficulty becomes the prospect that my "will Present" may have changed during the interim and ceased to be my "will Present" come the due date. This conundrum is resolved by that alphabetic curiosity, the signature, which attests to the fact that my "will Present" is always the same regardless of the date on which the contract is consulted. More importantly, however, it secures itself as the figment through which "I" establish my "self" as that to which the mark refers. It confirms that "I" am always "I" regardless of the date. We concluded the previous chapter on Plato by considering the necessity of a fixed and unchanging self that abides through time. Culturally, we have long since accepted "the premise that there is a 'me', a 'self', a 'soul', a consciousness which is self-governing and which discovers the reason for action in itself" as opposed to the collective.[6] When Nietzsche suggests that the promising animal must enact a "continuous willing of that which once has been willed, a specific *memory of will*"[7] we may argue that writing produces just such an artefact. The signature comes to play the part of the "memory of will," as the actionable proof through which I become identical to myself on the date I sign the contract, just as I am identical to myself at the later date; hence, the notion of *identity*. The concept of identity ensures that I am identical to myself in all cases (I am myself, myself is I). Only by positing a substance that *never changes* and therefore underwrites my signature as my "will Present" can a contract-based society secure its necessary foundations in each and every individual.

Havelock suggests this must be in spite of, and likely to the detriment of, the social whole, which becomes an aggregate of solipsists, as discussed previously. So, despite the unmistakable experiences of fluctuation and disruption, the "I" must always remain the same. A signature functions as a mark that proclaims my abiding personhood from one period to another and across multiple contracts. A vacillating bundle of sense impressions and moods does not honor a contract. Only a stable "I" can keep a Covenant.

Hobbes may well be agnostic on this point: so long as the Covenant is kept, the question of the existence of an abiding soul is irrelevant. In other words, I am obliged *to act as if* I am still of the same will at the designated time in the future; I am obliged to act as if I am still the same person (i.e., bear the same identity as the one who left the signature), whether or not this is actually the case. I am literally forced to do so.[8] Nietzsche cites violence, and Hobbes the fear of it, as that which make men promising animals. Of parties to a contract, Hobbes writes,

> But if there be a common Power set over them both, with right and force sufficient to compell performance; it is not Voyd. For he that performeth first, has no assurance that the other will performe after; because the bonds of words are too weak to bridle mens ambition, avarice, anger, and other Passions, without the feare of some coercive Power.... But in a civill estate ... there is a Power set up to constrain those that would otherwise violate their faith.[9]

Hobbes and Nietzsche both recognize that there can be no stable will across time. It is only with "some coercive Power" that persons can be counted upon to exist as unchanging agents who adhere to the social contract, and the multiple individual contracts it enables. Though they may "promise," Hobbes argues, human animals are not capable of keeping Covenants on their own and will do so only under constant forms of duress. The violence of "meer Nature" has simply changed forms on the way to the "civill estate." One could even say that violence in the "civill estate" is vaster, more far-reaching, more complete—which is to say, *more violent* than the state of Nature—though much of this violence exists *in potentia*. Hobbes would nonetheless claim that the civil estate is far preferable because it extends life and makes it less nasty and brutish.

As opposed to the state of Nature, in a civil society promises can be made and enforced. The threat of violence secures the identity of persons over time. "I" enter into a covenant; the same "I" will honor the contract or else be punished. In a social order built upon and organized by the contract, it is the *continuity* of the promising animal herself that matters. It makes little difference to the "civill estate" if this animal or that animal keeps her promise. It is only important that she remain *one and the same* animal across time, for then she can be held to account if she doesn't, in addition to taking on more contracts.

And it is in the interests of keeping contracts that social acts such as "naming" and "signing" draw their impetus.

Though Hobbes and Nietzsche emphasize the "time to Come" and the future orientation of the contract, respectively, Derrida stresses its quality of a permanent now *[maintenant]*.[10] Both are manufactured forms of temporality. *All writing*, not only the signature, creates a permanent now, whereas the nature of the contract is more about the interim rather than the now. A contract constructs a "now" only in the service of the time to come. I am a self today; I will (en)forceably be the same self on the date of collection. The periodic due dates are always in the future; the contract captures and confines "now" so as to construct identity over time. Now is only important insofar as it is when I sign; it is the fact that in so doing I launch a span that is significant. The span itself becomes enriching to the lender.

As the signatory, "I" am always "I" regardless of when you inquire. Derrida writes, "The general *maintenance* is in some way inscribed, pinpointed in the always evident and singular present punctuality of the form of the signature."[11] The signature as an instance of perpetual "now" resolves the problem of a potentially shifting will on the part of the signatory. So, while Derrida is correct in suggesting that the signature is of the order of nowness (Hobbes's "the will Present"), it is in fact the span or temporal lag that constitutes the debt relation. The past is of interest, indeed only arranges itself into existence, strictly by the fact that it is the point at which the debt was incurred. There is nothing before it. Tracking [debtors] only tracks itself back to what is alphabetic, that is, to the signature, to the drawing up of the contract itself. This is its only use for the past. What past existed prior to alphabet is not of any concern; neither is it even "knowable" as alphabetic objects are knowable. It is also in this (Platonic, colonial way) that the past is somehow ignoble. Time becomes the time of spans, of spanning. It cannot go "backward" but only forward; it is (recti-)linear motion. Plato rejected the (oral cultural inheritance of) the past and Aristotle was the first to develop the theory of time as a line.

In *Signs of Writing*, Roy Harris takes issue with Jack Goody's claim that in a writing culture "the signature effectively becomes a substitute for the person."[12] Harris believes the signature is "actually much better than the person. For the person can hesitate, prevaricate, renege: the signature cannot."[13] Far more than the performativity of spoken language (contra Austin), Roy Harris argues that it is true of no other sign apart from the signature that "its formation—the signing itself—*identifies* the signatory."[14] The act of this particular inscription reifies the identicalness of earlier self with later self and so it takes a noun (identity) and makes of it a verb (identify). This noun and verb converge in the signature and mutually comprise the identical site ("I") upon which debt is incurred and resolved, or defaulted upon and compounded. The alphabet is needed to perform the work of hypostasizing the debt and, at one and the same time, hypostasizing the *debtor*.

While writing in the non-alphabetic sense is far older than the Greek invention, there is little scholarly disagreement about its original purpose. It was a means of taking inventory (counting), and thereby also a means of tracking debt (accounting). If the subject is forged in guilt, as Nietzsche maintains, then so is she forged in debt. Both are forms of the demand for "repayment." Indeed, guilt is a monetary concept; it is turned

> first of all against the "debtor," in whom bad conscience will now establish itself, eat into his flesh, extend, and polype-like branch out into every depth and breadth until at last, in the conception of the irredeemableness of guilt, the idea of its unpayableness (*everlasting* punishment) is also conceived.[15]

Schuld signifies both guilt and debt. Despite my standing, good or ill, with the creditors, I must still be continually trackable. Having a fixed name that instantiates its referent makes all persons dwell in a state of "unpayableness." The name names a permanent state of indebtedness. The name creates a fixture to which the lifespan can be regularized by debt relations.[16]

NUMERACY

The Greeks were the first to use their alphabet to devise a system of mathematics, putting one system of abstraction into the service of developing another.[17] Put to mathematical use, the first letter of the alphabet would function as equivalent to "one" (*alpha*), "two" (*beta*), "three" (*gamma*), and so on. This secondary, mathematical use of the alphabet involved the same shapes, including the twenty-four letters, three "strange and antique" additional letters refigured for the purpose, and a shape resembling "M."[18] In his *History of Mathematical Notations*, Florian Cajori claims that this change was for the worse because it required the use of many more symbols. The Herodianac system, by contrast, which had been in use since the time of Solon (roughly 600 BCE) contained only six: '1,' '5,' '10,' '100,' '1000,' and '10,000.' Between 470 and 350 BCE, however, the new system derived from the alphabet came into wider use. Cajori's lament that the alphabetic system bears a significantly larger number of signs fails to recognize the extent to which alphabetic letters had already been routinized and internalized by an increasingly literate population. The cognitive burden was actually lighter because literates could make use of the same set of signs for dual purposes. Cajori admits that mathematical expressions had been painfully long in the Herodianic tradition, whereas alphabetic versions were much more concise.

Once the alphabet was ingrained as a *fixed sequence*, its letters (qua numbers) could easily be used to determine value based on the position relative to others in the series. When letters double as numbers, and the series is combined with the Hindu-Arabic invention of *the principle of position*, reading numbers is not unlike reading the alphabet. One scans a (alpha-) numerical sequence backward, that is, from right to left, against the direction of alphabetic reading, in order to determine value. To notate a numerical expression, that is "to achieve any other number, two or more of these are placed in a visible row . . . in order to assign to the individual figures ascending values in multiples of ten, these being governed by the relative distance of any figure from the end figure in the line."[19] Whereas the Babylonian system of computation was superior to Greek mathematics (apart from its geometry), it had not cut down to a mere handful the number of signs in play (as had the Hindu-Arabic system), so that deciphering the calculations it produced was slow and strenuous.[20] Its use of ideograms, and the uncertainty arising from the absence of a symbol for zero—that is, a way to indicate vacant places in the series—contributed to its restrictiveness. Like a syllabary, its territorialization remained limited. The Greek system combined dual (alphabetic) signs with "alpha to theta" signifying one to nine, with the eventual addition of the letter, "omicron," to distinguish between the end of one series and the beginning of another.[21] According to Havelock, "modern enumeration" depends on a like system that utilizes both the rule of position and dramatically reduced signs. This is what makes them quickly relatable, one to another, through processes of "addition, subtraction, multiplication, and division." [22] It is also what makes them international in scope. Consider the Romans, who used only seven of their letters as numerals, and who included operations such as subtraction from within the expression itself, an example being XXIV as the (Arabic) numeral 24.

Both alphabetics (writing) and numeracy (another form of writing) manipulate "signs of signs." This goes some way toward explaining their congruence, and in some instances, their interchangeability. Signs for positional value (itself an abstraction) substitute for things that are likewise abstractions (i.e., imaginary measures of quantity). The convertible nature of alphabetic letters as they stand in for numerals is still discernible in such current concepts as "alphabetic order," which denotes positional value. This is also the case with the meaning of "alpha" as not only "one," but also "the beginning" and with "omega" as "the end." *Alpha beta,* or "one, two"—with the "and so on" implied—is the name of the Greek invention, though it will eventually come to be known, of course, by its contraction, alphabet. Alpha beta as ("a," "b,") and alpha beta (as "1," "2") similarly imply a trajectory that is enacted by the inscription itself (not unlike a signature).

The Babylonian system could not be as readily converted to other times, places, and uses as could the fully abstract version developed in Greece.[23] The Greeks styled an order, it should be emphasized, which could, along with their alphabet, be used to notate any numerical value it was possible to conceive.[24] What the Babylonians, by contrast, had not managed was "to reduce and simplify the required number of signs and so arrange a convention which, by simple combination, could produce a value for any number whatever, just as a combination of alphabetic signs could produce a value for any linguistic sound whatever."[25] And "reading" an infinitely combinatory series of numeral-arrangements becomes a parallel operation to reading an infinitely combinatory series of letter-arrangements. A hypothetical unit based on biomechanical positions can take the form of a mark (a letter). A hypothetical quantity can also materialize from invisibility to visibility in the form of a mark (a numeral), indeed, the same one used backward. We should not be surprised to find that a hypothetical unit of value will also take material form in Greece in the shape of coined money around 600 BCE.[26]

In the shift to coinage, two intertwining aspects stand out: money becomes fungible, and it becomes fiduciary. That coinage must be fungible is an aspect of its being fiduciary. Fungibility demands that each coin be perfectly uniform and interchangeable, one for another. This in turn means that a quantity x of these identical coins can be transformed into anything else it is possible to purchase: a quantity y. Without alphabetic writing preceding the invention of fungible coinage, value "itself by itself" (Platonic *auto kath auto*)—that is, as an intangible, invisible notion, of which each individual, stamped portion of metal supposedly takes part—would have been unintelligible and unrealizable. As with the example of the apples in the previous chapter, and the philosophical question as to what it is that all apples possess in their appleness, the notion of value is also rendered abstract. What things are held to be valuable in terms of their particulars (i.e., the specifics of ceramics, oils, animals and so on) can never lead to the definition of value "itself by itself." It must be presented as an abstraction, a Form, as that to which all valuable items are referred and in which they all to different extents participate. If anything it is possible to *say* can be captured by the alphabet, then anything it is possible to quantify can be captured by numerals, and anything it is possible to obtain can be captured by coinage (abstract value). Greek money "was something that could turn into everything . . . . Gold, shaped into coins, is a material substance that is also an abstraction"; this is also the case for alphabetic or mathematical inscriptions.[27] A coin is "both a lump of metal and . . . a unit of currency which . . . could be exchanged for absolutely any other object whatsoever."[28] Greece becomes the first fully monetized society in history because it is the first fully alphabetic society in history.

Like the alphabet, money transcends the situation in which it is produced and inclines toward non-situations, which is to say, any situation. As opposed to perishable wealth, coinage can be stored or hoarded. Unlike grains, for instance, which must be redistributed regularly or else decompose, and unlike the sacrificial animals which, once slaughtered, had to be ritually parceled out in the form of feasting so as not to decay—money can be accumulated. (Both inventories and utterances can be accumulated with an alphabet in a manner that is outside the scope of a non-alphabetic society.)

Aristotle writes, "For future exchange, if one should not need anything now, *since there will be a time when he will need it*, money is a sort of guarantor for us, for it must be possible for a person who gives it to get something."[29] Like Hobbes's covenant, money is oriented toward the future and thus concerns itself with an unknown, non-existent state of affairs. Whereas for Hobbes, "I" may be unknown, for Aristotle, the situation will be unknown. When Aristotle names money a "guarantor," he refers to the fiduciary nature of coined money. Of the guarantee, Richard Seaford explains, unlike Babylonian silver, Greek money "was not just a generally exchangeable commodity: rather, it had a conventional value that depended on communal confidence (and in that sense was a kind of IOU), and so prefigured modern money, which is merely transferable credit."[30]

While my signature fixes the "I," and enables the Covenant, so does money fix a social guarantee and enable exchange. Both the I and the guarantee are fictional, but so are they both maintained by violence or the threat of violence. They are more apparent than actual. When one is "stamped" with a name, that name refers to a static referent (a soul or self), just as a "stamped" fragment of gold bespeaks a guarantee (not to mention an abstract realm of value). The stamp makes the thing stamped substitutable for or interchangeable with other items thusly stamped. Not because they are truly identical and thus indistinguishable, but because the "extra value" contained in the *having-been-stamped* provides a basis on which unlike things can become momentarily commensurable. What is fundamentally new about money as coinage is the existence of this "extra value"; Greek coins were "both valuable pieces of metal and at the same time something more . . . . Ancient coins were always worth more than the gold, silver or copper of which they were composed."[31] The something more refers to a posited stratum—not unlike the invented unit, "phoneme," which is nothing in itself, as there are no cuts in a stream of sound—but serves as a fantastical means by which to facilitate substitutability and circulation. We referred to it as a "hypothetical plane" in an earlier chapter. By "making visible" these imaginary units such as "extra value" and "phonemes," unlike things can be compared and exchanged, converted, and translated. "Stamping" the metal began as a means to inscribe a guarantee that the piece contained a trustworthy ratio of gold to silver, as opposed to, for example, an uncertain alloy. Yet this "guarantee" also works on a different plane, one that parallels the alphabetic tendency to attribute a greater measure of "truth" to something that is written down, simply because it has been transcribed into the alphabet.

Modern consumers maintain an almost mystical belief in coinage as "guaranteed" by the state, even though the guarantee itself will never be "redeemed." The fungible is necessarily interwoven with the fiduciary. One coin is identical to the last one, not (only) because of their material similitude, but because both are equally beholden to the accountability of the issuing state. Moreover, fiduciarity—which stems from "trust"—must function in a double register: in order to circulate, it must encapsulate both trust in the issuer and trust that it will be accepted in the *agora*. I must trust that the money is genuine, and I must also trust that *you* trust that the money is genuine, and that you will accept it in exchange for commodities. Yet even the fiduciary sense of money as "guarantor" is more virtual than actual. If the issuing state experiences a crisis and the currency is debased, as happened regularly in Rome,[32] then there is no *actual* guarantee. Devaluation makes explicit the fact that the guarantee was only ever hypothetical anyhow. In other words, the metal with which an ancient coin was minted would have been "worth" something on its own, but it could not be as much as the "extra value" with which it was stamped, since otherwise it could not circulate in the marketplace which was its sole function. You as a vendor will not accept an unstamped lump of gold otherwise similar in value to a stamped coin because it would lack this "extra value." The total value is both actual and imaginary, with the imaginary bearing the greater proportion of total value represented in each token.

Furthermore, the fiduciary signifies the guarantee that is purportedly to come, not strictly speaking from the issuing authority, but more so from what Lacan would call *le grand Autre* or the big Other. Just as the big Other guarantees "sense" to the alphabetic inscription in the form of the Symbolic Order, so does the big Other confer all value, since ultimately sense and value are expressions of the same thing. This is why Marx and Saussure use "signifiers" in the alphabetic sense to operate as analogues to money in the sense of carriers of value. The big Other is the final overseer, though one who is not entirely coincident with the state. Neither is the big Other another word for the gods, the power of which are already declining at this stage, nor even the one God of monotheism, who will soon be in ascendance. He is not even the literal Father—though the Name of the Father coincides with one's entry into the Symbolic Order. (Lacan presumed this entry to be based in *language*, whereas arguably it is rather an entry into alphabetics.) *Le grand Autre* is the intangible function of all these things combined. The big Other does not really exist, just as the guarantee itself does not exist, for what became of those Romans who found themselves, quite suddenly, with stores of worthless currency? To whom did they turn for the recompense they must have known would not be forthcoming? The big Other is the name of the omnipresent "issuing authority" who promises and who guarantees. Despite our knowing at some level that there can be none, we behave as if the guarantee were genuine and thereby provide the Other with a "reality" it does not otherwise possess. The big Other enjoins us to "pretend" that things are other than they are in a way that makes social lubrication, that is, the circulation of signs, possible. During public emergencies, according to David Graeber, the Greek city-states would "strike coins made entirely of bronze or tin, which everyone would agree, while the emergency lasted, to treat as if they were really made of silver."[33] Yet this is always how money operates, state of emergency or no, as the Chinese are the first to engineer: mere paper can suffice as the circulating symbol of value. The money token has largely disappeared altogether, or rather it has become digital, so that apart from numbers on screens, it no longer needs a material incarnation at all. As a dematerialized substance—itself an oxymoron—the abstraction becomes more "real," which is to say that what mattered in Greece, and what matters today, is not the material realm but the hypothetical one that orders it.

The difference between coinage and unstamped metals is also the difference between the alphabet and the syllabaries. The latter were "weighed down" by the history of themselves that they announced through the acrophonic, or otherwise conspicuous (rather than arbitrary), nature of the letters. By having no prior semantic entanglements and no historical sediment of any kind, the letters, as the coins, are unencumbered and uniquely able to circulate (as well as increase the host range). Because they act neutrally and without context, they are "free" to enter into, and back out of, any context whatever. As Schaps explains, "Coins would not be countable if they were not essentially identical. They had a value in exchange, but the value was not tied up with their history. They said nothing about their owner, and the items bought with them were similarly anonymous."[34]

As with the user of coinage, anonymity (or decontextualization) becomes foremost. In previous social formations, there had been codes and cues that enabled our trade patterns but also limited their remit, confining their large-scale coordination in terms of geographical space, historical relations, extent of "trust," and their various spatiotemporal boundaries. The fungible nature of coinage, by contrast, allows it to exist outside of any recognizable context. (The only other item of which this can be said is the alphabetic, or numerical, text.) At the same time, fungibility—that is, exchangeability—will be facilitated still more if the space in which exchange is to occur itself has no context, and no reason to exist except to render exchange more conducive. Once coinage is struck, Schaps notes, the *agora*, which had previously functioned as a site loosely set aside for association and public debate (and likely poetic recitations), almost immediately became synonymous with "marketplace." In Homer's time, there was no verb "to buy" and the people who gathered in the *agora* did so in order "to adjudicate a dispute," not to engage in commerce.[35] Schaps claims that by the classical period *agora* refers only to a space of economic transactions and no longer a political gathering point.[36]

Historians of ancient Greece debate the extent to which the centrality of the market becomes *disembedded* from social and cultural norms and at which point it does so definitively. None of them doubt that it takes place. Disembedding is an important aspect of becoming "context-free" in that it also indicates the growing distance from responsiveness to the needs of the group, as opposed to those of the individual. The *agora* supplies the primary site, and the concrete instance, of a *disembedded, emptied space* upon which the individual can operate in isolation from the oral-cultural group, strictly in her own interests: "The salient characteristic of a disembedded economy is probably *the anonymity of economic transactions* . . . . The extent to which such a transaction can be subordinated to noneconomic social norms is minimal."[37] In many ways the *agora* exists as counter to the group, in that it is a site of complete removal from oral-cultural concerns. It provides the necessary spatial circumstances to minimize and marginalize those "noneconomic social norms" of the collective. We should remember, however, that there is no such thing as a neutral, unfilled space in oral culture. The prototype of its appearance is, as De Kerckhove makes clear, and to which we return, *the theater stage*—the artificial site in which a sort of blank non-space is filled with the imaginary constructions of the alphabet. Coinage—and the alphabet—engineer the first appearance of what Benjamin might call "empty, homogeneous" space.

The *agora* becomes the baseline set of circumstances upon which multiple *items-without-context* display themselves, circulate, and change hands. The corollary to such a space is the autonomous subject who is herself dis-embedded. The *agora* provides a Platonic zone in which each autonomous individual can profitably and persistently "resist the urge to melt back into the fluid oral sensory network of the tribe [*sic*], and to detach [herself] gradually from the unconditional involvement demanded by the tribal [*sic*] situation."[38] Autonomous individuals enter the *agora* without names: anonymity is the mark of the decontextualized exchange process. It sits uneasily with the pressure of the contract-holder to be named, to wield her signature. Yet being named is not being "*known*"; it is being "*fixed.*" Both the named and unnamed are anonymous in the sense that I have been released from my obligations to reciprocity, or a duty of care, and so on, in regard to the oral-cultural group. All persons who are disembedded from their contexts are "equivalent" in this state of anonymity.[39] Aristotle argued that currency itself, or decontextualized money (coinage), "equalizes not only the goods but also the *parties* to the exchange."[40] Money homogenizes commodities as well as *users*:

> Firstly, it facilitates the kind of commercial exchange that is disembedded from all other relations: the only relation between the parties to such exchange is commercial, and *from the perspective of this relation* the parties are identical to each other . . . .[41]

In the history of the European west, this disentanglement from the needs of the group in favor of the primacy of the individual is seen as a triumph. It is here that the *demos* as an agglomeration of individuals can fully emerge. Yet this is not experienced as "liberatory" for many, neither when it takes place in ancient Greece, nor when the process is replicated in the colonies.

Anonymous individuals come to populate the Greek city-states and present themselves at the *agora*. Ste. Croix reminds us that the intellectual splendors of the city rely almost entirely on vast amounts of manual labor performed by the growing influx of Greek peasants. With the advent of money as coinage, there emerges a new category of laborer, the wage-earner. Homer occasionally speaks of *thetes*, laborers who work temporarily for basic maintenance (food, shelter) though not necessarily for what would be recognized as wages. In *The Odyssey*, Achilles claims the life of a *thes* is far worse than that of a slave: "A *thes*, not a slave, was the lowest creature on earth that

Achilles could think of."[42] According to the classicist, M. I. Finley, *thetes* were "unattached propertyless laborers who worked for hire [. . .]." In his view, "the terrible thing about a *thes* was his lack of attachment, his not belonging."[43] Though the appearance of *thetes* in the Homeric age is unusual,[44] the invention of coinage makes wage-labor much more widespread. The implication is that whereas the slave is provided with shelter and sustenance and a measure of stability, the *thes* must acquire these things as best he can with the equivalent coinage, introducing a (greater) element of precariousness, as *thetes* are typically homeless. At the same time, numerous scholars have suggested a continuity between slaves, *thetes*, and wage-laborers—such that the differences are of degree and not kind.[45]

Prostitution is greatly enabled by the advent of coinage.[46] Brothels and bordellos spring up around the *agora* and they house "slave-girls" as well as young men.[47] Prostitutes are "under compulsion" though they may also be compensated.[48] Each brothel is an extension of the larger *agora* nearby, in that it likewise constitutes an emptied space with no purpose other than to facilitate the exchange. They are "public" in that the cubicles in which the *pornai*, or prostitutes, sit and receive buyers can be freely accessed from the streets and are open to any individual with enough money. In fact, Seaford notes a long-standing trope about the continuity of purpose between money and prostitution. He considers the development of the fiduciary promise to be the most significant aspect of the parallel, since the big Other replaces oral-cultural connectedness. He writes,

> The guarantee provided by coinage tends to enable fleeting transactions with complete strangers. Money (especially as coinage) tends to promote an indefinite network of indiscriminate exchange that transcends the defined personal relations to be found within family, within various social groupings.[49]

He describes both money and prostitutes as "impersonally promiscuous" and attributes a unique symmetry to this particular exchange in that both elements ("coitus and money") are by definition non-selective and anonymous.

Higher-priced companions, known as *hetaerae*, are distinguished from *pornai,* or brothel-slaves. Patrons of *pornai* would be compelled to leave their private residences to enact the exchange, whereas *hetaerae* entertained at one's domicile.[50] *Pornai* could also be distinguished from the *hetaerae* "by the number and anonymity of her partners, as well as by the fact that she could not choose them; she sells herself to anyone who wishes [to have] her."⁵¹ Rampant prostitution—the ancient Athenian conditions of which are described by one historian as "abject" and "slavish"⁵²—provides the most complete example of the annihilation of context. Money must first be made non-perishable—that is, capable of being accumulated, with enough of it to become disposable—before it can be exchanged for coitus quite so systematically. Structures adjacent to the *agora*, such as the labyrinthine edifices of cubicles or large rooms in Athens,⁵³ will have to be erected for the purpose. Finally, the *pornai* themselves will have to become sufficiently without context to exist in this manner. Though Graeber is not addressing prostitutes or *thetes* here but slaves, he describes them in similar terms, as "equivalent," anonymous persons. According to Graeber, a "slave" is someone who has been torn out of her context. Her very status as slave indicates that she is unusually subject to violence. He writes,

> To make a human being an object of exchange, one woman equivalent to another, for example, requires first of all ripping her from her context; that is, tearing her away from that web of relations that makes her the unique conflux of relations that she is, and thus, into a generic value capable of being added and subtracted and used as a means to measure debt. This requires a certain violence.⁵⁴

The circulation of people and things resembles the orphaning of the text of which Plato spoke: alphabetic writing meanders through the streets without a Father to claim or defend it. Graeber further compares slaves to orphans as a result of the drive to forge equivalence and commensurability:

> To make something saleable, in a human economy, one needs to first rip it from its context. That's what slaves are: people stolen from the community that made them what they are. As strangers to their new communities, slaves no longer had mothers, fathers, kin of any sort . . . . A man could buy a slave, a woman kidnapped in a raid from a distant country. Slaves, after all, had not parents, or could be treated as if they didn't; they had been forcibly removed from all those networks of mutual obligation and debt. . . . This was why they could be bought and sold.⁵⁵

This violent dislocation from context Marx termed the "prehistoric stage of capitalism"⁵⁶ in which masses of agricultural dwellers were expropriated from the land so that they became free and "unattached"[57]—which is to say anonymous and without context. In the final sections of *Capital Vol. I*, Marx adds a brief history of the legislation regulating wage laborers. The *thetes* and *pornai* of Athens are the precursors to Marx's "vagabonds." Marx explains that once the peasants were separated from their means of subsistence, they could not be immediately integrated into the structures and disciplines of wage labor, yet neither did they have a means to sustain themselves. He writes,

> The proletariat created . . . by the forcible expropriation of the people from the soil . . . could not possibly be absorbed by the nascent manufacturers as fast as it was thrown upon the world. On the other hand, these men, suddenly dragged from their wonted mode of life, could not as suddenly adapt themselves to the discipline of their new condition. They were turned *en masse* into beggars, robbers, vagabonds.[58]

In order to establish control over the influx of now landless workers, the crown would rely on "bloody legislation" that treated them as "'voluntary' criminals."[59]

During the reign of Henry VIII, "sturdy vagabonds,"—those who are capable of physical labor but have no situation—will be "tied to the cart-tail and whipped until the blood streams from their bodies," at which point they will be forced to swear an oath that they will return to their places of birth and "put themselves to labour."[60] Yet the reason they are dislocated is because their birthplaces have been expropriated and enclosed; there is nowhere to return. On the second offense they will receive another whipping "and [have] half an ear sliced off." [61] On the third they will be put to death. By the time of Edward VI's reign, the law maintained that "All vagabonds shall be branded."[62] These methods of branding would also take place upon returning the vagabond to his birthplace, as though laborers are both required to "circulate"—as anonymous—yet also prohibited from doing so for the same reason. Branding inscribes the vagabonds, not with names but permanent "identity markers" all the same:

> If it happens that a vagabond has been idling about for three days, he is to be taken to his birthplace, branded with a red-hot iron with the letter V on the breast and be set to work, in chains, in the streets or at some other labour. If the vagabond gives a false birthplace, he is then to become the slave for life

of this place, of its inhabitants, or its corporation, and to be branded with an S.[63]

The "S" may be branded either on the back or the forehead. If branding is not enough to keep track of him, "every master may put an iron ring round the neck, arms or legs of his slave, by which to know him more easily and to be more certain of him."[64] For while decontextualization fosters circulation and anonymity, this also means the appearance of strangers who may or may not be trustworthy. Iron rings and branding provide the information that context has removed. In the reign of James I, the tradition of branding was continued to include an "R" on the left shoulder for incorrigible rogues. "R" for rogue; "S" for slave; "V" for vagabond.

Marx cites these protracted processes of overt violence as *preparation* for the discipline of wage-labor, something we assume developed in Western Europe spontaneously or as the evolution of thrift and self-denial. Marx describes similar laws in France, in which "every man in good health from 16 to 60 years of age, without means of subsistence and not practicing a trade, is to be sent to the galleys."[65] The Netherlands and the United Provinces exact the same control. According to Marx, the "equivalence" of persons, especially in the contractual relations between those who must sell their labor-power on the market and those in a position to purchase it, is always one of extensive and long-standing violence.

The logic of alphabet reaches its full expression in capitalism, but it is already operating in germinal form from the so-called Axial Age. We see the continuations of the Platonic Forms in the words of Marx on value: "The price or money-form of commodities is, like their form of value generally, a form quite distinct from their palpable bodily form; it is, therefore, a purely ideal or mental form."[66] And we can connect coinage itself to this principle—coinage being converted into the money-form to constitute price. As discussed previously, coinage is different from earlier types of money because it operates as a material substitution for the immaterial "true" value it represents, and which exists elsewhere in an incorporeal condition. It participates on both the theoretical and actual planes. Whatever the state of disrepair of the physical object, and its minimal actual worth, it will still be accepted as valid, that is "honored," by the big Other in whose name it has been minted. Greek letters are random shapes; that random shapes can "refer" to anything at all requires the same basis of an ongoing, implicit guarantee from the big Other to secure its functioning.

Though such "values" are invisible, they are expressed through their "equivalence" to another commodity which does not circulate in the same way as the others, but only reflects itself back onto itself. Money, too, becomes a commodity: "But money itself has no price. In order to put it on an equal footing with all other commodities in this respect, we should be obliged to equate it *to itself as its own equivalent.*"[67] This operation must be confined to the imaginary realm. Marx even says that the price, or value, exists only "in the heads" of the commodities and has to be materialized by affixing price-tags to their bodies.[68] Value is hypothetical. No matter the imaginary value a commodity may bear in the form of a price-tag, that amount remains theoretical, until the point at which the merchant actually sells it to someone else and completes the transaction. Marx stresses that there is no guarantee of this ever taking place, in which case "value" remains unrealized and unexpressed.

The Greek letters are also symbols of themselves as their own equivalents. They stand only for a unit that does not exist independently of the exercise, that is, phonemes, just as the "value" or price of commodities does not exist independently of their comparison to other commodities (or a single commodity in isolation, such as gold). Both operations—valuation and alphabetization—are strictly imaginary in this way, as Marx points out, and both have to be forced into a material incarnation they otherwise lack.

The formula C-M-C (Commodity-Money-Commodity) is not unlike the localized use of a Hebrew syllabary. The syllabary could stand in for the middle term, "M," because it is simply a "medium of circulation." Marx discusses how C-M-C begins and ends with a commodity and that this, like the use of a syllabary, is self-contained, extinguishing itself as it occurs. I decide that a pair of shoes (C) has lingered too long in my closet. I sell it on eBay. With the money (M) deposited in my account by the buyer, I take my friends out that evening for vegan sushi (C). Marx states, "The circuit C-M-C starts with one commodity, and finishes with another, which falls out of circulation and into consumption . . . [this] is its end and aim."[69]

The point at which money becomes not a medium of exchange but a self-impelling movement marks its transformation from coinage into capital: "The circuit M-C-M, on the contrary, commences with money and ends with money. Its leading motive, and the goal that attracts it, is therefore mere exchange-value."[70] In the equation, C-M-C, I begin with shoes and end with vegan sushi. (I accept money from the buyer on eBay and promptly pass it along to the sushi proprietor, who passes it along to someone else).

With M-C-M, however, I begin and end with the same substance, what Marx terms, "the shape assumed by its own value."[71] As Marx points out, a person would never launch the circuit M-C-M if she began and ended with the same *quantity* of money. For example, "To exchange £100 for [vegan sushi], and then this same [vegan sushi] again for £100, is merely a roundabout way of exchanging money for money, the same for the same, and appears to be an operation just as purposeless as it is absurd."[72] A portion of money is only distinguishable from another portion by the amount. I begin with £100 and buy vegan sushi. Rather than consume it, I sell it and end with £110. Marx explains that at this point, I do not extract the additional £10. It is not as though the £100 and the £10 are separated and move in different directions. Instead, the process begins over again but now with a different, incrementally larger, quantity (£110).

Because the process merely instantiates itself in order to begin again, it has no endpoint. The added value (£10) is in effect non-discrete; it simply combines with the original value (£100) to become the new starting point (£110) of yet another transaction: "The value originally advanced, therefore, not only remains intact while in circulation, but adds to itself a surplus-value or *expands itself*. It is this movement that converts it into capital."[73] This movement, and this movement alone, is the key: "For the movement, in the course of which it adds surplus-value, *is its own movement*, its expansion, therefore, is automatic expansion. Because it is value, it has acquired the occult quality of being able to add value to itself."[74]

Eric Havelock locates the "magic" of the universalizing impulse—or what he calls the "technological secret" of alphabetics—in the invention of the "phoneme" since deploying a system which "could identify the phonemes of any language with accuracy" thus presents the possibility of "placing two or several languages within the same type of script and so greatly accelerating the process of cross-translation between them."[75] Both alphabet and capital are designed to forge commensurabilities; they spread and thereby assimilate to themselves all that is analphabetic and non-capitalist. Both do this through a process of translation or conversion. It is no coincidence that coinage and alphabet are invented at roughly the same time and in roughly the same place.

Similarly, we could argue that writing does not ensure the eventual end of writing. Rather writing is self-perpetuating. No matter with what insight, what precision or what finality one writes, there will always be more to write—not because there is inherently more that "must" be written, but because writing, like capital, "begins and ends and begins with itself again," and in this respect, always entails its own continuation. Every act of writing is its own "spontaneous generation."[76] A generalized "writing" that does not and cannot end is much more important than any specific thing that is ever written. Very little that is written "needs" to be written. Likewise, commodities themselves are perfectly irrelevant to the real action, which is incessant movement. Marx says as much:

> The circulation of capital, suddenly presents itself as an independent substance, endowed with a motion of its own, passing through a life-process of its own, in which money and commodities are mere forms which it assumes and casts off in turn. Nay, more: instead of simply representing the relations of commodities, it enters now, so to say, *into private relations with itself.*[77]

Alphabetic signs always incline toward doing away with referents altogether; the sign does not need the referent because *it is a substitute for it.* The sign effectively supplants the referent, to the extent that it ever marked a correspondence in the first place (perhaps a nominal one). As Saussure notes, there is no natural connection between the word "sister" and the female sibling to which it ostensibly refers; there is nothing sister-like about "sister." Furthermore, "the idea of 'sister' is not linked by any inner relationship to the succession of sounds . . . . It could be represented equally by just any other sequence."[78] In fact, the existence of a concrete reality from which signs draw their meaning need scarcely even be maintained. Likewise, commodities and money fluctuate and constantly change their forms from one into the other and back again, only because capital has long since entered into "private relations with itself." The circulation of capital is not driven by "demand" or even "supply," not the desires of consumers, or the improvements of technology, or the satisfaction of human needs, or any other reason apart from a movement that generates more movement: "The circulation of money as capital is [. . .] an end in itself, for the expansion of value takes place only within this constantly renewed movement. The circulation of capital *has therefore no limits.*"[79] This is akin to saying that "the movement becomes *interminable.*"[80] To begin and end with money is, therefore, "never to end at all."[81]

Persons under such conditions adjust to this chronic movement accordingly. They learn to relate not to a world of referents, or as Ong says, "the plenum of experience," for this has little bearing on "real" social activity.

What is "real" takes place through those incarnations of "ideas in the mind" that are alphabetic texts and money. One relates signs to other signs, commodities to other commodities. It is this realm of the fantasy "real" that Marx describes as generating relations between persons as a "form of a relation between things,"[82] which is to say, between commodities qua signs. Is this not in part why Lacan says, "a signifier is what represents a subject for another signifier"?[83]

Both sign-relations and commodity-relations are products of the Greek code.

Interlude

KUBRICK, REDUX

Let us return briefly to the scene in which Moon-Watcher, accompanied by the blare of the tone poem, comes to apprehend the tapir bone as a tool. In Kubrick's allegory, the emergence of the tool is at one and the same time the emergence of the weapon. We might also expand on the ways in which the tool-cum-weapon functions as a "model" or as the stimulus to a multiply-branching virtual set of realities. In one, Moon-Watcher ignores the weapon. In another, he stores the weapon, but he does not use it. In still another, he carries it in case of an attack by a big cat, but he uses it to no other end. In yet another, he carries it for protection against big cats *and* uses it to turn tapirs into meat, but he hesitates to turn it on other apes. And finally, he defends himself against attack, gorges on fresh tapir and uses it at will on others of his own species. This array of simultaneous, possible worlds does not exist prior to the apprehension of the tool. Yet Moon-Watcher, once fully developed into *Homo sapiens,* will retroactively posit himself as the originator, the source of mastery over all other creatures, including those like himself. But he will be in error. The *tool* (or at best, the reflexive interaction between tool and ape) is the "originator," but its emergence is neither necessary nor even likely. It is pure accident.

If we switch points-of-view to that of the other troop at the waterhole, what can be said of the sudden incursion of murderous violence upon their own *Umwelt,* their creaturely lifeworld? Prior to the appearance of the tool-bearers, there had been antagonistic relations, to be sure, but the troops had not degenerated into direct physical harm. Writing (here, the analogue to Kubrick's tool-weapon) provides the means to concoct a proliferation of virtual models and then to physically instantiate one or another of them. Only the final two possibilities outlined above involved the obliteration of the "competing" realities. *2001: A Space Odyssey* implies that through choosing the final possibility—which affirms the Dawn of Man in and through nonessential violence (against ourselves)—we have negated the other four possibilities. They are not just non-actualized lines of potential, which are still possible but suspended. They are actively foreclosed. *The last is the only reality irreconcilable with any of the others.* As such, it is the extreme version, which may account for the divergence of Man from all other organisms. Yet so was this choice the fatal error: "Once upon a time, says Nietzsche, in a cosmos glittering forth innumerable solar systems, there was a star on which 'clever animals invented knowledge . . . [however] after nature had drawn a few breaths the star grew cold, and the clever animals had to die.'"[1]

In choosing violence through the prostheses of technology, so do those prostheses engender violence in turn. Eventually, Kubrick suggests, they will turn against the very ones who animated them. The will to expansion, technology, and violence undercuts its own persistence, and even seems to overwhelm survival itself. When HAL sings "Daisy Bell"—"*Daisy . . . Daisy . . . Give me your answer, do*"—the childishness of the tune hearkens back to our own elaborate programming in childhood. For a future society that has come to suppress and deny its inaugural aggression—witness the beautifully orchestrated conversation between Dr. Heywood Floyd and the Russian scientists at the international space station, in which conflict is sublimated through politeness and formality—the breakdown of HAL 9000 signifies the failure of techno-capitalist expansionism to rectify itself and to carry on: "*2001* is a film about a world where all aggressive behavior is everywhere suppressed, policed and erased, and where it coldly comes back to haunt us through Hal's madness."[2] Kubrick's Nietzschean trajectory extends a long way, from the cradle of the hominids to the apex of civilization. What Zarathustra did not foretell, however, was that it would end in HAL's erratic and self-destructive final stages. The written—the coded—realm would have to collapse under the weight of its own contradictions before Dave Bowman could proceed through the "birth canal" of the stargate.

6

Letters of Blood and Fire

Writing was granted literally universalizing and literally textualizing functions:
it wove a discourse that encompassed or generated mankind as a whole.

—FRIEDRICH KITTLER, *DISCOURSE NETWORKS 1800/1900*[1]

A virtual reality is not so much a predicative statement about the world as a
formative experience.

—RONALD SHUSTERMAN, "VIRTUAL REALITIES AND
AUTOTELIC ART"[2]

And the history of this, their expropriation, is written in the annals of mankind
in letters of blood and fire.

—KARL MARX, *CAPITAL, VOL. I*[3]

In *How to Do Things with Words*, J. L. Austin seeks to replace the assumption
that utterances are statements that "describe" a state of affairs, and do so
either truly or falsely, with the notion that utterances are performatives that
do things, either felicitously or infelicitously. We can take Austin's approach
to mean that all utterances are performative in one way or another. They
all intervene or act upon situations, rather than simply make observations
about them. Though on occasion he includes "written words" within the
scope of his argument, he deals almost exclusively with the occasions of
speech-acts. What Austin does not acknowledge is the degree to which writing must have already laid the foundation for each one of his examples, well
in advance of their execution, in order for them to have any performative

force at all. Without the structural support provided by writing, the performative would fail. What Austin mistakes as the performativity of *speech* is an aftereffect, a kind of echo, of the much more formidable performativity of *writing*.

His examples of the performative are as follows:

(E. a) 'I do (sc. take this woman to be my lawful wedded wife)'—as uttered in the course of the marriage ceremony.

(E. b) 'I name this ship the Queen Elizabeth'—as uttered when smashing the bottle against the stem.

(E. c) 'I give and bequeath my watch to my brother' as occurring in a will.

(E. d) 'I bet you sixpence it will rain tomorrow.'[4]

Austin's point is that language is never just reporting something but is actively involved in shaping it. But what of the prior literate and literary infrastructure that imparts meaning to these speech acts, that is, that endows them with their performative power? Without the multiform written pillars for these acts at every stage, they are not acts but games. Games conform to rules and conventions, but they have no performative social power. Austin unwittingly obscures the notary publics and the officiants; the issuers of marriage licenses and marriage certificates; the inheritance and estate lawyers; the probate attorneys; the bills of sale, the titles, and their preparers; the proof of loan payments; even social gambling laws and their enforcers. In the conversation about performativity, one must acknowledge the multitude of writers and writing and written artifacts that have gone into producing the state of affairs in which it is necessary and customary to utter the phrase, "I do,"—without which, "I do" is no more binding (that is, no more performative) than children engaging in make-believe.

On rare occasions when Austin does inquire into the conditions of existence surrounding or preceding the circumstances of utterance, he does not mention writing but only vague "essentials":

Speaking generally, it is always necessary that the *circumstances* in which the words are uttered should be in some way, or ways, *appropriate* . . . . Thus, for naming the ship, it is essential that I should be the person appointed to name her, for (Christian) marrying, it is essential that I should not already be married . . . .[5]

Without writing to erect the "essential" circumstances beforehand, the performativity of the *speech act* is marginal, inconsequential, even perhaps a formality after the fact, when compared to the enormity of alphabetic performativity.

Austin has not grasped the extent to which writing has already *modelled* a world in which speech-acts could bear sufficient performativity. Even Hobbes appreciated the fact that Covenants were only valid because of a preexisting (literate) infrastructure that would readily enforce them. Nietzsche, too, spoke of "promising"—not as a self-contained speech act, even within felicitous conditions—but as an orientation onto the future which already presupposed a certain type of subject, one which was itself forged through various methods of discipline and guilt. Of modelling, the semiotician Juri Lotman explains, "*Modelling activity* is human activity in creating models. In order that the results of this activity could be taken as analogues of an object, they have to obey certain (intuitively or consciously established) rules of analogy and, therefore, be related to one modelling system or another."[6] One way to think of the performativity of alphabetic writing is as a modelling activity. The alphabet is a "secondary modelling system"[7] that is premised on the idea that spoken language is yet another model (a primary modelling system) on which the secondary system is predicated. What is unusual about the alphabet is the extent to which it creates the object it supposedly represents at the same time that it duplicates and replaces it. Every time the model iterates itself again (reiterates), it expands.

In his description of models, Lotman uses the phrase "play-type" model to refer to children's activity, though not exclusively, and we may note the doubled valence of the term "play" as evoking a theatrical production as well. Lotman writes, "In a play-type model, each of its elements and the model itself as a whole, being identical to itself, is more than just itself."[8] The "more than just itself" is partly an instance of the fact that "play models randomness, incomplete determination, the probability of processes and phenomena."[9] The model extends itself by first replicating itself (the model models itself as a whole) and then by opening onto the "more." This is loosely related to the contemporary coding activity known as "defensive programming."[10] Models program themselves defensively in order to provide for what they cannot yet foresee ("incomplete determination") and for what they will never foresee ("randomness"), but for which they can still provide code (either as vacant "space," a placeholder, etc.). Each execution of the model is itself plus a quantity q. In this way, the model is never "fin-ished," especially insofar as it purports to model the world.

What Lotman describes in modeling activity is also a form of recursion. The alphabet is recursive, as opposed to only repetitive or iterative. Derrida argues that iterability is the most characteristic feature of writing: "both the possibility and the impossibility of writing [is] its essential iterability."[11] Per-haps because Derrida does not recognize a difference between alphabetics and every other form of writing, he omits *recursion* from his discussion. Iter-ability tends toward homeostasis not expansion. In this, iterability is not so different from repetition. Corballis gives the example of repetition by not-ing the first line of Chapter 9 in A.A. Milne's *Winnie the Pooh*: "It rained and it rained and it rained."[12] Though it contains the potential to repeat "and it rained" forever, it is not recursive in that each additional "and it rained" is not impelled or "driven by the previous one; it is simply added at the dis-cretion of the writer."[13] Iteration is sometimes mistaken for recursion, and in mathematical terminology, it indeed falls under "general recursive func-tions."[14] However, iterability tends to draw upon previous input but then to discard it in the output. This creates a looping effect, but it is a loop that does not enlarge itself. Repetition, iteration, and recursion all have the potential to continue forever. But only recursion uses the prior instance of itself to then *expand*. A common definition of recursion is that "it is a procedure that calls itself," which is to say, it "takes its own output as the next input."[15] Human language may contain recursive structures;[16] the simple definition of recursion is that it is "a constituent that contains a constituent of the same kind."[17] Theoretically, this form of embedding within speech could also take place endlessly, but as we have seen, the cognitive constraints of working memory eventually limit how long such a thing could go on. With writing, however, recursion need never stop. As opposed to iterative looping, recur-sion creates "a loop that can be extended indefinitely to create sequences or structures of unbounded length or complexity."[18]

We may note the resemblance between the alphabet as a recursive (modelling) activity and Marx's description of capital as value increasing itself by becoming "world-embracing": "The modern history of capital dates from the creation in the 16th century of a world-embracing commerce and a world-embracing market."[19] From within the model of global capitalism, "the appropriation of ever more and more wealth in the abstract" becomes the "sole motive" of its practitioners. The movement, "the restless never-ending process of profit-making alone,"[20] is what drives the expansion, the "world-embracing" imperative, of the model. Even individual capitalists function merely "as capital personified and endowed with consciousness and a will."[21] (In a similar vein, we might say that writing writes itself and that literate subjects are nodal points for the self-extension of the alphabet.) The formula M-C-M works in precisely this way, since it is in fact, as Marx indicates, "M-C-M$_1$, where M$_1$ = M + D M = the original sum advanced, plus an increment."[22]

Deleuze and Guattari describe the ceaseless movement of capital as it seeks to encompass the globe with the verbs "displace and enlarge."[23] Likewise Marx states, as if to describe a model:

Value therefore now becomes value in process, money in process, and, as such, capital. It comes out of circulation, enters into it again, preserves and multiplies itself within its circuit, comes back out of it with expanded bulk, and begins the same round ever afresh. M-M$_1$, money which begets money.[24]

Deleuze and Guattari note that

capitalism is continually confronting limits and barriers that are interior and immanent to itself, and that, precisely because they are immanent, let themselves be overcome only provided they are reproduced on a wider scale (always more reterritorialization—local, world-wide, planetary).[25]

This would suggest that the parameters of the model are not deterred by their internal obstructions but are in fact invigorated by them. That a model should allow for the unknown in advance creates something of a paradox and yet this is the source of its strength. It patterns and allows for numerous enough (imagined) contingencies—as Lotman says, it works through probabilities of processes—that it can successfully defer its own demise for another length of time and another.

As soon as it is invented, the alphabet begins cataloguing possible scenarios and correlating them to possible outcomes. When it does so in a way that is beautiful, it becomes literature. When it does so in a way that analyzes scenarios that have already taken place, it becomes history. When it does so in a way that categorizes and predicts natural phenomena, it becomes science, and so on and so forth. The Greek alphabet is a secondary-modelling system that maintains within itself the idea of a primary modelling system that it simply reflects—and that with each iteration, it reflects more faithfully and with greater accuracy that which it models. The alphabet, moreover, allows for memorizing only its code, and not the data—the iterations of itself—that it generates, which is part of the radical nature of the technology. This is how it avoids the "storage" problem of individual memory. Once the code is learned, and the decoding and encoding behavior habituated to the point of automaticity, working memory ceases to be an issue. A non-literate culture, meanwhile, cannot duplicate or maintain this explosion of information. The digital age sees an exaggeration of this effect: an exponential multiplication of data, the effects of algorithmic and unmitigated branching. And it is simply the culmination of a trajectory that was already launched from the time of the Greek invention.

The Greek technology allows for memorizing only itself, not information, as that is suddenly available at all times. Alongside the alphabet, "the nature of memory must have changed: you did not memorize [information], you memorized a code that gave you instant and permanent access to [that information]."[26] Plato argued that writing would destroy memory, but arguably all of (alphabetized and digitized) human memory is currently accessible.

The alphabetized brain does not have to "remember" much, once it is fully inscribed, that is, programmed, with the twenty-six letters. (Rather than remember, it *runs*.) Instead, it constantly carries out imaginary scenarios which it never stops doing, not even in sleep. For this reason, Daniel Dennett calls our popular understanding of consciousness the "Cartesian Theater," since it is the "stage" whereupon one watches the endless scenarios run.

We have argued that the Greek theater operated as a means to process and domesticate the disruptive new technology. Much can be understood about Western alphabetic consciousness, Derrick de Kerckhove contends, from examining the Greek stage. In the following passage, Lotman refers to "play" as an embodied simulation activity within the model. We might say that Lotman describes *late literacy* whereas De Kerckhove is interested in early literacy, before certain norms have become interiorized. To *internalize* play-type models, one must have learned how as a result of repeated exposure to experiential, interactive and imaginary versions. Lotman's mention of death situates play within an ambivalent spectrum that has "consequence-free" activity on the one hand and extremely high stakes, simulated or not, on the other. Consequences are always partly corrected for and partly indeterminate in the model:

Play has great importance in learning a type of behavior, as it permits the modelling of situations where the participation of an unprepared individual would put him in a risk of death, or situations, the creation of which does not depend on the will of the learning individual. Here, a conventional (playful) situation is a substitute for a non-conventional (real) one. This is extremely important. First, the learning individual gets the possibility to freeze the situation in time (change his move, "move again"). Second, he learns to model the situation in his consciousness, as he will envisage a certain amorphous system of reality as a game, the rules of which can and must be formulated. Related to this is another important feature: play gives a person the chance of a conditional victory over an unconquerable (for instance, death).[27]

Lotman's description equally well describes combat simulation for the soldier about to be deployed and the recess activities of small children. In the case of the latter, we may note her already-literate orientation, such that she understands herself as able to "freeze time" and to replay it again. Oral cultures have no such mechanism. The literate "player," meanwhile, becomes a "natural" at "envisaging a certain amorphous system of *reality as a game*." The outcomes may be dire (i.e., one's own death) or they may be inconsequential or even amusing. The important thing is that one becomes adept at *playing them all*, playing out each imaginable scenario, before they actually occur. De Kerckhove regards the scenarios of the Greek theater as precisely such "similes of social interactions" which are "played out" before the eyes of the spectators "on a symbolical plane." In addition to providing imagined, didactic scenarios for the literate and the non-literate alike, the Greek stage featured "images of experience" which could be "tried out before they were actually lived." Consequently,

The stage could be conceived as a rehearsal area for many prototypes of experiences, attitudes, emotions and mental processes which were incarnated by the actors or the chorus and would become the basis for the Western way of life. The stage and all its contents would eventually be interiorized individually by each spectator and become what we call 'consciousness.'[28]

This is to take "consciousness" to mean the interpolation of the Cartesian theatre.

As with the term "play" and for that matter, "model," Lotman uses "art" broadly. He sees it as fundamentally mimetic. All these terms inform one another and work interchangeably. For "art" one could easily substitute "alphabetic writing" since for Lotman the primary criteria for "art" (as for writing) is that it acts as a secondary modelling system that refashions and enlarges a primary modelling system. His explanation delineates important features of the modeling activity of the European west:

> Therefore, art is always an analogue of reality (of an object), translated to the language of the given system. Therefore, art is always conventional and, at the same time, must be intuitively recognized as an analogue of a certain object, that is, it must be "similar" and "dissimilar" at the same time. Emphasizing only one of these two inseparable aspects breaks the modelling function of art. The formula of art is: "*I know that it is not what it depicts, but I clearly see that it is what it depicts.*"[29]

The theater semiotician, Keir Elam, refers to the use of "modelled" items that appear on the stage in terms of what he calls "sign-vehicles."[30] A "sign-vehicle" is a term for any object appearing onstage, be it an actor, a prop, scenery, a mask, etc. An object presented on a stage is automatically a symbol, though it is also an everyday object. For instance, a costume covers the body. But the specific choices that make up the costume also signal many other things besides. Though Elam does not say so, the sign-systems on stage exhibit a direct correlation to the structure of the alphabet. This is the case because of the limited "repertory of sign-vehicles," which he attributes to the essential "semiotic economy of the theatrical performance."[31] By reducing the number of sign-vehicles, one does not circumscribe the potential for meaning; she encourages it to multiply. Deliberately or not, fewer sign-vehicles function as a means "to generate a potentially unlimited range of cultural units, and this extremely powerful generative capacity on the part of the theatrical sign-vehicle is due in part to its connotative breadth."[32] It is not just what it is (denotation), it is everything it could possibly symbolize as well (connotation).

One theorist charted the illustrious careers of a handful of recurrent Western stage props: the Communion wafer, the skull, the bloody handkerchief, the fan, and the gun.[33] By utilizing only twenty-six letters, the ambiguity and resulting proliferations of interpretation impart to alphabetic writing the illusion of vast regions of "meaning," and the satisfying endlessness of positing related theories. What Elam refers to as the ever-present denotative-connotative dialectic at work in all sign-vehicles is only possible in alphabetic cultures.[34] We saw how verbal precision increases dramatically in literate societies and how such increases are institutionalized through the creation of orthography. Dictionaries are literate inventions that place an emphasis on using some words to describe other words (denotation), while simultaneously establishing a profound basis of ambiguity at the root of all inscription. This indeterminacy and plurality converge to form connotation, or as Elam writes,

> This accounts, furthermore, for the polysemic character of the theatrical sign: a given vehicle may bear not one but n second-order meanings at any point in the performance continuum (a costume, for example, may suggest socioeconomic, psychological and even moral characteristics).[35]

Let us consider further how the dual-register of objects on a Greek stage can function as simple objects as well as complex symbols, that is, as themselves concretely and themselves in the abstract. Short for stage "property," a "prop" denotes a bolster or material aid for the modelling project: "Performance props can 'animate' the plot, provide a 'visual shorthand,' they can 'characterize' stage figures, they can 'resemble' their referents, and they can 'anchor scenes in dramatic reality.'"[36] In no previous historical circumstance, we might argue, had objects—free-floating, that is, as fully separated from subjects—been transplanted onto a context-free zone (the empty container of the stage) as themselves context-free.

We may take for example several uprooted trees, potted and densely situated on the stage. They are still trees, though now they "stand for" a forest through which the characters may amble and deliver their lines. These objects announce that they are themselves in addition to a reduced (symbolic) instance of a fuller circumstance that exists elsewhere: "*I know that it is not what it depicts, but I clearly see that it is what it depicts.*" Instead of meaningfully arranging foliage on a stage, consider what would happen if the audience and the players simply took themselves to a nearby (real) forest and enacted the drama there. This would inevitably be disappointing in that the trees in a forest are simply themselves and nothing else, whereas a tree on a stage is itself, that is, "identical to itself and more than just itself."[37] Literate persons are accustomed to the "more than just itself." So are persons who live under capitalism.

In this way, stage props are not unlike commodities. A commodity is itself but also a symbol of a (vast, unlimited) value-structure that is elsewhere, all-encompassing, and invisible. Props are material and yet they are seemingly abstract, context-free, circulating, mysterious—just like commodities. We prefer the symbolic instance to the fuller "real" instance, though which is which may shift, particularly on the stage. The symbolic somehow appeals to the audience to the extent that the "real" can either be "real" or "unreal." Whichever one it ends up being (real or unreal) is ultimately of no consequence or even interest:

> Even these real objects are not viewed by the audience as real things, but only as signs of signs, or signs of things. If, for example, an actor playing the role of a millionaire wears a diamond ring, the audience will regard it as a sign of his great wealth and not care whether the diamond is real or a fake. . . . It is interesting that on the stage a real thing, for example, a real diamond, is often only a sign of a sign of a thing (for example, the sign of the wealth of a character) and not the sign of the thing itself. On the other hand in a theatre performance the most schematic sign of the most primitive scenery can denote the thing itself.[38]

Splashes of green paint can suffice for a forest and in some respects, will operate more effectively in the economy of sign-vehicles than actual greenery would. As with the relocation to a literal forest for a theatrical performance, the "real" thing can be far less captivating or appealing than the symbol. A fake diamond in a play, exaggerated for effect, can be more mesmerizing than a real one which has been borrowed for the performance. The crude symbol is compelling; in many respects, it becomes *more real* within the diegesis of the play than the non-symbolized thing itself.

Mapping is yet another alphabetic, modelling activity in which the most "schematic signs" and "primitive scenery" may actually be preferable to more "realistic" depictions. Maps do not have to be terribly specific in order to serve their purposes. The roughest outline of a bush suggests vegetation, and nothing more than a thin wavy line is perfectly adequate to designate a river. It is often the case that the more detailed a map becomes the more difficult it is to read *as a map*. Recall Baudrillard quoting Borges on the preposterous nature of a map so excellent that it becomes the same size as the territory itself.[39] Maps are a form of alphabetic writing and they resemble theatrics in the sense that their symbology is limited—even scant. Again, they suppose space is akin to Benjamin's time: "homogeneous" and "empty."[40]

As with alphabetics, literates are willing to sacrifice much for the brevity and mobility of the twenty-six letters. A map conceives of space in a highly specific way; it offers a theory of space. The map draws upon and produces the very territory it supposedly charts, just as a play (as Lotman's "text within a text") draws on the "real life" beyond the stage, from which it differentiates itself *as theatrical.*

Lotman observes how such interaction with objects (sign-vehicles) provides a double (temporal) register through which the alphabetic subject is expected to realize herself. Doubling does not depict (iteration), it generates (recursion). "Players" in the play-type model operate at the level of the concrete and the abstract at one and the same time:

> Play is the *simultaneous* realization (not their *alternation in time!*) of practical and conventional behaviour. The player must simultaneously remember that he is participating in a conventional (not real) situation (a child knows that the tiger in front of him is a toy and is not afraid of it), and not remember it (when playing, the child considers the toy tiger to be a real one). The child is only afraid of the living tiger, the only thing he is not afraid of is the stuffed tiger; he is *slightly afraid* of a striped gown thrown on a chair and *representing* a tiger in the game, that is, he *simultaneously* is and is not afraid of it.[41]

Lotman insists that the spectator/actor—she will be both in turn—does not shift back and forth in time between "reality" and "symbolism." His remarkable conjecture is that she must maintain both (self-cancelling propositions) at once. The play-type model is not reserved for "play" alone—that is, for the diversions of children—but as a training ground for alphabetic and capitalist life, in which players must "remember" and "not remember" at the same time. The only way to do so successfully is to assume, in every situation, that there are only symbols and behave accordingly. Because to behave as if there were no symbols is to be functionally disabled. It is safest to behave as if the real things had been substituted with the not real. Substitution is the mark of the model: "A model is an analogue of an object of perception that substitutes it in the process of perception."[42] This suggests one need not ever distinguish because the substitution has happened already in the act of perceiving. The mode of the model is to expand, which is to say, produce. It not only substitutes but substitutes "productively." Because the secondary model (alphabet) duplicates itself as the primary model (language), the oscillation itself, the movement, enlarges the model, however slightly, through every permutation. The child must learn to manage such movement if she is to keep up as an adult. The point of Lotman's scenario is that "the ability to play means mastering such twofold behavior."[43] If one does not understand that the uprooted, potted and purposely arranged plants on the theater stage *stand for* the "forest" then she cannot comport herself in alphabetic, capitalist culture. By contrast, if I never acknowledge that there are "real trees" in "real forests" to which the theatrical props correspond, I am not unduly hindered in my full-fledged participation in alphabetic culture. In order to thrive within the model, I should always err on the side of behaving as if the real were not real. In this way, I master twofold behavior by making it a single behavior.

We might ask, what is the status of the actual tiger? Not the toy, nor the idea, nor the fantasy, nor the striped gown, but the animal? In the model, strictly speaking, referents effectively do not exist. They needn't. When *tiger* appears in the play-type simulations of children, it is as a composite symbol called up to elicit excitation in the form of fear, thrill, adventure, exoticism, nature. If we were to encounter the rather desolate creature behind bars in the city zoo, even *it* would be a composite symbol—rather than a sentient being, because that is the only way it can figure in the model. We may perceive the tiger as "real" (she is breathing, she is blinking, we can identify her genus and species, we "know what we are looking at" when we encounter her), but she is also *not real* (we have only a vague sense of her "consistency," her persistence in time when we are not looking at her, and so on). She is in effect on a blank stage, and this is not so different from looking at her in a photograph on a different stage. When we fix our gaze on the next animal in the following cage (the orangutan, for example), the tiger has ceased to exist, insofar as she did, for those few moments when we perceived her, admired her majesty, felt sorry for her, and walked away. "Tiger" is not real but not entirely unreal; its "reality," therefore, is "virtual."

This tiger is an amalgamation built of things we have encountered through the alphabet *about* her. It is not possible to apprehend her without the alphabetic apparatus producing our view, either in person or otherwise. Our gaze was already alphabetized before she entered our field of vision and thus already crowded with alphabetic facts and interpretations and connotative meanings about her. The role of the actor on the Greek stage is to present a composite "Man" just as the tiger in another setting will provide the composite, "wild animal."

Literate persons in the model become accustomed to understanding themselves as avatars on a virtual stage who ceaselessly observe themselves and make adjustments accordingly. This derives from Greek theatrics, according to De Kerckhove, who describes the function of the actor as being "primarily to project a detached, personalized and homogenous image of the human body . . . ."[44] By this, we may take him to mean an image of the human body as an extractable unit, a unit unto itself, severed from the oral-cultural whole and presented as a self-directed entity, *acting* (as in both pretending and imposing his will) upon an image of absolute space. Modern notions of cartography, geography and topography derive from Ptolemy, and Aeschylus is the dramatist of burgeoning ideas about "Man" as a self-conscious entity, loosed upon the world—that is, as a "player" upon a "stage." The actor or agent originates in Greek theatre, where

> a sort of imaginary 'self' predominantly visual in its representations will begin to invade *a perpetual montage* of experiences played and replayed before and after the actual interaction with the environment and with other persons.[45]

From the point of view of consciousness as an internal theater introjected by alphabetic writing, we may regard the actor, astride a "world" composed of absolute space, and engaged in repetitive simulations, as a defining feature of Western "Man."[46]

What of other persons in the model? What, for example, are non-Greeks? As the model spreads from alphabetic Europe to the rest of the world, what becomes of the non-alphabetic?

Real and not real.

IN ILLUSTRATION

Apropos of Austin's speech act theory, we could point to the extreme performativity of various written enunciations by the major European empires, such as Spain. One alphabetic act which became binding (and highly performative) as of April 30, 1492, was that of King Ferdinand and Queen Isabella, who accorded to a Genoan sailor, Cristobal Colón, those "privileges and prerogatives" associated with discovery and conquest.[47] Their signatures bore witness and would continue to do so in the absence of their royal bodies, with the words: "I, the King; I, the Queen." Cristobal Colón had been enacting and reenacting the scenes of his discovery of trade routes, riches, and generalized conquest since he was able to conceive them, and he convinced King Ferdinand and Queen Isabella to do the same.

Columbus conceived of his project to extend the model and find a route to the Indies because of the things *he read*. The historian Hugh Thomas imagines Columbus had encountered Seneca's assertion that one could sail from Spain to the Indies in a very short time. This was confirmed for him by Pierre d'Ailly's *Imago Mundi* which, because the author had read the same passage, implied that the size of the world was modest: "the Atlantic was narrow, [and] Seneca had been right to say that with a favorable wind one could cross it in a few days."[48] Apparently, Columbus wrote in the margins: "There is no reason to believe that the ocean covers half the earth." Thomas also mentions *The Description of Asia*, by Pope Pius II (Aeneas Silvius Piccolomini) who likewise believed one could gain passage to Asia by travelling west, and who characterized all seas as "navigable and all lands habitable."[49] And finally a letter by the Florentine Paolo del Pozzo Toscanelli to King Afonso V's chaplain included a map on which a path to China had been traced along a westward route.[50] Even more performative than the contents of Columbus's library, or the initiatory documents of Ferdinand and Isabella, would be the Papal Bull of 1493. It changes a vast expanse of the globe into the Spanish Empire through a few written words: "All islands and mainlands found and to be found, discovered and to be discovered towards the west and the south" become, in the Papal act of inscription, Spanish, and by extension Catholic, territory. The act of writing is also the

> drawing and establishing [of] a line from the Arctic pole, namely the north, to the Antarctic pole, namely the south, no matter whether the said mainlands and islands are found and to be found in the direction of India or towards any other quarter, the said line to be distant one hundred leagues towards the west and south from any of the islands commonly known as the Azores and Cape Verde are likewise the possession of Spain forever.[51]

Spain is already a litigious society, the lawyer-class being that from which many conquistadors, including Quesada and Cortés, are drawn. It should not surprise us that the conquerors were above all *writers*, that the Spanish conquest is one of the most written in human history, and that the demand for *relaciones* and *probanzas* creates an enormous alphabetic feedback loop between the administrators of the colonies in the Americas, the royal court of Sevilla, and the burgeoning literate publics of Western Europe. These documents are distributed widely and published in five languages for audiences that cannot consume enough of them.

The monarchy and papacy confer a performative title on Columbus, in the form of the *adelantado,* whereby he becomes "Admiral of the said Islands and Continent you shall so discover and conquer; and that you be our Admiral, Vice-Roy, and Governour in them, and that for the future, you may call and stile yourself D. Christopher Columbus . . . . By this our letter, [we] bestow on you the employments of Admiral, Vice-Roy, and perpetual Governour forever."[52] The paper is a license, again profoundly performative, which confers on the owner the status of *adelantado*, a medieval military title that literally meant "advance man" or "invader." It signified an implicit promise that the bearer would in all probability become a governor of whatever province he subdued and settled. Yet the *adelantado* itself is but the prompt, the incipit. The *probanza* engenders a true profusion of alphabetic writing, founding a new genre entirely, proto-autobiographic in form. Ostensibly addressed to the King and Queen from the Americas, thousands of *probanzas* fill the imperial archives at Seville, Madrid, Lima, Mexico City, and elsewhere. Most have likely never been read.[53] Bernal Díaz alone penned over six hundred pages detailing the Conquest of Mexico in addition to several *probanzas* he wrote in previous years.[54] Only the most elite and well-connected conquistadors' work was likely to be read, but still he must write them. As part of his duties all conquistadors were required to pen their *probanzas*, the purpose of which was twofold: firstly, it was a means to

> inform the monarch of newly acquired lands, especially if those lands contained the two elements most sought as the basis of colonization—settled native populations and precious metal. The other purpose was to petition for rewards in the form of offices, titles and pensions. Hence the Spanish name for the genre *probanza de mérito* (proof of merit).[55]

Almost all writing by conquistadors falls under this genre, either as letters (*cartas*), reports or accounts (*relaciones*), or hybrid forms of the two, *cartas de relación*.

The fact that the conquistadors were all equipped to record everything in alphabetic writing and did so voluminously—some, such as Cortés, with remarkable prose styles—speaks to a misperception that still clings to the conquistador myth, namely that these figures were outlaws, mercenaries, or "hard men" of some form or another. In fact, they were overwhelmingly low-level civil servants, university educated, and as such, they belonged to a literate elite. Even the later colonization of Panama, Peru, and Colombia (1519–1543) was effectuated to a great extent by lesser nobility, "aides, secretaries, and similar employees," professionals, ecclesiastics, notaries and royal officials. Those who did not write as part of their professional lives used numbers instead of the alphabet, though they still kept books (slave owners, horse owners, merchants, rentiers).[56] As the historian Enrique Florescano argues, the genre produced, (though paradoxically, because it is a functionary's genre), "a new protagonist of historical action and narration: the conquistador."[57] The amount of Empire-writing was copious.

If, as has been suggested in previous chapters, the subject is forged in guilt and in debt, the *probanza* constitutes a noteworthy genre, because proof—that is, proof of merit—can never really be established once and for all. (Quesada spent twelve years in litigation with the Spanish monarchy, trying to augment his standing and his spoils.) Columbus's announcement of the discovery hovers somewhere between a carta (*letter*) and a probanza (*proof of merit*). Several noteworthy features of non-alphabetic as opposed to alphabetic cultures come immediately to the fore. The first is Columbus's adherence to a religion-of-the-book, a subject to which I return in the next chapter. Secondly, the Tainos (the indigenes Columbus encounters first) are persons who do not leave their own contexts. The implications of this are enormous. Columbus writes, "Everything they have or had they gave for whatever one gave them in exchange, even taking a piece of glass or broken crockery or some such thing, for gold or some other thing of whatever value."[58] For Columbus and his sailors, these (ten thousand)[59] acts bespeak a profound naïveté. We could also argue that the objects themselves, from the Taino point of view, form only a small, and possibly insignificant, part of a larger fabric of relations, much as Ong argued that words merge with a dozen other environmental cues in any given oral-cultural situation. Talk of "exchange" is also misleading because it suggests equilibration, yet without the notion of a third commodity that both stands for itself (i.e., gold) *and* for a measure of all other commodities in comparison (i.e., prices as various gold-magnitudes), "exchange" as Columbus understands it, is not a goal. For Columbus, by contrast, owing, earning, and favorable exchange are the very structure of his existence. To the sovereigns, he writes

[. . .] In seven years from today I will be able to pay Your Highnesses for five thousand cavalry and fifty thousand foot soldiers for the war and conquest of Jerusalem, for which purpose this enterprise was undertaken. And in another five years another five thousand cavalry and another fifty thousand foot soldiers, which will total ten thousand cavalry and one hundred thousand foot soldiers; and all of this with very little investment now on Your Highnesses' part in this beginning of the taking of the Indies and all that they contain.[60]

He also asks for a cardinalate for his son even though that son is underage, and also that his crew member and good friend, Pedro de Villacorta, be named "paymaster of the Indies."[61]

Columbus is not without empathy. We cannot say that he tortures and enslaves the Taino because he does not see them as human. He remarks upon mutual "sadness" when they cannot communicate with one another, and he acknowledges "much friendship from the king of that place, who prided himself in calling me and having me for a brother; who (also) appeared to accept everything as the greatest boon in the world, as I said."[62] For Columbus, the indigenes are both *real* ("the Indians [. . .] had become friendly with me"),[63] and they are *unreal* ("In the westernmost part (of Cuba) [. . .] everyone is born with a tail").[64] This is the case for all the Spanish literates.

And this "unreality"—or virtuality—of persons in the model cannot be separated from the extremes of violence committed against them. That the conquistadors were capable of such extreme violence is not a deviation from their literate orientation, but a logical extension of it. In their "Remarks on a Virtual World," Harrison, Haruvy, and Rutström point out that "The word virtual simply means something that is similar to something else but without some of the properties of that to which it is similar."[65] In other words, it is a model. This quality of unreality accounts in part for Tzvetan Todorov's explanation of a typology of new violence in the Americas.[66] The very presence of a dislocated observer (the alphabetic writer) who either appears on the beach at San Salvador, or overlooks the precipice above the Tenochtitlan valley, means that person is operating outside of his received context. One aspect of virtual worlds "is the elimination of real geographic distance."[67] In such situations, according to Todorov, actions find justifications not from the context—to which the decontextualized figure, by definition, does not belong anyhow—but only from themselves. In the colony, as opposed to the metropole, "one wields the saber for the pleasure of wielding the saber, one cuts off the Indian's nose, tongue, and penis without this having any ritual meaning for the amputator."[68] Dictionaries are collections of words which define any given word by pointing only to other words. Decontextualized violence is countenanced only by itself, by its previous iterations on the one hand and the iterations to come, on the other. One act of decontextualized violence occasions another, particularly when the victims are concrete enough to appear in the model and virtual enough to destroy: "The more remote and alien the victims, the better: they are exterminated without remorse, more or less identified with animals."[69]

Recall the condemnation of Joseph Conrad's Heart of Darkness by the Nigerian novelist, Chinua Achebe, who accused the imperial author of being a "bloody racist."[70] Achebe took particular umbrage at a passage in which Conrad describes "natives" in a self-induced trance as writhing in a "frenzy." The "frenzy" should have been explained as a complex ritual behavior with component parts, a history, practitioners of various degrees of expertise, and so on. For Achebe, Conrad's inclusion of these details, presumably as a measure of cultural respect, would have mitigated his claims to "racism." What Achebe does not appreciate is that for Conrad, the "natives" would also have been *virtual*, no matter how sensitively—as opposed to how dismissively—he described them. Conrad, Achebe contends, should have recognized—as did Picasso, Gauguin, and other visual artists—the richness of African forms, as they used it to rejuvenate moribund European art in the twentieth century. As Lotman writes, "In relation to a logical model homomorphic to it, a play-type model is not perceived through the antithesis, 'true—false,' but as a 'richer—poorer' (*both of them true*) reflection of life."[71] We know, for example, that Cortés greatly admired the Aztec civilization, and genuinely believed it was more "civilized" than any European capital at the time. He described Tenochtitlan and Montezuma's palace in great detail. Yet this did not deter him from slaughtering the Aztec leader, torturing his family member, and reducing the glittering city to rubble.

Of the work of model-building, Slavoj Žižek writes,

> If we want to simulate reality within an artificial (virtual, digital) medium, we do not have to go all the way: we just have to reproduce those features which will make the image realistic from the spectator's point of view. For example, if there is a house in the background, we do not have to program the house's interior, since we suspect that the participant will not want to enter the house; or, the construction of a virtual person in this space can be limited to his exterior—no need to bother with inner organs, bones, etc.

We just need to create a program which will promptly fill in this gap if the participant's actions necessitate it (say if he plunges a knife deep into the virtual person's body).[72]

It is as if Achebe believes that Conrad should have "programmed" the internal organs, the beating hearts and the coursing of blood through the veins—as though this would have made him personally more sensitive and less racist. Todorov suggests that the colonial position itself inhibits familiarity; otherwise, the violence of massacre would become murder. Murder is something that takes place in the home country, whereas massacre is reserved for less real inhabitants of the model. Of the slaughter of indigenes in the colonies, Todorov notes, "The individual identity of the massacre victim is by definition irrelevant (otherwise his death would be a murder): one has neither time nor curiosity to know whom one is killing at that moment."[73] We arrive again at the alphabetized duality of being named and being anonymous; one is named and perhaps even admired (Montezuma) on the one hand, and the greater number left anonymous (massacred "Indians"), on the other. Yet both are *less real* within the model than the authors of that model. Even today, we do not know, and are not curious to know, the practices or preferences of the South Asian children who stitch our clothes or the Chinese workers who assemble our iphones, because then we would be harder pressed to use them as slaves. We should not like, in other words, to restore to them a context—but even if we did—they would still remain virtual.

Violence is not "virtual" in an oral culture. Where it exists, it is likely ritualized, which means contained, structured, and limited, never *unlimited*, never self-begetting. When Todorov mentions the Spaniards' absence of ritual meaning, it confirms their dramatic remove from oral culture, wherein actions are made meaningful, that is, contextualized, within a collective field of social norms. A parallel thus emerges between sacrifice, which is a religious killing, and the new modern violence of massacre, which Todorov calls "atheist"—despite the conquistadors' loud proclamations of their Catholic faith. Todorov remarks that even the lust for gold cannot explain such violence:

We cannot justify the massacre at Caonao by any form of greed, nor the hanging of mothers from trees, and children from the mother's feet; nor the tortures in which the victim's flesh is torn off with pincers, bit by bit; slaves do not work better if the master sleeps with their wives over their supine bodies.[74]

It is purposelessness in and of itself, Todorov claims, that drives the cruelty of this violence which is therefore enacted elsewhere, that is, "far from the central government, far from royal law, [where] all prohibitions give way, [and] the social link, already loosened, snaps."[75] An extension of this line of reasoning would be that violence becomes virtual in the Americas because it is uniquely without consequences. Just as one kills with impunity inside a digital, gaming virtual world, so one kills with impunity where there is similarly no means of sanction or repercussion. The big Other does not exist in this place. (Not until Bartolomé de las Casas does the voice of conscience enter into this alphabetic maelstrom, and few are as prolific as Las Casas. However, his compassion extends only as far as the Indians, for whom he becomes a stalwart champion; he advocates their replacement by sturdier black African slaves.)

Massacre is unacceptable, according to Todorov, because its social function, "is not recognized."[76] It is not recognized as a functional goal as exercised *in the metropole* (because the victims there, having determinable identities, would be murdered, not massacred). As Cortés was well aware, however, massacre is extremely functional *in the colony*. Massacre does not conflict with any of the conquistador's goals; rather it will prove the most efficient means to their achievement. Such violence, though free from ritual meaning, is not, thereby, purposeless.

The alphabetic network from Western Europe to the Americas, well-travelled as it is, is also limited. The participants share basic assumptions. Even Las Casas, who is the great defender of the indigenes and critic of Spanish excesses, still uses the same postures, the same arguments, the same tools of communication, worships the same God—who is revealed through the alphabet—as the others. Alphabetic literacy, like any "occult" system, is originally limited to the monarchy, the aristocrats and the clergy first of all, with their functionaries and scribes following. *Amongst themselves* the writers and readers of this rather rarefied discursive network are in tacit agreement as to the social function performed by massacre. They are in a unique historical position produced by alphabetic decontextualizations to both acknowledge and not acknowledge the social functions of such violence.

Pope Alexander, King Ferdinand, Queen Isabella, and the myriad investors have already inadvertently blessed whatever happens. And they have always already "run" scenarios of their own: If the conquistadors are lost at sea the monarchy is out very little, only the investors lose; if the conquistadors find gold, the monarchy collects between 70% and 90% of the spoils; if the conquistadors enslave large populations and turn them into vassals, who must pay regular taxes and tributes, the income stream is endless; and if those vassals kneel down as subjects to the Spanish crown and additionally, convert to Catholicism, then the Empire and Church are exponentially enlarged. As one historian notes, "To some extent, all participants were investors in commercial ventures that carried high risks but also the highest of returns. The Spaniards called these ventures "companies" [. . .]. The conquerors were, in other words, *armed entrepreneurs*."[77] We should eschew the myth that they were driven by a love of adventure or a passion for discovery. The violence of massacre, which Todorov claims was invented by these Spaniards—though other European nations will quickly follow suit—is not a defect of the model but a salient feature of its drive to replicate and extend itself.

There is a well-known rendering of Alvarado's massacre in the Great Temple of Tenochtitlan reproduced in Todorov's book (see Fig. 1).[78] It stands as one of the few counterexamples to the barrage of alphabetic writing that flowed from Cortés and the other conquistadors. In the second letter to King Charles V, Cortés described the Aztec Temple as a place of unholy savagery in vivid and ornate prose. It is a site he condemned as a heathen place where he had personally witnessed the dried blood of humans on the walls.

Non-alphabetic cultures have not been running scenarios; this is the source of their "vulnerability." Whereas Todorov has suggested that the Aztecs were masterful at ritual communication, the Spaniards succeeded because they were gifted at "improvisation." Yet as we can see in the Aztec depiction of events, the Spaniards are not improvising; they are doing the opposite. They have been "rehearsing" and running "mental" models for a very long time. Though one could argue that this is only the perception of the artist and not a faithful rendition, the impression is certainly one of "surprise" for the Aztecs on the one hand and a certain "foreknowledge" for the Spaniards on the other. One sure indication of this is that the latter are covered literally from head to toe in armor. They wield massive steel blades which are larger than the bodies of the conquistadors themselves. Only two carry (relatively small) shields as if to express confidence in their preordained inviolability. The outsized nature of the swords speaks both to the artist's view of the weapons as gruesomely lethal, and to the fact that—unlike European art—the perspective

Fig. 1: The Alvarado massacre in the Great Temple of Tenochtitlan from the Durán Codex

is not derived from an imaginary neutral observer, the point-of-view usually cast at eye-level. The vantage point is not that of an individual watcher. If perspective entails a singular view, if it must presuppose a separated voyeur, then the Aztec pictogram shows no "perspective" at all. The archways seem to open outward and lay flat; they are too diminutive in size for humans to fit through. "Any idea of linear perspective," Todorov comments, "and hence of an individual viewpoint, is absent."[79]

In sharp contrast to the militarized dress and attitude of the Spaniards, the Aztecs are barefoot and naked apart from the lengths of cloth draped over the shoulder and around the loins. The posture of each Aztec is supine, even that of the sole figure who may not yet have been attacked. The posture of each Spaniard, meanwhile, is erect and suggests an agile, almost casual mastery, the facial expressions ranging from vexed to bemused. There are *three times* as many Spaniards as there are Aztecs. The abandoned objects on the ground suggest that the Aztecs are occupied and interrupted in the midst of something absorbing that commanded their attention. They have been caught unawares.

In fact, they were conducting a temple festival. The *Florentine Codex* by Sahagún includes oral responses from witnesses, collected shortly after the massacre. The first one killed was a musician (a drummer) whose hands were severed, presumably to stop him drumming, then his neck.[80] Other survivors note, "Of some they slashed open their backs: then their entrails gushed out. Of some they cut their heads to pieces . . . . Some they struck on the shoulder; they split openings. They broke openings in their bodies."[81] The Aztecs had "very precise rules about violent assaults on the body" and they had no conceptual place for "preemptive massacres."[82] The dismayed and dismaying attempts to discover "the sense in the Spaniards cuttings and slashings"[83] is apparent in both the oral transcripts and the pictogram. Perhaps the conquistadors, who were not professional soldiers, behaved so for precisely that reason. The descriptions recall the behavior of the neighborhood butcher; Alvarado and the others at the massacre may well have been more used to gutting animals than killing opponents in battle. At the same time, the prevalence of "butchery" is fitting, because there was no war. The Aztecs had not known they were "conscripted" and had no grievance. Neither did the Spaniards.

The existence in the pictogram of not simply blood and death, but of dismemberment, beheading, and the gouging of the eyes, that is, *mutilation*, signifies what Todorov characterizes as the (new) typology of violence. The victims were "unarmed warrior dancers."[84] The Spaniards have not simply killed their "enemies," who were not in fact "enemies"—as Montezuma received them according to ambassadorial protocols—but only potential obstacles to the procurement of more gold. We can see how Todorov finds these strains of violence more purposeless than purposeful. As it is without purpose, so is it without end. It calls to mind the words of Las Casas in regard to another massacre at Caonao in Cuba, which both he and Cortés witnessed: "[They began] to kill as many as they found there, so that a stream of blood was running, as if a great number of cows had perished."[85] The only blood spilled in the pictogram is Aztec.

Cortés used his slaves and vast estate as collateral to fund his expedition into the interior of Mexico. He had already been in the Americas for fifteen years, so the notion that he was seized by a certain bloodlust, a kind of temporary madness, is untenable. On the way to the Aztec capital, he executed two fellow Spaniards who wanted to call it off and turn back. Upon landfall in Mexico, he burned the ships that had carried them from the Caribbean so that no one could retreat. Cortés will go on to kill Montezuma and torture his nephew in order to find the mother lode of gold which, it turns out, does not exist. The violence of massacre is sloppy and brutal because its goal is not to win a war; it is to guarantee a return on investment. Secondarily, it seeks to create an alphabetic platform from which the writer inscribes a doubled and aggrandized version of himself. Historians concern themselves with what sort of man Cortés was, and he dutifully supplied them with copious clues; they repeat his self-assessments: "Given the necessity to demonstrate his own indispensability, it is unsurprising that along the way Cortés should claim 'the art of adaptation and improvisation' as the very 'principle of his conduct.'"[86] Yet just as with the conquistadors at the Alvarado massacre, Cortés is not one who adapts and improvises. All moves and countermoves had been formulated and reformulated in advance.

The monarchs are eager to lay claim to what they understand through reading and maps to be the "world": a form of autonomous space in which there appear "some islands and Continents in the ocean."[87] A principal agent such as Cortés—who understands himself as performing upon a stage where he comprises himself and stylizes his actions—narrates himself as protagonist of a great alphabetic drama. He performs his role. Posturing before the big Other (*back home*), becoming truly him-self in the conquest of Mexico and engendering this true self as he writes it, he is confident that the King and Queen of Spain, and the Pope alongside them, will sit in awe and congratulate him as they read of his deeds. Indeed, the better written *relaciones*, letters, and *probanzas* enjoyed wide circulation in print for public consumption. In this way, large swathes of literate Europe "spectate" and absorb each brave act of the conquistador as if they were living it themselves. This autonomous subject already entails a permanent, stable separation from the environment, as well as an internalized perceptual apparatus (the "Cartesian Theater," the alphabetized brain) that continually affirms this separation and writing reinforces it.

Indeed, because Cortés enacted the scene of conquest over and over again in the Cartesian Theater, by the time it was actualized, he probably experienced it, or saw himself experiencing it, as a familiar and somewhat subdued echo, a muted copy of the imaginary original, seen after a succession of mentally reproduced scenes and counter-scenes. Perhaps the conquest was even an anti-climax at the time of its occurrence—an out-of-body screening of something deferred and unreal except insofar as it will feature as proof of merit in his written description to the King.

Todorov makes the same comment about Columbus, who can only see what he already expected to find, which is even true of the items he did not expect to find: the indigenous people who flee from him. He had expected a coterie of emissaries. His vision is remarkably confined to the determinations of his expeditionary mission and the alphabetic genre in which it materializes. We see him fashioning his perception of the New World as he encounters it along lines already fixed by the expectations of his sponsors and readers. This must always be the case with alphabetic writing, since as Walter Ong argues, "the writer's audience is always a fiction."[88] Columbus must fictionalize the reception of his letter by fictionalizing (imagining beforehand) what he believes his readers (the sponsors, the investors, the monarchy, and later a paying literate public) would have wanted him to find, and so finding it.

Columbus keeps a diary which—like the conquistador narratives—founds a new genre; he keeps a daily record from his "small cabin on the *Santa María*," which was "itself a radical change, for such diaries were unknown before."[89] Of the "Letter to the Sovereigns," the historian Margarita Zamora expresses incredulity at Columbus's "unabashed" discussion of "personal concerns, even self-interest, the lingering bitterness of his earlier humiliation [when his venture was multiply rejected], his pride in the success of the endeavor, his rather arrogant demands for compensation, and so on."[90] Yet it was incumbent upon the writer to show that he had fulfilled the contractual obligations laid out in the *adelantado*, which would eventually contain clauses regarding breaches, the penalties for which included imprisonment (Sebastian de Benalcázar and Hernando Pizarro were jailed in the 1540s) and fines (Juan de Oñate was fined 6,000 ducats in 1614).[91] Columbus is the subject who is formed in debt—that is, named, sponsored, party to a contract, and cast upon the seas as an "avatar" who supervenes in the autonomous space of the globe. He is further consolidated as a subject as he attempts to release himself from these debts (with diaries, self-aggrandizing missives, inventories of slaves and lists of commodities rendered in tribute and in payment). Aren't all literates obliged to perform like acts as assiduously and as often? Is there not a sense in which all writing is along the lines of the *probanza de merito*? Or at least a form of inventory, either of deeds or of commodities?

Montezuma is easy to kill. When he finds out about the impending arrival of the Spaniards, he sends his emissaries to present them with gold and twenty young women as a gesture of good will and in the hope that they will leave. It is not a naïve act, but a belief that value is context-bound rather than cumulative and endless. "Have these gifts; you are welcome to them" does not automatically mean, "There is more; come and take what remains," which is what the Spaniards understand. Unlike the Spaniards, Montezuma has not already secured victories hundreds of times on a hypothetical plane. That he is not able to strategize "appropriately" may account for his enigmatic behavior.

He does not act and appears almost paralyzed. When he hears word that his gifts have not sufficed and that the breach of the city borders by the Spaniards is imminent, he falls into a state resembling catatonia. One account states, "Montezuma lowered his head, and without answering a word, placed his hand upon his mouth. In this way he remained for a long time. He appeared to be dead or mute, since he was unable to give any answer."[92] Montezuma, of course, has never been alphabetized; he cannot extricate himself from his lived environment and contemplate himself and his options from one remove. He has no neutral, staged second space available at the ready. He cannot "vacate" his body and enact all the possibilities for a response within an immaterial realm of abstract space. He is not an avatar—one whose image is redoubled and available for surveillance. Montezuma's ability to act is drawn from his surroundings alone. His attempts to draw meaning from his situation and become oriented fail, in part because the situation itself has been authored *ex nihilo* by the Spaniards. He does not even know for certain who the Spaniards are or what they want. At some level, he understands it is "gold," yet there is no notion of a universal equivalent, and the desire remains incoherent. When asked why they so desperately want this gold, Cortés answered that they eat it: "Cortés, apparently, had offered this explanation: the Spaniards need gold as the cure for a sickness. The Indians, who identify gold with excrement, find this difficult to accept."[93]

Montezuma's hesitations are usually regarded as a character flaw, as proof that he was effete and poorly equipped to lead. Seen as too melancholy or too philosophical, he languished instead of responding boldly to the Spanish incursion. In the *Florentine Codex*, he is likewise depicted as immobilized by the news of the invaders: "When he heard this, Montezuma merely lowered his head; he remained in this attitude, and did not speak at all, but remained a long time full of affliction, as if he were beside himself."[94] Ironically, perhaps, it is just this failure to be "beside himself" that seals his defeat. He cannot cast himself fictively beyond his body and think as a "self" would, which is to operate over and against his people. It is not that he would have chosen self-preservation, but like a captain sinking with his ship, he valiantly rejected the notion. Rather the idea of "saving his skin," as Clendinnen glibly puts it, at the expense of the known world, simply makes no sense. The Spaniards do not understand this any more than the histo-rians who sift through the writings afterward. Montezuma cannot make recourse to an analogue state in which he would become separate from his setting, his network of relations, his cosmology and so on, and exist quite apart from it. For this, too, would be a kind of death.

The phenomenon of "massacre" is intimately tied to alphabetic writ-ing. Without writing, the displacements that brought the Spaniards to the New World and engendered the actions undertaken there could never have occurred. Writing models the world; writing takes Cortés to the Americas; and writing is what he sends back. In many respects, he massacres the Aztecs *in order to write about it*, in order to narrate his victory, in order to chronicle how resplendent they were. Writing is meant to "explain" what is inexpli-cable until it is no longer inexplicable, no longer appalling. Had we been in attendance, there would be no need to write, and had we been in atten-dance, we would still be appalled. Writing always comes to us from at least one degree of spatial and temporal remove. Whatever event is written about is both elsewhere and in the past, which is to say, *not here* and *not now*. The written world is always virtual.

In the end, the written world is practically the only world we *know*—that is, we know things because we have read about them. Our actual experience of almost anything at all is negligible by comparison to our "experiences" and knowledge-gathering through writing, and media enabled by writing (internet, film, television, etc.). The range of our physical encounters is infinitesimal compared to what we have "encountered" in forms of fiction. As Ong notes, written artefacts create a "distant past," or a very recent one for that matter, from which puzzles with strange words (since fallen into disuse) come to us.

"Virtuality" is compounded by this temporal and spatial remove. In comparison to what we have learned from written information, there is almost literally nothing that we glean from actual experience: "The world in which our consciousness at each moment situates us is the expression of our reading and not the summary of our direct experience, so restricted in comparison."[95] We even learn to speak as though we were writing, that is we "speak literately."[96] Everything on which we base our everyday existence is, to a greater or lesser extent, fictional—virtual.

The alphabetic protagonist is not a marginal or an unusual figure. We should look on the victor, Cortés, as "revealing not a primitive nature, the beast sleeping in each of us, but *a modern being, one with a great future in fact*, restrained by no morality and inflicting death because and when he pleases."[97] The cultural descendants of Cortés inhabit a world that is literally of their own making. This is the sense in which writing is performative. The Spanish conquest of the Americas was a literary endeavor, or at least an enterprise of letters, of encoding, decoding, transcoding, translating, and endless composition, from the outset. The literate elites of Southern Europe set about building a model. The performativity of this model extends far beyond the christening of ships or the enunciating of "I do." It is the construction of the very universe in which those things occur. As Anthony Pagden writes, "The answer to Todorov's question, 'Did the Spaniards defeat the Indians by means of signs?' is clearly yes."[98] When Todorov argued that it was above all signs that decimated the native peoples of the Americas, he should have specified the alphabet.

7 The Subject Is Always Alphabetized

Writing is in a way the most drastic of the three technologies. It initiated what print and computers only continue.

—WALTER ONG[1]

Printing was God's highest act of grace.

—MARTIN LUTHER[2]

As commodity production develops and becomes the typical form of production, man's imagination grows more and more separate from his actions and becomes increasingly individualized, eventually assuming the dimensions of a private consciousness.

—ALFRED SOHN-RETHEL[3]

There is no subject apart from the alphabetized subject.

In *A History of Reading*, Steven R. Fischer argues that two types of reading have "apparently always obtained: literal or mediate reading (learning), and visual or immediate reading (fluent)."[4] Fischer suggests that when one is learning to read, the early step of correlating the (hypothetical) sound to the arbitrary sign is difficult, labor-intensive, and thus subject to delay, that is, "mediate." Over time, however, as fluency builds, the reader can bypass the step of correlating the letters to hypothetical sounds—since she has already forged those pathways—and move directly from "sign to sense, bypassing sound altogether." The reading that fluent, adult readers perform is thus "immediate." Though the adjectives "mediate" and "immediate" are used by

Fischer to convey a shorter or longer temporal lag, they also, and in more literal terms, suggest the presence or absence of an "interface." As I learn to read, it is not simply that I decode the signs more quickly, which I do, but also that the *interface* between my brain and "sense" appears to vanish. One definition of an interface calls it an "agitation" or "friction between different formats."[5] By "removing" the friction of alphabetic letters through habit and repetition, a fluent reader is not aware of mediation at all but rather grasps information as if directly. An "immediate medium" is an oxymoron. Yet the notion has a history as long as the alphabet itself; there is meaning, and the alphabet supplies the transparent means to its conveyance. Being too aware of the medium, however, means one cannot access the message without dissonance. We have been attempting to "lose" the alphabet in this way for a long time.

We could even say that the material "detour" of alphabetic letters on the route from sound to sense is no longer strictly speaking necessary, since computers read for us—and much faster, of course—so that we no longer need to expend what energy it once took to scan the lines of letters and decode them. The computer "reads" prior to, and thus outside of, our conscious awareness and simply delivers up the contents of a pre-processed message, usually in the form of images and sounds.

In her discussion of what she calls the "cognitive nonconscious," N. Katherine Hayles notes the discrepancy between computed algorithmic time and the time it takes a human brain to process information: "By contrast, computer algorithms (in automated stock trading, for example) can operate in the one to five millisecond range, about three orders of magnitude faster than humans."[6] Though she stresses that "computational media operate in microtemporal regimes inaccessible to humans," arguably there has been a modality of information processing that is more or less "inaccessible" since the dawn of the alphabet.[7] Computational media merely quicken—or drive further into unconsciousness—what was already unavailable to consciousness. Reading that was, in Fischer's sense, "immediate" has now become even more so—immediate to a degree of a "missing half-second."[8] Also immediate in that the content arrives immediately in the sensorium and takes little processing at all. "Reading" is also immediate in that it does not even require (or perhaps permit) my creative internal production of characters and scenes and events any longer. In the reading of a novel, for example, there was a gap of interplay in which, although the writer was providing me with "instructions" for my hallucinations, I still maintained a measure of "creativity" in terms of the audiovisual contents my brain produced in response. When reading becomes pre-processed in the form of films or television or videos, for instance, those "choices" have been made for me by someone else. Though reading, and thus supplying the material for the Cartesian Theater myself, required a certain amount of cognitive labor, it also afforded me an amount of shared creation, and thus possibly counter-interpellation, that is now foreclosed. When we hear stirrings about the death of reading and the decline of literacy, we should not assume a coming state of the post-alphabetic. Far from it. We have merely become hyper-alphabetized. The process of reading is done, even more so than before, *on another scene*—algorithmically, non-cooperatively, and thus invisibly.

Let us consider Havelock's assessment of the alphabet in its infancy. He marvels at the brilliance of a self-launching code which is automatically executable on any prepared human brain. Computational media simply build on a state which was always manifest in the alphabet; reading (or logging on?) is a species of sending an "electric current to the brain." There is also a measure of prescience—he has provided a precursory explanation of wetware—in his report on the symbiotic connectivity between brain and alphabet:

> The acoustic efficiency of the [alphabetic] script had a result which was psychological: once it was learned *you did not have to think about it*. Though a visible thing, a series of marks, it ceased to interpose itself as an object of thought between the reader and his recollection of the spoken tongue. The script therefore came to resemble an electric current communicating a recollection of the sounds of the spoken word directly to the brain so that the meaning resounded as it were in the consciousness without reference to the properties of the letters used. The script was reduced to a gimmick; it had no intrinsic value in itself as a script and this marked it off from all previous systems.[9]

While Havelock remarks on the elision of letters and meaning resounding in the consciousness through the spoken word, he does not mention the simultaneous resort to visuality that the sounds evoke. This is perhaps even stranger than the experience of an "electric current"—the fact that decoding generates audiovisual hallucinations in the reader. Though confined to the visual field—where they do and do not appear to the organs of sight—"letters" are sound-cues. "Acoustic memory" is Havelock's phrase, but which memories are being accessed? How does one remember things she has never seen, events that did not occur, people she has never met, and so on? The alphabet creates hallucinations in the form of memories *that never took place.*

We visualize the things being "told" to us by the authorial voice as if they corresponded to the real world. They are apparitions assembled in the "mind's eye" per the writer's commands, her blueprints, her conjuring, her séance, with one's Cartesian Theatre as the setting. As real as these visions seem they cannot be construed as "audiovisual" because they do not derive support from the actual scopic or auditory field. The reader is experiencing an intense audiovisual encounter which is entirely hypothetical. Despite watching, despite "seeing it" very clearly, it is neither visual nor oral, because one has no eyes or ears inside her head with which to see or hear. The actual scopic field is occupied in the scanning of letters and the auditory register has become at least partially deadened to stimulation. If one is reading with concentration, she is likely to block out sounds that would compete for her attention. Her eyelids may become as slits, and the eyes themselves constantly saccade back and forth across the page, in a strangely mechanized manner, while the rest of the body becomes almost completely inert. Either the body is possessed, or it is vacated; it is hard to say which. In either case, the person is no longer "at home."

Friedrich Kittler rightly connects reading with hallucination, as it entails hearing voices from absent speakers and seeing things that do not exist, often in a state resembling mesmerism. This description of reading accords with records from the early scientific literature regarding hallucination. An 1832 definition by Esquirol stated that the "person hallucinating 'ascribes a body and an actuality to images that the memory recalls without the intervention of the senses.'"[10] If the events, bodies, and images did not have a certain *level* of actuality for the reader, she would not be compelled to continue. She could not be constantly aware of the fact that what she was reading is "not real" at the same time that she immersed in it. If she refused to indulge the scenarios at all, then she would not be able to read.[11] A more recent definition understands hallucination as "any percept-like" experience that happens "in the absence of an appropriate stimulus," but which nevertheless produces "the full force or impact of the corresponding actual (real) perception," as though "not amenable to direct or voluntary control by the experiencer."[12] It is up for debate whether or not black scratches on white paper constitutes an "appropriate" stimulus for all manner of audiovisual material to project itself into my "mind's eye," though I will certainly respond with emotion, and once I have submitted to the "show," I will feel that I am not terribly in control of what unfurls there. (Though more so than when the writing is done by cinematograph, or photograph, as opposed to typograph, as above.) I am reading "directions" for the performance after all, to which I could theoretically make willful substitutions, though the incentive to do so is minimal, since it would almost certainly create "agitation" and "friction."

We imagine that whether or not we hallucinate is "up to us." We can always shut the book or turn off the monitor. We assume we could easily judge the difference between hallucinating and not hallucinating by looking to the forms and objects around us to confirm whether or not they existed. And this would be easy enough if that was all there was to it, if hallucination had to do with perception of the external world. As one early twentieth-century psychologist put it,

> The usual definition of illusion and hallucination is with regard to the external object. Illusion is defined as fallacious perception of some actually existing object, while hallucination is perception of a non-existing object . . . . From a strictly psychological standpoint illusions and hallucinations cannot possibly be differentiated from other psychic states by the presence or absence of external objects. External objects can hardly be regarded as constituents or necessary ingredients of psychic states.[13]

Whether or not objects exist in my field of vision makes no difference when it comes to the spectacle unfolding inside my head. The presence or absence of the *percept* is irrelevant to my immersion in hallucination, which is, after all, the "perception of a non-existing object."

The sight of a person engaged in hallucination would be disconcerting if it were not so common. Though many painters have accorded it a certain charm, it can also uncannily resemble a state of catalepsy. In his book about (digital) reading practices, Manuel Portela examines aspects of the body reading, especially as they have been depicted in nineteenth and twentieth century European paintings. He discusses how the reader makes a good "sitter" for the artist because of her postural immobility. If she weren't reading, she might be inclined to use her body: to stretch, shift positions, gesture, or distort her features by speaking. By giving her a book, he has offered her a mode of egress such that while her unmoving body remains, she can go elsewhere. Even though the act of reading is embodied, "constituted by eyes, hands, head, body, codex, and the processing of signs," it nonetheless appears as a practice of profound disembodiment. Apart from a flick of the page at steady intervals, the body enters a state of near muscular paralysis and stays more or less frozen throughout. The painter may well favor that sitter who has exited from her body so to speak—and left behind a comely shell—as did Matisse when he painted his daughter Marguerite and produced *Interior with a Young Girl (Girl Reading) 1906*. Of Marguerite Matisse, Portela writes, the "temporary unawareness of the space around her is transmitted by showing her eyelids completely engaged in the reading and is underlined by the sitter's unawareness of being depicted."[14]

Does Marguerite know that she is hallucinating? Not while she is doing so. (Or perhaps as with the diamond prop in the previous chapter, she neither knows nor cares whether it is "real" or "unreal".) She does not even know that she is the subject of a painting, according to Portela, or that her father is present or that he is engaged in activity that involves her. Even if she chose to distinguish between "real" and "unreal," when she is actively engaged in hallucination, she is not "available" to make the distinction, but has become fully engrossed in the imaginary vision. Marguerite Matisse does not know she is being represented, because her environs have no attraction when compared to the seductions of hallucination. Painters, her father among them, "have represented reading as a deep immersion in the virtual world maintained by the symbolic power of signs."[15]

We can imagine without much difficulty that Marguerite Matisse, in the course of having been painted, experienced something like Havelock's "electric current" to her brain. Havelock's use of the word "gimmick" is significant ("The script was reduced to a gimmick; it had no intrinsic value in itself as a script and this marked it off from all previous systems"). Dating from 1920s era America, the word referred to "a piece of magicians' apparatus." Though the origin is unknown, "gimmick" is thought to be a rough anagram of "magic."[16] Hearing sounds from absent speakers and seeing images based on what the absent speakers say is to partake of a kind of magic. It is to be transfixed in ways magic is said to transfix: through enchantment, hypnotism, trance-induction, spellbinding, possession. Like all magic, the magic of writing effaces its own workings in order to be effective. The alphabetic medium is duly erased by the protocols of reading such that the reader may more vividly hallucinate, for if one reads in the right way, "a real, visible world" will "unfold within" her "in the wake of the words."[17] With practice, this happens without "even having to think about it." As with any form of magic, why or how it works is beyond the reach of the participant or the bystander, and the possibility of gaining such understanding is deferred by the procedure itself.

We might imagine that the arbitrary letters of the Greeks would have appeared bizarre and conspicuous upon first being introduced. Yet over time, their invisibility was actually ensured by this very recourse to arbitrariness, since they would only draw attention to themselves in the early stages of proficiency. By the time their patterns had been internalized, they would cease to appear, in the conventional sense, at all. How does the brain render something from the audial register through a visual channel, which itself becomes non-visual (i.e., effectively invisible)? And how does the "thingness" of alphabetic letters, which always have a material incarnation, eclipse itself and become pure "sense"? Fischer suggests that the brain occults the sound on the way to sense, though this must also entail an effacement of visual materiality.

And what of the situation in which there is a failure in some part of the hallucinatory sequence, so that the letters do not vanish and "cease to interpose themselves?" Is this not an apt definition of dyslexia? Proficiency in the skill of decoding letters is measured by how easily a reader becomes unaware that she is engaged in the act of reading. Dyslexia, by contrast, names a general difficulty with decoding alphabetic signs, such that the reader cannot fully accomplish this "unawareness" because the shapes continually intrude upon her field of vision. Rather than disappearing, as happens with successful reading, the letters continue to reassert themselves. They appear as clumsy and random. This prevents the flow of hallucination "in all its glowing colors, shadows, and lights [that] 'hit the favorable reader as if with an electric shock.'"[18] A full twenty percent of the U.S. population is dyslexic.[19] For the non-dyslexic, on the other hand, the alphabet is almost miraculously invisible. When one reads, she does not see but looks *through* the letters. One of the most peculiar aspects of the alphabet is that the ocular basis of the letters does not, cannot, register, even though the act is profoundly visual. Otherwise there could be only the repeated stumbling over a succession of shapes, a maelstrom of Kittler's "black squiggles on white paper."[20] Children whose brains have not sufficiently adapted the visual system to "map onto spoken sounds and words" are considered learning disabled. Unlike the sitter in *Girl Reading*, dyslexics cannot display the "functional unawareness" of the letters that would enable them to become successful readers, though dyslexia also encompasses other alphabetic "failures," such as those involving spelling (orthographic dyslexia), mathematics (dyscalculia) and handwriting (dysgraphia).

In his description of the exchange relation in capitalist society, Alfred Sohn-Rethel elucidates an equally complex semiotic maneuver, one which like reading entails an "evacuation" procedure in addition to "functional unawareness." As noted previously, the materiality of money must elide itself and become invisible, forming a purely abstract and functional "blank" in our experience, before the exchange of commodities can take place. Sohn-Rethel explains that if we became aware of the reality of money at the point of exchange—if we suddenly understood that there is no actual value to hand but only a worthless semiotic artefact, a thin leaf of special cloth, dyed, stamped with insignia, imprinted with a number, and in fact worth only about five cents—we would be unable to execute the transaction. The smooth functioning—what he calls the "social synthesis"—of contemporary capitalism requires that each actor engage in a recurrent, even habitual, *self-absenting* procedure. Either the money must register as a void in the perceptual field, or the actor must be "unaware" of herself acting. What actually transpires is a version of both at once: "The abstractness of that action cannot be noted when it happens, since it only happens because the consciousness of its agents is taken up with their business and with the empirical appearance of things which pertains to their use."[21] He might also have added that the *empirical thingness* of the money-sign cannot be noted either, or else the operative abstraction could never take place before the actual trade, when the commodity purchased is also an oxymoronic abstract-thing. This active not-noting occurs at the level of the unconscious through every phase of the exchange process. Sohn-Rethel describes this "absentness" of persons (and signs) at the scene of exchange, or the activation of what Žižek calls the "signifying chain that persists on 'another Scene,'"[22] as follows:

> One could say that the abstractness of their action is *beyond realisation* by the actors because their very consciousness stands in the way. Were the abstractness to catch their minds their action would cease to be exchange and the abstraction would not arise.[23]

We can substitute Sohn-Rethel's words relating to exchange with concepts relating to alphabet and the meaning of the passage remains the same: "The abstractness of [alphabetic reading] cannot be noted when it happens, since it only happens because the consciousness of its agents is taken up with [hallucinating] . . . . Were the abstractness to catch their minds their action would cease to be [reading] and the abstraction would not arise." The complex problem of "*real abstraction*" in the exchange relation is one and the same as the alphabetic paradox of an "immediate medium." The media persist, in both cases—the black letters, the money-signs—yet one must behave as if they did not. The "virtual" or as Sohn-Rethel prefers, the abstract, must intervene at several points in the act of exchange while occulting knowledge of itself from the conscious awareness of all parties involved.

The dyslexic is too conscious of the materiality of letters and their linear arrangement on a page to shift into abstraction. This surplus of awareness causes her failure to decode. In order to read, or to participate in an exchange society with an abstract general equivalent (money), she must remain *unconscious* of the paradoxical nature of the symbol, which is both "real" (a string of letters) and not-real (a hallucination of meaning). This failure to absent oneself—the failure to achieve a state of effective unconsciousness—becomes devastating in a high-literate, capitalist culture. We can easily imagine a parallel "disability," a dyslexia of capital, in which the sufferer at the scene of exchange sees only cotton-weave paper stamped with the greenish visages of dead presidents. Try as she might, she cannot understand how the shift from semi-worthless paper to universal equivalence should take effect. To her eyes, there is no magic function embodied in the special paper, but only a few cents worth of tinted rectangular fabric. She is unable, moreover, to perform that equilibrating function (this equals that much of the third thing) necessary for life under capitalism. The vast majority of socialized adults perform these and other acts of abstraction continuously and without mental effort. Hence Havelock's admiration for the efficiency of the Greek code: "once you have learned it, you no longer have to think about it."

Indeed, difficulty only arises when one *does* think about it. The fully literate brain is automatically equipped to operate through those chains of infinite substitution that comprise both alphabetic writing and exchange relations. To think about it is to become conscious at the scene of exchange or at the site of reading and thus derail the process. When one hears about the crisis of Western education, what is being critiqued is the failure of automaticity, the unconscious mastery over the technology. For ones such as the author and the reader of this text, meanwhile, the well-wrought neural pathways of alphabetization, forged in infancy and another two decades and then some, are reactivated every time the arrangement of letters is seen. This in turn reinforces the architecture of the synapses. In terms of the general equivalent, the "decision" to consume is made prior to (or elsewhere than) the scene of exchange, where "real abstraction" happens without thinking on the part of the actors.

Consider another episode of alphabetic failure, as it may only be through failure that we can become aware of what is otherwise unconscious. In his study of a subject with an eidetic memory, *The Mind of a Mnemonist*, A. R. Luria discusses his encounters with an anonymous subject whom he calls "S." According to Luria, S. could remember lists of random numbers fifteen years after he recited them.[24] Luria provided him with lists of numbers and letters of up to seventy characters, which he could recall in reverse order as easily as the original order. Luria writes, he could "readily tell me which word followed another in a series, or reproduce the word which happened to precede one I'd name."[25] In this ability, there was apparently no difference between nonsense syllables, meaningful words, sounds, or numbers. According to Luria, S. incurred more problems trying to forget than with trying to remember.[26] Between various careers, S. performed these feats of memory for a living. His brain was apparently so attuned to the materiality of the shapes that he could not make the move to unconscious abstraction required of alphabetic reading.

Curiously, perhaps, S. could technically read. He could decode alphabetic letters and display a level of comprehension, but he was quite unable to effectuate the second operation, which is to hallucinate. As the dyslexic is shamed as "disabled" in a high-literate culture, S. seems similarly ashamed of his disability, stating, "The things I see when I read aren't real, they don't fit the context."[27] What S. does not realize is that this is an insight, not a deficiency. The things one "sees" when she reads *are not real*—they are audio-visual hallucinations—and they fit no context, since alphabetic writing is created to perform as its own "context," as a context unto itself. S. apparently means he cannot conjure a context-free context which is what the alphabet presupposes, but only his actual surroundings. S.'s inability to forget concretes, which is to say to *eclipse* them, makes performing cognitive abstractions such as substitution and generalizability impossible. He fails to visualize the composite, virtual reality created by the alphabet. He cannot manage to cognitively produce *memories he has never had*. While the act of reading is, he states, technically possible with much mental exertion, as it is for many dyslexics, it holds out no means of seduction. Because he cannot hallucinate, neither can he *read*. He states

If I'm reading a description of some palace, for some reason the main rooms always turn out to be those in the apartment I lived in as a child . . . . Take the time I was reading *Trilby*. When I came to the part where I had to find an attic room, without fail it turned out to be one of my neighbor's rooms—in that same house of ours. I noticed it didn't fit the context, but all the same my images lead me there automatically. This means I have to spend far more time with a passage if I'm to get some control of things, to reconstruct the images I see. This makes for a tremendous amount of conflict and it becomes difficult for me to read. I'm slowed down, my attention is distracted, and I can't get the important ideas in a passage. Even when I read about circumstances that are entirely new to me, if there happens to be a description, say, of a staircase, it turns out to be in a house I once lived in. I start to follow it and lose the gist of what I'm reading. What happens is that I just can't read, can't study, for it takes up such an enormous amount of my time.[28]

Without hallucination, reading becomes uninteresting, laborious, and to a large extent, impossible. S. would clearly like to be able to imagine the grand palace in *Trilby*. He is frustrated by the "inappropriate" memories of architectural features from his own life as they repeatedly intrude. They are (actual) memories and not hallucinations. By noting S.'s reaction, we can better appreciate the extent to which a so-called (successful) reader is both aware and unaware of being deceived. A reader may know there is no corresponding referent for the grand palace, and yet she also believes that there is, or that there could be, or that there may be, or that there once was—in order to immerse more pleasurably in the story.[29] Reading inaugurates a state in which the successful reader *forgets to remember* that what she is encountering is not real. If she could not suspend her disbelief in this way she could not be captured, nor *captivated*, by the process of reading, as S. clearly cannot be. There is a profound confusion between belief and disbelief in the act of reading—such that reading convokes a state in which *there is no disbelief to suspend*.

When we are actively hallucinating, we do not know that we are doing so. "We" are not really "on hand" to make the distinction, since the cognitive faculties are occupied at the moment in question. One can only ever know that she was hallucinating afterward. In the nineteenth-century, when such research was becoming widespread, Edward Gurney argued in *Phantasms of the Living* (1886), that hallucination is only recognizable as such *after the fact*, and never during the episode. Another thinker on the subject, Hippolyte

Taine, offers a complementary assessment: "Whenever the objects of imagination engross the attention wholly, they produce a temporary belief of their reality."[30] Gurney came to the conclusion that one does not so much hallucinate as conclude that she "had been hallucinating."[31] Gurney writes, "The definition of sensory hallucination would thus be *a percept which lacks, but which can only by distinct reflection be recognized as lacking, the objective basis which it suggests*."[32] It may well be the case, however, that the moment of "distinct reflection" never actually comes. Who is to say that my reflection will be "distinct," my conclusion along the order of "recognition," or that my judgment will be "objective"? One might protest that she always maintains a semi-conscious sense of "having been hallucinating," albeit shortly before being ensnared by another signifier. This state of semi-awareness regulates a coherent, if blurred and shifting boundary, between hallucinating and not-hallucinating. Yet some scholars, such as Taine, argue that the distinction itself is specious, and so *never* coherent enough to locate or verify. We are always hallucinating.[33] Not only can the "watcher" not remove herself from the symbolic chain, but the "watcher" herself is produced by, and appears as the effect of, an accumulation of (alphabetic) signs. Lacan writes, "The Other is the locus in which is situated the chain of the signifier that governs whatever may be made present of the subject—it is the field of that living being in which the subject has to appear."[34]

The alphabetized brain never stops hallucinating. This is ultimately the case, *even without a text*, as though it were quite impossible to stay "with" the body, to discontinue the constancy of self-exiting. Lacan calls this, after a fashion, aphanisis. Aphanisis means one "leaves" her body to "appear" elsewhere, that is, in the Symbolic order, the field of the Other. She succumbs to "fading" in the physical register, the better to immerse in her representations. Indeed: "How can one deny that *nothing* of the world appears to me except in my representations?"[35] Lacan references the kind of subject born of such an orientation as: *I see myself seeing myself.* [36] The "self" I see myself seeing has very little to do with my corporeal incarnation—which is often in a state of disuse anyhow—and everything to do with the "imago" I have internalized and carry around in my mental theater space. A moment's reflection confirms this split from my body, since I never "look down" when I am engaged in seeing myself. Neither am I equipped to perform most of my daily routines in front of a mirror, though the sense of the specular is profoundly present within the paradigm of *I see myself seeing myself*. For Lacan, as for Gurney and Taine, the world is thereby "struck with a presumption of idealization, of the suspicion of yielding only my representations."[37] Taine describes perception along the lines of other paradoxes such as "real abstraction" or "immediate medium." He calls it "true hallucination";[38] *all perception*, he argues, consists in "illusions and rectifications of illusion— hallucinations and repressions of hallucination."[39] In the course of everyday perception, illusion and rectification of the illusion "follow so closely that they are confused into one."[40] This is yet another sense in which there is no disbelief to suspend.

To better explain the alphabetic paradox of "immediate media" and "true hallucination," and to establish a genealogy of the hallucinating subject, we turn to a time of rupture within the early modern Christian church. In late medieval England, Christian scripture dealt extensively with the gory materiality of the crucified body. The Middle English verse poem, "The Long Charter," used the controlling metaphor of an alphabetic text to signify Christ's physical sacrifice. The crucified body is depicted as a kind of charter (with the seal authenticated in His blood) to be handed in ("redeemed") at the appropriate hour, thus admitting the owner/believer into the kingdom of heaven. Of the poem, Laura Ashe explains, "[the] metaphor is fully, and perhaps for modern tastes excessively, developed such that Christ's skin has been stretched on the cross to make the parchment, the scourges of the attackers the pen, his blood (and sometimes the spittle of the Jews) the ink, the wound in his side the seal."[41]

Enjoying common currency, the metaphor also connected the parchment which was fastened onto a child's hornbook (from which she learnt her alphabet) to Christ's body nailed on "the tree of the rood." Christ's nailed hands and feet are akin to "the ABC nailed on its wooden panel."[42] Margaret Aston cites the following passage from a poem in which the "savior's wounds become the red letters limned on the vellum."[43] Vellum itself is the *skin*, usually derived from pigs, on which alphabetic material, including the Gutenberg Bibles, was printed, so the comparison is not inappropriate:

Come hither, Joseph, behold and look,
How many bloody letters ben written in this book.
How many letters thereon be
Read and thou may wite and see.[44]

"Wite" is a Middle English synonym for "see." The imperative to take in the savior with one's eyes already obtains—hence "behold," "look," "read," "wite," and "see"—and is tantamount to absorbing divine presence. An identity between reading and taking in the divine has already been established, however tenuously, and both confirm the ocular orientation that accompanies high literacy. Children adopt this epistemological outlook. Yet the comparison of Christ's flesh to alphabetic textuality—and the scene of a blood-soaked crucifixion as template and writing surface for the Gospels—is problematic to the extent that, though vivid and intense, it (bleeding flesh) does not promote automatic reading. In Havelock's words, the alphabet must cease to "impose itself as an object of thought," it must *fail* to be spectacular. In retrospect, it was a misjudgment to so readily entwine letters with the fleshly wounds of an embodied Savior. Perhaps there is something salient to the notion that the Protestant Reformation in Germany was considerably more successful than previous English efforts, because it had the benefit of the printing press.

The alphabet depends on its ability to "disappear" into its apprehension by the reader; the code erases itself as it effectuates its decoding. As the historian of the printing press, Elizabeth L. Eisenstein, writes, "One might compare the effects of listening to a Gospel passage read from the pulpit with reading the same passage at home for oneself. In the first instance, the Word comes from a priest who is at a distance and on high; in the second it seems to come from a silent voice that is within."[45] The most powerful idea is to imagine that God is speaking directly to me: that His voice is resounding in my head, and that I soak up his meaning *without mediation*. This is impossible, of course. There is always a material incarnation of the alphabet; yet the "agitation" and "friction" may be so deftly obscured as to seem inexistent.

With the advent of the printing press, Luther and his contemporaries had the advantage, in their crusade against the Catholic Church, of the ability to efface—to a far greater extent than ever before—the concrete medium from the field of consciousness in the act of reading. Much of the movement of Protestantism consists in the struggle to eliminate the "medium." The Catholic hierarchy stands in the way of direct access to God, just as a conspicuous medium draws attention to itself *as medium* and thus weakens spiritual union. Though all major religions of the Book are chirographic, the Protestant Reformation may be judged as particularly influential because it was typographic.

If one wanted to obscure a medium, how might she do so? To begin with, she would make each letter identical in height and width. Each letter type would consist of a "uniform rectangular body."[46] It would be so cast as to encourage "proper juxtaposition to one another in free combination."[47] They would be interchangeable.[48] The spacing would be uniform. Margins would be strictly set and make judicious use of white space. The distance between words would be exact, though they would differ from the distance between letters within the same word. All would be left-justified. Like the tidiest furrows in a well-ploughed field, the lines—and the non-lines or white lines that would separate one row from another—would be highly standardized and inked evenly. They would bear no trace of an individual copyist, his unsteadiness of hand, for instance, or his imperfectly straight lines. They would not be copied, in other words, but produced by a moveable metal type printing press. They would be printed.

The invention of the printing press and the uniformity and ubiquity of print made the German Reformation more successful than earlier English efforts (i.e., Lollardy). And though Wyclif and his followers lacked the printing press, we can still detect certain strategies on their part, perhaps unwitting, to obscure the alphabet in other ways. One is to regard the Bible as a sacred object, rather than an ordinary book or other manufactured thing. For Wyclif, "Holy Scripture is defined not as any physical book or expression in a particular language but as the Eternal Word or Book of Life that transcends any individual exemplar."[49] Such notions of an "Eternal Word" and a "Book of Life" are, of course, thoroughly alphabetic. Jesus exists between and through letters: "Moreover, Wyclif regards Christ both as the hermeneutical key that guarantees true interpretation of scripture and as scripture itself."[50] Though they constantly invoke it, the reformers do not draw attention to the *act* of reading. That is, they regard both the act and the Book as something which involves no decoding or mediation. In a single gesture—summed up in the phrase, *sola scriptura*—the Reformers both exalt the alphabetic text and minimize, if not erase, it.

None is more adept at effecting this paradoxical gesture than Martin Luther. Luther succeeds in convincing people that reading has nothing to do with deciphering a peculiar code, but rather communing with the Divine. The Catholic clergy can only stand in the way of this access. (This strategy is also behind his translation of the Bible into the vernacular.) The elimination of the priests indeed removes *one* layer of "friction" between God and believer. The Protestant remedy presents a kind of proxy solution to the actual (unsolvable) problem of alphabetic mediation (and also ambiguity, as we shall see). It is a sizable obstacle for a religion wholly dependent upon the book, and one seeking to become even more so by stripping itself of all other benchmarks (hierarchy, tradition, liturgy, iconography, and so on). By ridding oneself of a corrupt and insidious clerical structure, one appears to have rid oneself of the difficulties of mediation, without accepting, of course, that the real contradiction is elsewhere. Why, for example, does the monotheistic God choose to incarnate himself through an obscure, pagan-Greek technology? God preexists the text but chooses to reveal Himself alphabetically.

If authority is located in the author and the author is God, and if the question of what the Scriptures "literally" mean is in fact an admonition to refer back to the alphabetic letters, then we have traveled in a circle. Rather than retreating from such tautologies, Luther accepted them as proof of the self-corroborating nature of the text. The heart of the message of the famous speech at Worms can be summarized as follows: "Scripture was the sole authority. It was even the authority on its authoritative interpretation. Scripture, Luther insisted, interpreted itself."[51] It is the authority on its own authority. What better means to address the uncanniness of the alphabet than to insist that it is the incarnation of God Himself. *Jesus is a self-interpreting alphabetic text.* In this way, the gimmick—or perhaps, the magic—inherent in reading becomes its virtue rather than a point of weakness. It elicits the faith of the faithful. Because it *is* God, the alphabet is more than capable of sustaining the paradox of an "immediate medium"—or more precisely, a medium *which is not one.*

A hand-copied manuscript, in contrast to a printed one, was difficult to read. The words were not spaced uniformly across the page but ran together. One strained to read a hand-copied manuscript. She remained aware of the distinction between one copy and another, such as the illuminations, for example, and the unmistakable and unavoidable "presence" of the copyist on virtually every page, calling up *this* monk, in *this* cloister, at *this* time period, and so on. (It is too much "context".) Though there would have been little lay reading or circulation of such manuscripts, the hand-copied text proclaims itself in terms of what might be called its "use value": its embeddedness in a set of expectations and purposes. This "use value" undermines its status as a fetish object. The supply, moreover, is strictly limited by the length of time and level of difficulty it requires for a single monk to produce a single Bible. From 1455, however, the Bible is printed, and from the moment it "steps forth as a commodity," Marx tells us, the object "is changed into something transcendent."[52] How much of the fetish character of a commodity is residual from this origination in mass-produced Bibles? There is a direct alphabetic logic to capitalist (mass) production:

> [Print] embedded the word itself deeply in the manufacturing process and made it into a kind of commodity. The first assembly line, a technique of manufacture which in a series of set steps produces identical complex objects made up of replaceable parts, was not one which produced stoves or shoes or weaponry but one which produced the printed book. In the late 1700s, the industrial revolution applied to other manufacturing the replaceable part techniques which printers had worked with for three hundred years.[53]

Henry Ford will simply accelerate the techniques derived from Gutenberg. The printing press had long since existed in China, though the Chinese printers molded characters, while the Korean and Uigur Turks molded words, not letters.[54] Ong tells us that the alphabetic letterpress, in which "each letter was cast on a separate piece of metal, or type, marked a psychological breakthrough of the first order," because it made words more "thing-like," though it also served to generalize the notion that the letters of the alphabet *preexist* the words they combine to make.[55] Likewise God preexists the words into which He will make himself known in the Bible.

The minimum, according to the central tenets of the Reformation, is that each person should be able to read (the Bible) by him or herself. In the decades following Gutenberg's invention, literacy rates rise accordingly, showing a "radical increase" from the 1520s throughout the remainder of the century and beyond.[56] Literacy reached an "epochal culmination" during the Reformation, as it placed "new primacy on reading and mass schooling."[57] Unsurprisingly, Luther became a "tireless advocate for schools."[58] Though Gusdorf calls it a "significant coincidence" that the "very same group of people who decide in 1536 to adopt the Reformation in Geneva likewise enact compulsory public education,"[59] there is, of course, no coincidence at all. The Protestant admonition to universal literacy—which has in fact become the *compulsory literacy* we know in the West today—affirms the principle that solitary reading provides the basis for a religious experience that is both sufficient and *preferable to* the material-ritual, collective experience of all prior religions. Never before had there been a religion which could be practiced completely alone, and homologically, neither had there been a religion so deeply beholden to an alphabetic text. As Eisenstein suggests, what could be more powerful than God communicating with me directly? The "silent voice" is another alphabetic contradiction, yet God is fully capable of contradiction: the "silent voice that seems to come from within" would likely have seemed to be God Himself "speaking" to me alone.[60] The fallible priest, and even the presence of other parishioners, can inspire little confidence or appeal when compared to the (alphabetic) voice of God that I can "hear" resounding, apparently *inside* me, as I read. Print only escalates this effect, because the monk-copyist's presence no longer interferes with my hallucinations of divine unification, and the texts themselves are plentiful and inexpensive.

It is not surprising, then, that at this historical conjuncture, greater and greater numbers of people experience the (religious) *hallucination* as more compelling and more attractive—indeed more "real"—than anything they encounter in the flesh. Indeed, the dullness of the quotidian must have been unbearable by contrast. We may note that of the Solae of the Protestant Reformation, each entails a strictly *mental* disposition; they are: *sola scriptura* (the Bible alone), *sola fide* (faith alone), and *sola gratia* (grace alone), with *solo Christo* (Christ alone) and *soli Deo gloria* (glory to God alone) following later. Each takes place within the realm of hallucination and is an avowed commitment to the priority of the hallucinated world.

A new kind of European religious practice is slowly instituted—the first that can be called radically self-contained—in which the main tenet is the solitary engagement with alphabetic writing. One reads and interprets the Bible *by oneself*. Lutheranism, and concurrent reformation movements such as Calvinism and Pietism, will redefine religious experience. A religion based overwhelmingly on *the solitary reading of a book* entails "practices" that would have been unrecognizable *as religion* up to that point, in part because expressions of religious devotion had never taken place primarily on an "interior plane." The social rituals that once defined religious activity were deemphasized and in many cases eliminated outright. The rejection of (c)atholic practice in favor of the Book, that is, solitary reading, solidifies the discourse of the individual who stands (alone) before God.[61]

The individual is alone before a God who interpellates him, inviting him to accept the call. Importantly, Althusser's well-known scene of interpellation is modelled on instances drawn from the Judeo-Christian religion of the Book. In the Biblical scene, as well as in Althusser's modified scene in which the individual is hailed by the officer of the law, it is not sufficient to be hailed, either by the Word of God, or the call, "*Hey, you there!*" One must "turn" and respond to the hail in order for the circuit to be completed; that is, for the subject to be recruited. Luther's description of himself on the streets of Wittenburg bears an uncanny resemblance to Althusser's scene of interpellation. In the following, he describes how to remove mediation (the obstacle of Latin) from communion with God, articulating his plan to formulate a vernacular German translation of the Bible by "considering the mouths" of lay people: "We have to interrogate the mother in her house, the children in the streets, the common man in the market, and consider their mouths to know how they speak in order to translate accordingly. Then they will understand and will note that we are speaking German with them."[62] Interrogation and interpellation are both forms of address in which a response is demanded, usually under the weight of authority on the part of the one who hails. His phrase, "Then they will understand," suggests persuasion, an elicitation of fellow-feeling, complementary to the demand for a reply. Interrogation requires a response as firmly as does interpellation. According to Althusser, the latter should be understood along the order of "Pascal's Christ [who] says, 'It is for you that I have shed this drop of my blood,' where what is required is the response, '*Yes, it really is me!*'"[63] The analogous structure is apparent in Althusser's use of the Old Testament version: "And it came to pass at that time that God the Lord (Yahweh) spoke to Moses in the cloud. And the Lord cried to Moses, 'Moses!' And Moses replied, 'It is (really) I! I am Moses thy servant, speak and I shall listen!' And the Lord spoke to Moses and said to him, '*I am that I am.*'"

All alphabetic forms, provided I have been made literate, are *addressed to me*. The letters, so long as I have been alphabetized, cannot block my entry into the hallucination, provided they are in a language I know. This is the case for every reader of the alphabet and every consumer of the other media it has enabled. I will find certain hallucinations more attractive than others, and I will divert my attention accordingly, but I am almost never *not hallucinating*. One of the first and most profound instances of the general address that is alphabetics comes through the Bible. Luther understood this: every (faithful) reader of the Bible knows that the words are addressed to him. The answer to the hail, according to Althusser—the turn—is the point at which the subject is inaugurated: "Why? Because he has recognized that the hail was 'really' addressed to him, and that 'it was *really him* who was hailed' (and not someone else) . . . . The one hailed always recognizes that it is really him who is being hailed."[64] The alphabet creates a universe of hallucination that in one way or another "recruits" subjects ("it recruits them all").[65]

I "turn" at all scenes of interpellation automatically, which is to say, I "read" before it occurs to me to refuse to read. Perhaps that sign or this message or that notice or this advertisement or that hail is not addressed to me, but I "read" it just to make sure it is not addressed to me. Either way, I read it. This is the sense in which the hail always gets it right. The alphabetized subject must be made to see not the letters, but rather the imaginary worlds of which they are simply the triggers. Once fully alphabetized, the literate subject no longer even requires a physical text to trigger hallucinations. In the absence of an alphabetic script, she will "read" her own projections, anxieties, fantasies, narrations, actions, perceptions, and responses in precisely the same way. One runs some scenarios—or replays others—almost ceaselessly. Increasingly, there is computational media as well, for which the effort of "reading" in multiple senses—that is, the agitation or friction of grappling with an interface—is almost reduced to nil. While there are versions of all such things in non-alphabetic cultures, of course, I would argue that they do not structure the lifeworld to such a profound extent that there is never a reprieve, and from which there can be no exit.

Today, "virtual" constructions order our lives so thoroughly that whether or not they are "real" or "virtual" has little bearing on our day-to-day interactions. We no longer find it worth it to make the distinction. In an early work exploring virtual reality, Giuseppe Mantovani differentiated two approaches to understanding VR. The first he called the "conventional" view, which posited the VR environment as an invented world with a reality of its own, though one which was distinguishable from the "real" world. Using the example of a love-making scene between Casey and Linda in "Neuromancer," he writes, "For supporters of this position, Linda is either Casey's girl in flesh and blood, or she is a simulation. They believe that, however efficient the simulation, we can always distinguish between the real and the simulated Lindas."[66] In contrast to the conventional view, there is the "cyber perspective": "In this case, knowing whether the Linda who is embraced is 'real' or simulated is not important, because the only difference, the physicality of her body, is a trap to be sprung." Advocates of the latter view seek to embrace a new orientation—"one in which warrantability is irrelevant, spectacle is plastic and negotiated, and desire no longer grounds itself in physicality."[67] Mantovani was writing seventeen years ago. Simulations were far more rudimentary and cursory than they are today. A term more appropriate to contemporary conditions may be Hayles's cognitive nonconscious—a term modified from Nigel Thrift's technological uncon-

scious[68]—a state in which the possibility for either challenging or confirming the distinction between real and virtual does not even arise. One example is the "soft-computing" of wearables, such as cellphones or more literally, Apple watches, which function as symbiotic appendages:

> "The goal of wearable computing is to produce a synergistic combination of human and machine, in which the human performs tasks that it is better at, while the computer performs tasks that it is better at. Over an extended period of time, the wearable computer begins to function as a true extension of the mind and body, and no longer feels as if it is a separate entity. In fact, the user will adapt to the apparatus in the same way that we adapt to shoes and clothing to such a degree that being without them would make most of us feel extremely uncomfortable."[69]

Many people are "extremely uncomfortable" without their smart-phones. Between soft-computing and "ubiquitous" computing, such as the "embedded sensors, smart coatings on walls, fabrics, and appliances, and RFID (radio frequency ID) tags"[70] that cover our environments—in addition to what Thrift calls "track-and-trace" positioning technology—it becomes quite difficult to differentiate a "real" from a "virtual" set of circumstances. In this respect, Mantovani was right (and Luther before him) when he noted in 1995:

> The less media-operated mediation is perceived, because the medium presents its fictional world efficiently, the more mediated experience *surreptitiously replaces* people's possible direct experience, without their becoming aware of the moment when direct and indirect experience might diverge.[71]

This is yet another way of saying, "there is no disbelief to suspend."

Nick Bostrom famously argued not only that we like to play simulation games but that it is quite likely we are complex self-aware avatars in an ancestor simulation game ourselves.[72] Even if Bostrom's thesis is not true, it is still true. Ever since the invention and widespread use of the alphabet, we have been the coded subjects of a contingent technology that operates by projecting the coordinates of its own virtual reality—by iterating and reiterating its (primary and) secondary modelling systems—and normalizing it as "real." One of the central ways of doing so is through the illusion of a self at the center of these hallucinations. According to the contemporary

German philosopher, Thomas Metzinger, the brain produces an internal model of the self and presents as transparent what is in fact a complicated illusion. In other words, the model does not know that it is a model (instead taking itself as "an actually existing entity"), which leads Metzinger to state "nobody ever *was* or *had* a self."[73] Inasmuch as we are indeed self-aware avatars in a simulated world, Bostrom is correct.

Perhaps we may better understand now why, as Frederic Jameson quipped, it is easier to envision the end of the world than it is to envision the end of capitalism. Both alphabet and capitalism are open systems, which means they have no end and can brook "no Outside."[74] Colonialism is the union and spread of both. Because the alphabetized subject is the locus of hallucinations, there are no means for her to investigate what non-capitalist social formations—or, alternately, oral cultures—were (or are) like, since she always brings the alphabet along with her. As Ong notes, there can only be apophatic descriptions of oral culture from our position of high-literacy. We can only know oral culture by what it was not. Yet to assess alphabetics (and capitalism) as violent systems—and certainly as much more systematically violent and destructive than non-alphabetic cultures—is not to "romanticize" oral cultures or to indulge in nostalgia. It is to try to understand a means of life that did not have a hallucinating subject at its center. If we accept the hallucinating subject as "natural," however, rather than as a social and historical aberration resulting from the Greek invention, then we, as Badiou suggests, may as well end all talk of "collective action."[75] *For either there is collectivity*, which I have tried to render here, *via negativa*, through glimpses of those non-capitalist oral formations in which *all of* human history was comprised prior to the Greek alphabet—or there is the individual immersed in her own self-obsessions.

At the conclusion of *2001: A Space Odyssey*, Dave Bowman arrives at the far end of the universe to find that he is inside of his own head. Beyond the stargate a banal domestic interior, decorated in the style of Louis XVI, materializes, along with mirror images and projections of other "Dave Bowmans." He is aware of organic life, perhaps, only by the sound of his own steady breathing. When Kubrick pairs the breathing with the odd shrieks of the Ligeti track, we understand that the monolith is not far. Past Pluto, at the edge of space and time, all that Dave Bowman discovers is the individual self, embalmed in its technological grip.

Notes

PRELUDE

1. Arthur C. Clarke, "The Sentinel," in *The Sentinel: Masterworks of Science Fiction and Fantasy* (New York: Berkley Books, 1983), 148.

2. Martin Heidegger, "Who Is Nietzsche's Zarathustra?," trans. Bernd Magnus, *The Review of Metaphysics* 20, no. 3 (1967): 413.

3. See David W. Patterson, "Music, Structure and Metaphor in Stanley Kubrick's *2001: A Space Odyssey*," *American Music* 22, no. 3 (2004): 444–74.

4. Stanley Kubrick and Arthur C. Clarke, *2001: A Space Odyssey*. Unpublished screenplay, 1965. www.archiviokubrick.it

5. Clarke, "The Sentinel," 142.

6. Susan White, "Kubrick's Obscene Shadows," in *Stanley Kubrick's 2001: A Space Odyssey: New Essays*, ed. Robert Kolker (Oxford: Oxford University Press, 2006), 127–46.

7. See Leroi-Gourhan discussed in Michael Haworth, "Bernard Stiegler on Transgenerational Memory and the Dual Origin of the Human," *Theory, Culture & Society* 33, no. 3 (2016): 151–73.

8. Michel Chion, *Kubrick's Cinema Odyssey* (London: British Film Institute, 2001), 135.

9. "The Invention of the Human" is the name of Part I of Bernard Stiegler's *Technics and Time, 1: The Fault of Epimetheus*, trans. Richard Beardsworth and George Collins (Redwood City, CA: Stanford University Press, 1998).

10. Most non-human primates eat meat only rarely, thus making the gorging on tapir meat doubly unnecessary. See David P. Watts, "Meat Eating by Nonhuman Primates: A Review and Synthesis," *Journal of Human Evolution* 149 (2020): 1–25.

11. André Leroi-Gourhan, *Gesture and Speech*, trans. Anna Bostock Berger (Cam-

bridge, MA: MIT Press, 1993), 184–85. He notes, "The human internal economy, however, was still that of a highly predatory mammal even after the transition to farming and stockbreeding . . . . In this way human society became the chief consumer of humans, through violence and through work, with the result that the human has gradually gained complete possession of the natural world."

12. Heidegger, "Who Is Nietzsche's Zarathustra?," 415.

13. Carl Freedman, "Superman among the Stars," review of *Kubrick's 2001: A Triple Allegory* by Leonard F. Wheat, *Science Fiction Studies* 28, no. 2 (2001): 297.

14. Friedrich Nietzsche, *Thus Spake Zarathustra*, trans. Thomas Common (New York: Modern Library, 1917), 6. He writes, "Ye have made your way from the worm to man, and much within you is still worm. Once were ye apes, and even yet man is more of an ape than any of the apes."

15. Heidegger, "Zarathustra," 414.

16. Friedrich A. Kittler, "In the Wake of the Odyssey," in *The Truth of the Technological World: Essays on the Genealogy of Presence*, trans. Erik Butler (Redwood City, CA: Stanford University Press, 2013), 286.

17. Kittler, "In the Wake of the Odyssey," 286.

18. Friedrich A. Kittler, "Universities: Wet, Hard, Soft, and Harder," *Critical Inquiry* 31, no. 1 (2004): 249. The full quote reads "The Turing machine, then, was, is, and will be the condition of possibility of all computers. Just as in ancient Greece where one and the same alphabet stood at once for speech elements, natural numbers, and musical pitches, our binary system encompasses everything known about culture and nature, which was formerly encoded in letters, images, and sounds."

19. White, "Kubrick's Obscene Shadows," 130.

INTRODUCTION

1. Claude Lévi-Strauss, *Tristes Tropiques*, trans. Doreen Weightman and John Weightman (New York: Penguin Books, 2012).

2. See, for example, Chris Johnson, "Lévi-Strauss: The Writing Lesson Revisited," *Modern Language Review* 92, no. 3 (1997): 599–612; and Peggy Kamuf, "Chris Johnson's Writing Lesson," *Paragraph* 43, no. 1 (2020): 114–21. See also Rodolphe Gasché, "The 'Violence' of Deconstruction," *Research in Phenomenology* 45, no. 2 (2015): 169–90.

3. Jacques Derrida, *Of Grammatology*, trans. Gayatri Chakravorty Spivak, 1st American ed. (Baltimore: Johns Hopkins University Press, 1976).

4. Lévi-Strauss, *Tristes Tropiques*, 345.

5. Lévi-Strauss, 347.

6. Lévi-Strauss, 346.

7. Lévi-Strauss, 346.

8. Lévi-Strauss, 348.

9. Lévi-Strauss, 352.

10. Lévi-Strauss, 348.

11. Lévi-Strauss, 342. Here he quotes from the report of an American Protestant Missionary.

12. Renée Koch Piettre, "Claude Lévi-Strauss," last modified January 14, 2018, https://prosopo.ephe.psl.eu/claude-lévi-strauss

13. Derrida, Of Grammatology, 56.

14. Walter J. Ong, Orality and Literacy: The Technologizing of the Word (London: Taylor & Francis e-Library, 2004), 83.

15. Spivak, Translator's Preface, Of Grammatology, lxxxiii.

16. Derrida, Of Grammatology, 110 (emphasis mine).

17. Derrida, 110.

18. Derrida, 109.

19. Derrida, 109.

20. Derrida, 110.

21. Derrida, 112.

22. Derrida, 37.

23. Sandra Gustafson, "Orality and Literacy in Transatlantic Perspective," 19: Interdisciplinary Studies in the Long Nineteenth Century 18 (May 9, 2014): 2, https://doi .org/10.16995/ntn.687. Gustafson writes, "For many years any critical analysis of oral genres risked being dismissed as unsophisticated phonocentrism, and while this burden has lightened somewhat recently, it is by no means entirely gone. This is a confused response to a major issue in literary studies, but an influential one none-theless."

24. Lydia H. Liu, "Scripts in Motion: Writing as Imperial Technology, Past and Present," PMLA 130, no. 2 (2015): 375.

25. Derrida is introduced to the philosophy community in the United States with his delivery of the paper "Structure, Sign, and Play in the Discourse of the Human Sciences" in 1966, though his influence in American literary studies, largely through the efforts of Gayatri Spivak, will be far more significant. Homi Bhabha, another major figure in postcolonial studies, is also profoundly influenced by Derrida. Edward Said favors Foucault in Orientalism, but with multiple qualifications.

26. Liu, "Scripts in Motion," 377.

27. Derrida, Of Grammatology, 90. But because Liu has removed power and vio-lence from her discussion of writing as an imperial technology, she is puzzled as to why the "Romanized script," i.e., the Greek alphabet, has taken over the world and more contemporarily, the internet in the form of the English language. Indeed, such questions are unanswerable if all scripts and writing systems are the same.

28. Havelock argues that the impressions Western culture holds of the glory and splendor of ancient Greece are taken from the oral period, that is, the period of com-plete non-literacy. Admittedly, Havelock and Ong also exalt what they see as the trea-sures of the Greek alphabet and do entertain the narrative of civilizational genius. But they do not attribute this to the "superiority" of the Greek people; rather, they just

so happen to be the ones among whom it occurred. It is a profound misunderstanding of their work to assume, as many have, that the celebration of the alphabet—by a life-long writer and a Catholic priest, no less—is equivalent to the simultaneous denigration of oral cultures. In fact, they regularly caution against such intellectual slackness. By affirming "literacy," they are not simultaneously devaluing orality. The same is less obvious, however, in more intemperate writers such as Marshall McLuhan and Friedrich Kittler. Havelock, Ong, McLuhan, and Kittler, though accused of ethnocentrism, nevertheless deliver valuable insights not generated elsewhere, even though one is forced to overlook the privilege and occasional condescension they are sometimes prone to express. See also the successors to Kittler who attempt to correct his excesses while retaining his insights in the compelling work of German Media Theory. Additional, related works of the Toronto School of Communication theory, such as Robert K. Logan's *The Alphabet Effect*, are neither circumspect in their Eurocentrism nor contain much of value to our current concerns.

29. Eric A. Havelock, *The Literate Revolution in Greece and Its Cultural Consequences* (Princeton University Press, 2019), 44, https://doi.org/10.2307/j.ctvbcd1d2. He refers to it as "a recent accident."

30. Derrida, *Of Grammatology*, 107.

31. Claude Lévi-Strauss, *Structural Anthropology*, trans. Claire Jacobson and Brooke Grundfest Schoepf (New York: Basic Books, Inc., 1963), 344.

32. Levi-Strauss, *Tristes Tropiques*, 351.

33. Vilém Flusser and Mark Poster, *Does Writing Have a Future?*, Electronic Mediations, v. 33 (Minneapolis: University of Minnesota Press, 2011). It is for this reason that his conjecture that *images* somehow correct or displace writing is mistaken.

34. Friedrich A. Kittler, *Discourse Networks 1800/1900* (Stanford, CA: Stanford University Press, 1990), 53.

35. Because they cannot "see" the alphabet, scholarly fields such as book history are promising, but ultimately insufficient to address these questions. Though they foreground materiality in important ways, they still unwittingly eclipse the theoretical areas that require investigation. They also partake in what we might call the ethnocentrism fallacy. German Media Theory, too, makes interesting use of the physicality of communication devices, but perhaps in a backlash against its main progenitor, Friedrich Kittler, it often downplays the uniqueness of the alphabet, as this would foreground European media and thus compound his perceived ethnocentrism. The work in this field is nonetheless useful as is related research in the fields of "the internet of things," media ecology, and media archaeology. Media archaeology would appear to be better equipped than some of the other paths of inquiry to incorporate philosophical and theoretical concerns. See, for example, Erkki Huhtamo and Jussi Parikka, eds., *Media Archaeology: Approaches, Applications, and Implications* (Berkeley: University of California Press, 2011).

36. N. Katherine Hayles, *My Mother Was a Computer: Digital Subjects and Literary Texts* (Chicago: University of Chicago Press, 2010), 49–50. She writes, "Code has

become arguably as important as natural language because it causes things to happen, which requires that it be executed as commands the machine can run. Code that runs on a machine is performative in a much stronger sense than that attributed to language."

37. Friedrich A. Kittler, *Gramophone, Film, Typewriter*, Writing Science (Stanford, CA: Stanford University Press, 1999), xl.

38. See Catherine Malabou, *Plasticity at the Dusk of Writing: Dialectic, Destruction, Deconstruction*, Insurrections (New York: Columbia University Press, 2010); Catherine Malabou, "The End of Writing? Grammatology and Plasticity," *The European Legacy* 12, no. 4 (July 2007): 431–41, https://doi.org/10.1080/10848770701396254

39. Claude Lévi-Strauss, *Tristes Tropiques*, 349.

CHAPTER 1

1. Marshall McLuhan, *Understanding Media: The Extensions of Man* (Cambridge, MA: MIT Press, 1994), 83.

2. Denise Schmandt-Besserat, *Before Writing* (Austin: University of Texas Press, 1992), 4. Schmandt-Besserat argues most educated people still believed the alphabet had been deposited on Earth by God well into the eighteenth century.

3. Eric A. Havelock, "Oral Composition in the Oedipus Tyrannus of Sophocles," *New Literary History* 16, no. 1 (1984): 185, https://doi.org/10.2307/468781

4. Eric A. Havelock, *Origins of Western Literacy: Four Lectures Delivered at the Ontario Institute for Studies in Education*, Toronto, March 25, 26, 27, 28, 1974 (Toronto: Ontario Institute for Studies in Education, 1976), 41.

5. Gita Bandopadhyay, "Bengal's Nonsense Rhymes," *India International Centre Quarterly* 17, no. 3/4 (1990): 265.

6. Eric A. Havelock, *The Literate Revolution in Greece and Its Cultural Consequences* (Princeton, NJ: Princeton University Press, 2019), 77–80, https://doi.org/10.2307/j.ctvbcd1d2. See Havelock's far more elegant explanation using "Jack and Jill." I have added a rhyme of non-European origin to express the colonial implications of alphabetic literacy—something with which Havelock was not expressly concerned, though in many ways, as I explain in the next chapter, the intrusions of literacy upon the Greeks themselves are revealing of its effects on other oral cultures.

7. Havelock, *Literate Revolution*, 78–79. To be exact, there must actually be subtraction with consonantal systems not (the) addition (of vowels), because the vowel sound is included with the consonant to form a syllable. For the first word "rock," we would encounter something like the symbols "ra ca" or "ru cu" or "ro co" and so on, so that we would have to make choices about where to keep the vowel sound, where to mentally cut it off and ignore it, as well as where the words within the phrase began and ended. Already the idea that the alphabet "adds vowels" is fallacious.

8. Bandopadhyay, "Bengal's Nonsense Rhymes," 266.

9. Havelock, *Origins of Western Literacy*, 42.

10. Havelock, *Literate Revolution*, 81.

11. Ferdinand de Saussure, *Course in General Linguistics*, ed. Charles Bally and Albert Sechehaye, trans. Wade Baskin (New York: Philosophical Library, 1959), 45.

12. Havelock, *Literate Revolution*, 80.

13. Havelock, 81.

14. The classification system of occlusives is also revealing. As Saussure explains, they are categorized according to the precise location in the orofacial region where they block the vibrating column of air. Those that are formed by the closing and sealing of the lips, as with "p," are called labials (i.e., p, b, m); those that include the opening and closing of the teeth in the modification of the vibrating column are known as dentals (i.e., t, d, n); those made by the constricting of the throat region are known as gutturals (i.e., k, g, ñ), and so on. The contemporary "points of articulation" have expanded to include more precise categories, including bilabials, labiodentals, alveolars, palatals, velars, uvulars, etc. There are also subgroupings according to the "manner of articulation," etc.

15. Henri-Jean Martin, *The History and Power of Writing*, trans. Lydia G. Cochrane (Chicago: University of Chicago Press, 1994), 31.

16. Havelock, *Literate Revolution*, 77.

17. Friedrich A. Kittler, *Discourse Networks 1800/1900* (Stanford, CA: Stanford University Press, 1990), 51.

18. Uzzi Ornan, "Phonemes and Their Realization in Hebrew," *Hebrew Studies* 57 (2016): 226.

19. Ornan, 225.

20. Ornan, 225.

21. Albertine Gaur, *Literacy and the Politics of Writing* (Bristol, UK: Intellect Books, 2000), 36.

22. Gaur, 36.

23. Havelock, *Literate Revolution*, 80.

24. Andrew Davidson, "Writing: The Re-Construction of Language," *Language Sciences* 72 (March 2019): 134–49, https://doi.org/10.1016/j.langsci.2018.09.004. Davidson provides a useful overview of this debate.

25. Walter J. Ong, *Orality and Literacy: The Technologizing of the Word* (London: Taylor & Francis e-Library, 2004), 47.

26. Ong, 2.

CHAPTER 2

1. Derrick de Kerckhove, "A Theory of Greek Tragedy," *SubStance* 9, no. 4 (1980): 35, https://doi.org/10.2307/3684038

2. Eric A. Havelock, *The Literate Revolution in Greece and Its Cultural Consequences* (Princeton, NJ: Princeton University Press, 2019), 45. He writes of interpenetration, noting: "Age-old habits of non-literacy were to be invaded by new habits of literacy, whatever those should prove to be."

3. Marshall McLuhan, *The Gutenberg Galaxy: The Making of Typographic Man* (Toronto: University of Toronto Press, 2008), 22.

4. See Tobin Nellhaus, "Literacy, Tyranny, and the Invention of Greek Tragedy," *Journal of Dramatic Theory and Criticism* 3, no. 2 (1989).

5. Mike Chappell, "Delphi and the 'Homeric Hymn to Apollo,'" *The Classical Quarterly* 56, no. 2 (December 2006): 331–48, https://doi.org/10.1017/S0009838806 00036X

6. Chappell, 344.

7. Michael Scott, *Delphi: A History of the Center of the Ancient World* (Princeton, NJ: Princeton University Press, 2014), 21.

8. Scott, 20.

9. C. Scott Littleton, "The Pneuma Enthusiastikon: On the Possibility of Hallucinogenic 'Vapors' at Delphi and Dodona," *Ethos* 14, no. 1 (1986): 77.

10. E. R. Dodds, *The Greeks and the Irrational* (Berkeley: University of California Press, 1951), 71.

11. Littleton, "The Pneuma Enthusiastikon," 77.

12. Rosalind Thomas, "Literacy in Ancient Greece: Functional Literacy, Oral Education, and the Development of a Literate Environment," in *The Making of Literate Societies*, ed. David R. Olson and Nancy Torrance (Malden, MA: Blackwell, 2001), 68.

13. Thomas, 68.

14. Thomas, 68.

15. Scott, *Delphi*, 43.

16. Plato, *Plato: In Twelve Volumes. 1: Euthyphro. Apology. Crito. Phaedo. Phaedrus*, trans. Harold North Fowler, Loeb Classical Library 36 (Cambridge, MA: Harvard University Press, 2005), 275e.

17. Scott, *Delphi*, 12.

18. Leonhard Schmitz and A. S. Wilkins, "Divinatio," in *A Dictionary of Greek and Latin Antiquities*, ed. William Smith, William Wayte, and G. E. Marindin (London: John Murray, 1890).

19. 'The Homeric Hymn to Apollo' quoted in Chappell, "Delphi and the 'Homeric Hymn to Apollo,'" 337.

20. Dodds, *The Greeks and the Irrational*, 72.

21. Scott, *Delphi*, 12.

22. Plato, 244b.

23. Plutarch, "The Obsolescence of Oracles," in *Moralia, Volume V*, trans. Frank Cole Babbitt, Loeb Classical Library 306 (Cambridge, MA: Harvard University Press, 1936), 350–51.

24. Plutarch, 350–51.

25. Aldo Bizzocchi, "How Many Phonemes Does the English Language Have?," *International Journal on Studies in English Language and Literature (IJSELL)* 5 (October 1, 2017): 36–46, https://doi.org/10.20431/2347-3134.0510006

26. Havelock, *The Literate Revolution*, 62.

27. Havelock, 61.

28. Havelock, 61.

29. Havelock, 71.

30. Plato, 275d.

31. Sophocles, Luci Berkowitz, and Theodore F. Brunner, eds., *Oedipus Tyrannus: A New Translation*, A Norton Critical Edition (New York: Norton, 1970), 18–19.

32. Plato, 275e.

33. Cedric H. Whitman, "Jocasta," in *Oedipus Tyrannus: A New Translation*, ed. Luci Berkowitz and Theodore F. Brunner (New York: Norton, 1970), 170.

34. Lorenzo Veracini, *The Settler Colonial Present* (Basingstoke: Palgrave Macmillan, 2015), 16.

35. Veracini, 18.

36. Sophocles, Luci Berkowitz, and Theodore F. Brunner, *Oedipus Tyrannus*, 3.

37. Marshall McLuhan, *Understanding Media: The Extensions of Man*, 1st MIT Press ed. (Cambridge, MA: MIT Press, 1994), 82.

38. McLuhan, 83.

39. Harold Bloom, ed., *Sophocles' Oedipus Rex*, Bloom's Guides (New York: Bloom's Literary Criticism, 2007), 29.

40. Bloom, 29.

41. Sophocles, *The Oedipus Casebook: Reading Sophocles' Oedipus the King*, ed. Mark Rogin Anspach and William Blake Tyrrell (East Lansing: Michigan State University Press, 2020), 33.

42. Sophocles, Berkowitz, and Brunner, *Oedipus Tyrannus*, 11.

43. Sophocles, Berkowitz, and Brunner, 10.

44. Sophocles, Berkowitz, and Brunner, 11.

45. Sophocles, Berkowitz, and Brunner, 12.

46. Sophocles, Berkowitz, and Brunner, 13.

47. Sophocles, Berkowitz, and Brunner, 12.

48. Sophocles, Berkowitz, and Brunner, 12.

49. Sophocles, Berkowitz, and Brunner, 12.

50. Sophocles, Berkowitz, and Brunner, 12–13.

51. Martha C. Nussbaum, "The 'Oedipus Rex' and the Ancient Unconscious," in *Sophocles' Oedipus Rex*, ed. Harold Bloom (New York: Chelsea House, 2007), 156.

52. Frederick Ahl, *Sophocles' Oedipus: Evidence and Self-Conviction* (Ithaca: Cornell University Press, 1991).

53. Jacques Derrida, *Of Grammatology*, trans. Gayatri Chakravorty Spivak (Baltimore: Johns Hopkins University Press, 1976), 138.

54. Sophocles, Berkowitz, and Brunner, *Oedipus Tyrannus*, 26.

55. Friedrich A. Kittler, *Discourse Networks 1800/1900*, trans. Michael Metteer (Stanford, CA: Stanford University Press, 1990), 51.

56. Sophocles, Berkowitz, and Brunner, *Oedipus Tyrannus*, 24.

57. Sophocles, Berkowitz, and Brunner, 24.

58. Sophocles, Berkowitz, and Brunner, 24.

59. Sophocles, Berkowitz, and Brunner, 25.

60. Sophocles, Berkowitz, and Brunner, 29.

61. Sophocles, Berkowitz, and Brunner, 24.

62. Slavoj Žižek, *The Sublime Object of Ideology*, Phronesis (London; New York: Verso, 1989), 43.

63. E. R. Dodds, "On Misunderstanding the 'Oedipus Rex,'" *Greece & Rome* 13, no. 1 (1966): 48.

64. Dodds, 48.

65. Žižek, *The Sublime Object of Ideology*, 43.

66. Žižek, 43.

67. Sophocles, Berkowitz, and Brunner, *Oedipus Tyrannus*, 22.

68. Sophocles, Berkowitz, and Brunner, 29.

69. Sophocles, Berkowitz, and Brunner, 29.

70. Gilles Deleuze and Félix Guattari, *A Thousand Plateaus: Capitalism and Schizophrenia*, trans. Brian Massumi (London: Continuum, 2011), 138.

CHAPTER 3

1. Sigmund Freud, *Three Contributions to the Theory of Sex*, trans. A. A. Brill (New York: Nervous and Mental Disease Publishing Company, 1916), 64.

2. Melanie Klein, "The Rôle of the School in the Libidinal Development of the Child," *The International Journal of Psycho-Analysis* 5 (January 1, 1924): 317.

3. Eric A. Havelock, *The Literate Revolution in Greece and Its Cultural Consequences* (Princeton, NJ: Princeton University Press, 2019), 62, https://doi.org/10.2307/j.ctvbc d1d2

4. Friedrich A. Kittler, *Discourse Networks 1800/1900*, trans. Michael Metteer (Stanford, CA: Stanford University Press, 1990), 30.

5. Eric A. Havelock, *Origins of Western Literacy: Four Lectures Delivered at the Ontario Institute for Studies in Education, Toronto, March 25, 26, 27, 28, 1974* (Toronto: Ontario Institute for Studies in Education, 1976), 20.

6. Walter J. Ong, *Orality and Literacy: The Technologizing of the Word* (London: Taylor & Francis e-Library, 2004), 67.

7. Havelock, *Origins of Western Literacy*, 39.

8. Havelock, 24.

9. Havelock, 24.

10. Philippe Ariès, *Centuries of Childhood: A Social History of Family Life*, trans. Robert Baldick (London: Jonathan Cape Ltd., 1962), 329.

11. Ariès, 329.

12. Ariès, 329.

13. Jacqueline Rose, *The Case of Peter Pan, or, The Impossibility of Children's Fiction*, New Cultural Studies (Philadelphia: University of Pennsylvania Press, 1993), 60.

14. Lewis Mumford, *Technics and Civilization* (Chicago; London: The University of Chicago Press, 2010), 176.

15. Mumford, 176.

16. Mumford, 176.

17. Susan Willis, *A Primer for Daily Life*, Studies in Culture and Communication (London; New York: Routledge, 1991), 144.

18. Willis, 144.

19. Willis, 144.

20. Willis, 143.

21. Willis, 143.

22. David R. Olson and Nancy Torrance, "Conceptualizing Literacy as a Personal Skill and as a Social Practice," in *The Making of Literate Societies*, eds. David R. Olson and Nancy Torrance (Malden, MA: Blackwell, 2001), 9.

23. Jean-Pierre Changeux, *Neuronal Man: The Biology of Mind*, trans. Laurence Garey (New York: Oxford University Press, 1986), 227.

24. Changeux, 227.

25. Bryan Kolb and Robbin Gibb, "Brain Plasticity and Behaviour in the Developing Brain," *Journal of the Canadian Academy of Child and Adolescent Psychiatry = Journal de l'Academie canadienne de psychiatrie de l'enfant et de l'adolescent* 20, no. 4 (November 2011): 265–76.

26. Mark S. Seidenberg, *Language at the Speed of Sight: How We Read, Why So Many Can't, and What Can Be Done about It* (New York: Basic Books, 2018), 4.

27. Walter J. Ong, *Orality and Literacy*, 12.

28. Kolb and Gibb, "Brain Plasticity and Behaviour in the Developing Brain," 265–76.

29. Jon Bardin, "Neurodevelopment: Unlocking the Brain," *Nature* 487, no. 7405 (July 4, 2012): 25, https://doi.org/10.1038/487024a

30. Bardin, 26.

31. Bardin, 26. He writes, "And structural brakes are considerably more difficult to release than functional ones."

32. Jean-Pierre Changeux, *Neuronal Man: The Biology of Mind*, 228. Emphasis mine.

33. Peter R Huttenlocher, *Neural Plasticity: The Effects of Environment on the Development of the Cerebral Cortex* (Harvard University Press, 2002), 175, https://doi.org/10.4159/9780674038936

34. Catherine Malabou, "The End of Writing? Grammatology and Plasticity," *The European Legacy* 12, no. 4 (July 1, 2007): 440, https://doi.org/10.1080/10848770701396254

35. David Harvey, "Greeks and Romans Learn to Write," in *Communication Arts in the Ancient World*, ed. Eric A. Havelock and Jackson P. Hershbell (New York: Hastings House, 1978), 74.

36. Harvey, 75.

37. Constantin A. Marinescu, Sarah E. Cox, and Rudolf Wachter, "Paideia's Children: Childhood Education on a Group of Late Antique Mosaics," in *Constructions of Childhood in Ancient Greece and Italy*, ed. Ada Cohen and Jeremy B. Rutter, Hesperia Supplement 41 (Princeton, NJ: American School of Classical Studies at Athens, 2007), 101–14.

38. Marinescu, Cox, and Wachter, 108.

39. Marinescu, Cox, and Wachter, 108.

40. Marinescu, Cox, and Wachter, 108–9.

41. Louis Althusser, *On the Reproduction of Capitalism: Ideology and Ideological State Apparatuses*, ed. Jacques Bidet, trans. G. M. Goshgarian (London; New York: Verso, 2014).

42. Radiah Smith-Donald et al., "Preliminary Construct and Concurrent Validity of the Preschool Self-Regulation Assessment (PSRA) for Field-Based Research," *Early Childhood Research Quarterly* 22, no. 2 (April 2007): 174, https://doi.org/10.1016/j.ecresq.2007.01.002

43. Smith-Donald et al., 174.

44. Andrew Davidson, "Writing: The Re-Construction of Language," *Language Sciences* 72 (March 2019): 138, https://doi.org/10.1016/j.langsci.2018.09.004. Emphasis mine.

45. Abercrombie quoted in Andrew Davidson, "Writing: The Re-Construction of Language," 138.

46. Klein, "The Rôle of the School in the Libidinal Development of the Child," 312.

47. Plato, "Laws VIII," *Plato in Twelve Volumes*, trans. R. G. Bury, vol. 10 & 11 (Cambridge, MA: Harvard University of Press, 1967), 838a–839a, www.perseus.tufts.edu

48. Klein, "The Rôle of the School in the Libidinal Development of the Child," 326.

49. Klein, 315.

50. Klein, 315.

51. Klein, 324.

52. Klein, 324.

53. Klein, 324.

54. Klein, 316–17.

55. Klein, 317.

56. Niemeyer quoted in Friedrich A. Kittler, *Discourse Networks 1800/1900*, 30.

57. Kittler, 30.

58. Harvey, "Greeks and Romans Learn to Write," 74.

59. Kittler, *Discourse Networks 1800/1900*, 30.

60. Kittler, 30.

61. Kittler, 50.

62. Dover quoted in Jesper Svenbro, *Phrasikleia: An Anthropology of Reading in Ancient Greece*, trans. Janet Lloyd (Ithaca, NY: Cornell University Press, 1993), 195.

63. See Debra Hawhee, *Bodily Arts: Rhetoric and Athletics in Ancient Greece* (Austin, TX: University of Texas Press, 2005).

64. Klein, "The Rôle of the School in the Libidinal Development of the Child," 60.

65. Michel Foucault, *Discipline and Punish: The Birth of the Prison*, trans. Alan Sheridan, 2nd Vintage Books ed (New York: Vintage Books, 1995), 137. Of the modern regimes of discipline, he writes, "They were different from slavery because they were not based on a relation of appropriation of bodies; indeed, the elegance of the discipline lay in the fact that it could dispense with this costly and violent relation by obtaining effects of utility at least as great."

66. Foucault, 138.

67. Foucault, 152.

68. Berry Mayall, "Children's Lived Bodies in Everyday Life," in *Sociology of the Body: A Reader*, ed. Claudia Malacrida and Jacqueline Low (Ontario, Canada: Oxford University Press, 2008), 201.

69. Mayall, 201.

70. Mayall, 202.

71. Doug Bolton, "Why It's Impossible for You Not to Read This Sentence," *The Independent*, February 18, 2016, www.independent.uk

72. Bolton.

73. Lidia Stanton quoted in Bolton.

74. Bardin, "Neurodevelopment," 26.

75. Louis Althusser, *Lenin and Philosophy, and Other Essays*, trans. Ben Brewster (New York: Monthly Review Press, 2001), 105.

76. Althusser, *On the Reproduction of Capitalism*, 145.

CHAPTER 4

1. Jasper P. Neel, *Plato, Derrida, and Writing* (Carbondale: Southern Illinois University Press, 1988), 75.

2. Georges Gusdorf, *Speaking (La Parole)*, trans. Paul T. Brockelman (Evanston, IL: Northwestern University Press, 1979), 110.

3. Gusdorf, 111.

4. Nelson Cowan, *Working Memory Capacity* (New York: Psychology Press, 2016), 1.

5. Gusdorf, *Speaking*, 111.

6. Nelson Cowan, "What Are the Differences between Long-Term, Short-Term, and Working Memory?," in *Progress in Brain Research*, ed. Wayne S. Sossin et al., vol. 169 (Elsevier, 2008), 2, https://doi.org/10.1016/S0079-6123(07)00020-9. Cowan considers the history of memory studies beginning with Ebbinghaus and James.

7. Walter J. Ong, "Writing Is a Technology That Restructures Thought," in *The Written Word: Literacy in Translation*, ed. Gerd Baumann (Oxford: Oxford University Press, 1986), 39.

8. Ong, 39–40.

9. Ong, 40.

10. W. V. O. Quine, *Ontological Relativity and Other Essays* (New York: Columbia University Press, 1969), 53.

11. See C. MacKellar, ed., *Cyborg Mind: What Brain-Computer and Mind-Cyberspace Interfaces Mean for Cyberneuroethics* (New York: Berghahn, 2019), 170.

12. Julian Jaynes, *The Origin of Consciousness in the Breakdown of the Bicameral Mind* (Boston: Houghton Mifflin, 1990), 290.

13. Jaynes, 270.

14. Jaynes, 270.

15. Jaynes, 270.

16. Jaynes, 270.

17. Eva von Dassow, ed., *The Egyptian Book of the Dead: The Book of Going Forth By Day*, trans. Raymond O. Faulkner and Ogden Goelet (San Francisco: Chronicle Books, 2015), 152. Ogden Goelet describes *ba* as usually depicted as a bird (a Jabairu stork) with the human head of the deceased. The special emphasis of *ba* is on its mobility, such that he invokes the phrase "free as a bird." *Ka* should not be translated as "soul," according to Goelet, because though it was one version that the "human personality" could take after death, it was often separated from the body while still alive and operated as a kind of Doppelganger or possibly a guardian. It would be "overhasty" to connect this "complex" word with "soul."

18. Goelet, in Eva von Dassow, *The Egyptian Book of the Dead*, 152.

19. Jaynes, *The Origin of Consciousness*, 291.

20. Plato, "Apology," in *Plato in Twelve Volumes*, trans. Harold North Fowler, Vol. 1, Reprinted, The Loeb Classical Library 36 (Cambridge, MA: Harvard University Press, 2005), 41c.

21. Plato, "Apology," 41c.

22. Plato, "Cratylus," in *Plato in Twelve Volumes*, trans. Harold North Fowler, Vol. 12 (Cambridge, MA: Harvard University Press, 1921), 400a–400b.

23. Plato, "Cratylus," 400b–400c.

24. John Burnet, *The Socratic Doctrine of the Soul* (London: Humphrey Milford, Oxford University Press, 1916), 14.

25. Burnet, 14.

26. Burnet, 14.

27. Plato, "Phaedo," *Plato in Twelve Volumes*, trans. Harold North Fowler, Reprinted, vol. 1, The Loeb Classical Library 36 (Cambridge, MA: Harvard University Press, 2005), 69e–70a.

28. Plato, "Phaedo," 70a.

29. Plato, "Phaedo," 77b.

30. Jaynes, *The Origin of Consciousness in the Breakdown of the Bicameral Mind*, 291.

31. Plato, "Phaedo," 79c.

32. Plato, "Phaedo," 79d. The dialogue continues: "But when the soul inquires alone by itself, it departs into the realm of the pure, the everlasting, the immortal and

the changeless, and being akin to these it dwells always with them whenever it is by itself and is not hindered, and it has rest from its wanderings and remains always the same and unchanging with the changeless, since it is in communion therewith. And this state of the soul is called wisdom. Is it not so?" "Socrates," said he, "what you say is perfectly right and true."

33. Neel, *Plato, Derrida, and Writing*, 75.

34. Jaynes, *The Origin of Consciousness*, 291.

35. Jaynes, 291.

36. St. Augustine, *Confessions* (Peabody, MA: Hendrickson Publishers, 2011), 116.

37. Henri-Jean Martin, *The History and Power of Writing*, trans. Lydia G. Cochrane (Chicago: University of Chicago Press, 1994), 33.

38. Jean Soler, "Why Monotheism," trans. Janet Lloyd, *Arion: A Journal of Humanities and the Classics* 14, no. 3 (2007): 57. As Soler writes, "Even at the beginning of our own era, the Temple of Jerusalem, said to be the one place where the cult of the Sole God could be celebrated, was reserved for the Jews alone."

39. Soler and Lloyd, 57. He adds, "However, from the moment, at the beginning of the fourth century AD, when a Roman emperor, Constantine, converted to Christianity, the deity known as God progressively turned into the God of first the Romans, then the Europeans and the peoples that they made their subjects. In other words, God once more became the mark identifying, no longer just one particular ethnic group, as is still the case in Judaism, but a whole collection of nations united by the worship of the Son of God."

40. See Derrick de Kerckhove, "Theatre as Information-Processing in Western Cultures," *Modern Drama* 25, no. 1 (1982): 143–53, https://doi.org/10.1353/mdr.1982 .0000; as well as Eric A. Havelock, *Preface to Plato* (Cambridge: Belknap Press, Harvard University Press, 2010).

41. Walter J. Ong, *Orality and Literacy: The Technologizing of the Word* (London: Taylor & Francis e-Library, 2004), 21.

42. Ong, 22.

43. Ong, 24.

44. George Steiner, *Language and Silence: Essays on Language, Literature, and the Inhuman* (New York: Atheneum, 1972), 177.

45. See Eric A. Havelock, *Preface to Plato* (Cambridge: Belknap Press, Harvard University Press, 2010).

46. Gusdorf, *Speaking*, 110.

47. Plato, "Republic," in *Plato in Twelve Volumes*, trans. Paul Shorey, vol. 5 & 6 (Cambridge, MA: Harvard University Press, 1969), 595b.

48. Milman Parry and Adam Parry, *The Making of Homeric Verse: The Collected Papers of Milman Parry* (New York: Oxford University Press, 1987), 329.

49. Parry and Parry, xxvi.

50. Samuel Eliot Bassett, *The Poetry of Homer* (Lanham, MD: Lexington Books, 2003), 18.

51. See Michel Foucault, "What Is an Author?," in *The Foucault Reader*, ed. Paul Rabinow (New York: Penguin Books, 1984), 101–21.

52. Bassett, *The Poetry of Homer*, 17.

53. Bassett, 14.

54. Kevin Robb, *Literacy and Paideia in Ancient Greece* (New York: Oxford University Press, 1994), 3.

55. H. T. Wade-Gery, *The Poet of the Iliad* (Cambridge: Cambridge University Press, 2013), 32.

56. Plato, "Phaedo," in *The Collected Works of Plato*, trans. Hugh Tredennick (Princeton, NJ: Princeton University Press, 1980), 65a.

57. Ong, *Orality and Literacy*, 24–25.

58. Ong, *Orality and Literacy*, 25. He adds, "The conflict wracked Plato's own unconscious. For Plato expresses serious reservations in the *Phaedrus* and his *Seventh Letter* about writing, as a mechanical, inhuman way of processing knowledge, unresponsive to questions and destructive of memory, although, as we now know, the philosophical thinking Plato fought for depended entirely on writing. No wonder the implications here resisted surfacing for so long."

59. Havelock, *Preface to Plato*, 4. He writes, "[Plato] opens by characterizing the effect of poetry as 'a crippling of the mind.' It is a kind of disease, for which one has to acquire an antidote. The antidote must consist of a knowledge 'of what things really are.'"

60. Havelock, *Preface to Plato*, 200. Emphasis mine.

61. Ong, *Orality and Literacy*, 73–77. The final section of Chapter 3 is called, "Words are not signs."

62. Ong, 12.

63. Alexander Romanovich Luria, *Cognitive Development: Its Cultural and Social Foundations*, ed. Michael Cole, trans. Lynn Solotaroff and Martin Lopez-Morillas (Cambridge, MA: Harvard University Press, 1994), 151.

64. Luria, 151.

65. Luria, 144.

CHAPTER 5

1. Henri-Jean Martin, *The History and Power of Writing*, trans. Lydia G. Cochrane (Chicago: University of Chicago Press, 1994), 36–37. Martin goes on to quote Jacques Gernet, who states, "It seems to me personally that there is a fairly strict relationship between the mentality that permitted the invention of a uniform money and the invention of the alphabet. It would seem that both could likewise be conceived as a 'measure of all things and a sort of common denominator.'"

2. Thomas Hobbes, *Leviathan*, ed. Crawford B. Macpherson (London: Penguin Books, 1972), 193.

3. Friedrich Nietzsche, "A Genealogy of Morals," in *The Works of Friedrich*

Nietzsche, ed. Alexander Tille, trans. William A. Hausemann, vol. X (New York: Macmillan, 1897), 65.

4. Hobbes, *Leviathan*, 194.

5. Hobbes, 194.

6. Eric A. Havelock, *Preface to Plato* (Cambridge: Belknap Press, Harvard University Press, 2010), 200.

7. Nietzsche, "A Genealogy of Morals," 64.

8. Julia Felsenthal, "Give Me Your John Hancock: When Did We Start Signing Our Names to Authenticate Documents?," Slate.com, March 18, 2011. In the 13th century, agreements were often "sealed" by a slap or some other act of violence so that both parties would "remember not only the injury but the accord that was reached on its infliction."

9. Hobbes, *Leviathan*, 196.

10. Jacques Derrida, *Limited Inc*, trans. Samuel Weber and Jeffrey Mehlman (Evanston, IL: Northwestern University Press, 1988), 20.

11. Derrida, 20.

12. Roy Harris, *Signs of Writing* (London; New York: Routledge, 1995), 83.

13. Harris, 83.

14. Harris, 80.

15. Nietzsche, "A Genealogy of Morals," 117.

16. Names, it should be remembered, do not become fixed until well into the alphabetic age. Within cultures that are not alphabetic, such as the Nandi, "a person will have acquired between five and nine anthroponyms by the time s/he reaches old age." See Susan Chebet-Choge, "The Case of Dead and Non-Used Nandi Anthroponyms," *AlterNative: An International Journal of Indigenous Peoples* 6, no. 1 (August 1, 2010): 46. In England and Scotland, persons often had two or three bynames during their lives and names were not necessarily hereditary. It was not until the 15th century in England and the 16th century in Scotland that most people had acquired "fixed, hereditary surnames." See David Hey, ed., *The Oxford Companion to Local and Family History* (Oxford; New York: Oxford University Press, 1996), 15. Only after the 1789 Revolution in France did a gradual shift from "relative laxness" to "fixedness" regarding proper names take place, and this due solely to status and property disputes. See Tiphaine Barthelemy, "Patronymic Names and *Noms de Terre* in the French Nobility in the Eighteenth and the Nineteenth Centuries," *The History of the Family* 5, no. 2 (2000): 181.

17. Florian Cajori, *A History of Mathematical Notations* (New York: Cosimo Classics, 2011), 23. There is some question as to whether it was actually a Hebrew version of alphabetical mathematics that the Greeks copied, though following our definition of alphabet as opposed to syllabary, only the Greek version would qualify. In any case, the Hebrew version was operative around the same time if not before.

18. Cajori, 23.

19. Eric A. Havelock, *Origins of Western Literacy: Four Lectures Delivered at the*

Ontario Institute for Studies in Education, Toronto, March 25, 26, 27, 28, 1974 (Toronto: Ontario Institute for Studies in Education, 1976), 79.

20. Havelock, 79.

21. Cajori, *A History of Mathematical Notations*, 28.

22. Havelock, *Origins of Western Literacy*, 79. He continues, "The system, considered as an invention which converts the invisible into the visible using an atomic system of ten elements, represents an intellectual achievement comparable to that of alphabet. And once again the symbols are so reduced in number that they can be taught by rote to children. The recognition of number can become as swift and automatic as the recognition of a sentence."

23. Havelock, 79.

24. Havelock, 78.

25. Havelock, 78.

26. David Graeber, *Debt: The First 5,000 Years* (Brooklyn, N.Y: Melville House, 2011), 244.

27. Graeber, 245.

28. Graeber, 245.

29. Aristotle quoted in David Schaps, *The Invention of Coinage and the Monetization of Ancient Greece* (Ann Arbor, MI: University of Michigan Press, 2015), 13.

30. Richard Seaford, "Coinage and Early Greek Thought," *Radical Anthropology* 1, no. 5 (2013): 3.

31. Graeber, *Debt*, 245.

32. Schaps, *The Invention of Coinage*, 31.

33. Graeber, *Debt*, 246.

34. Schaps, *The Invention of Coinage*, 120.

35. Schaps, 111.

36. Schaps, 112.

37. Schaps, 32.

38. Derrick de Kerckhove, "Theatre as Information-Processing in Western Cultures," *Modern Drama* 25, no. 1 (1982): 149, https://doi.org/10.1353/mdr.1982.0000

39. Roland Barthes, *Mythologies*, trans. Annette Lavers (London: Jonathan Cape Ltd, 1972), 139. See his comments on anonymity, which he specifies as "the anonymity of the bourgeoisie." He writes, "The whole of France is steeped in this anonymous ideology: our press, our films, our theatre, our pulp literature, our rituals, our justice, our diplomacy, our conversations, our remarks about the weather, a murder trial, a touching wedding, the cooking we dream of, the garments we wear, everything, in everyday life, is dependent on the representation which the bourgeoisie *has and makes us have* of the relations between man [sic] and the world."

40. Richard Seaford, *Money and the Early Greek Mind: Homer, Philosophy, Tragedy* (Cambridge, UK: Cambridge University Press, 2004), 151–52.

41. Seaford, 151.

42. M. I. Finley, *The World of Odysseus* (New York: New York Review Books, 2002), 53.

43. Finley, 52–53.

44. Schaps, *The Invention of Coinage*, 153.

45. Schaps, 153. According to Schaps several scholars have argued that "the service of a *thes* was not visibly different from that of a slave."

46. Seaford, *Money and the Early Greek Mind*, 156.

47. Graeber, *Debt*, 187.

48. Edward E. Cohen, *Athenian Prostitution: The Business of Sex* (Oxford; New York: Oxford University Press, 2015), 3–4.

49. Seaford, *Money and the Early Greek Mind*, 156.

50. Laura McClure, *Courtesans at Table: Gender and Greek Literary Culture in Athenaeus* (New York: Routledge, 2014), 15.

51. McClure, 15.

52. Cohen, *Athenian Prostitution*, 3–4.

53. Cohen, 4.

54. Graeber, *Debt*, 159.

55. Graeber, 145–46.

56. Karl Marx, *Capital: A Critique of Political Economy*, ed. Friedrich Engels, trans. Edward Aveling and Samuel Moore, Vol. I (Moscow: Progress Publishers, 1887), 508.

57. Marx, 508.

58. Marx, 522.

59. Marx, 522.

60. Marx, 522.

61. Marx, 522.

62. Marx, 525, n1.

63. Marx, 522.

64. Marx, 522.

65. Marx, 523.

66. Marx, 67.

67. Marx, 67. Emphasis mine.

68. Marx, 67.

69. Marx, 105.

70. Marx, 106.

71. Marx, 74.

72. Marx, 106.

73. Marx, 106.

74. Marx, 107. Emphasis mine.

75. Havelock, *Origins of Western Literacy*, 47.

76. Marx, 108.

77. Marx, 108.

78. Ferdinand De Saussure, *Course in General Linguistics*, ed. Charles Bally and Albert Sechehaye, trans. Wade Baskin (New York: Philosophical Library, 1959), 67–68.

79. Marx, 107. Emphasis mine.

80. Marx, 106. Emphasis mine.

81. Gilles Deleuze and Félix Guattari, *Anti-Oedipus: Capitalism and Schizophrenia,* trans. Robert Hurley, Mark Seem, and Helen R. Lane (London; New York: Continuum, 2012), 270. They write, "The introduction of money as an equivalent . . . makes it possible to begin and end with money, therefore never to end at all."

82. Marx, 48.

83. Jacques Lacan, *Écrits,* trans. Bruce Fink (New York, NY: Norton, 2006), 694.

INTERLUDE

1. Nietzsche quoted in Jakob von Uexküll, *A Foray into the Worlds of Animals and Humans,* trans. Joseph D. O'Neil (Minneapolis: University of Minnesota Press, 2010), 1.

2. Michel Chion, *Kubrick's Cinema Odyssey* (London: British Film Institute, 2001), 148.

CHAPTER 6

1. Friedrich A. Kittler, *Discourse Networks 1800/1900,* trans. Michael Metteer (Stanford, CA: Stanford University Press, 1990), 70.

2. Ronald Shusterman, "Virtual Realities and Autotelic Art," *SubStance* 22, no. 2/3 (1993): 120, https://doi.org/10.2307/3685274

3. Karl Marx, *Capital: A Critique of Political Economy,* ed. Friedrich Engels, trans. Edward Aveling and Samuel Moore, Vol. I (Moscow: Progress Publishers, 1887), 508.

4. J. L. Austin, *How To Do Things With Words,* ed. J. O. Urmson and Marina Sbisà (Cambridge, MA: Harvard University Press, 1975), 5.

5. Austin, 8.

6. Juri Lotman, "The Place of Art among Other Modelling Systems," trans. Tanel Pern, *Sign Systems Studies* 39, no. 2/4 (December 1, 2011): 250, https://doi.org/10.126 97/SSS.2011.39.2–4.10

7. Walter J. Ong, *Orality and Literacy: The Technologizing of the Word* (London: Taylor & Francis e-Library, 2004), 8.

8. Lotman, "The Place of Art among Other Modelling Systems," 256.

9. Lotman, 256.

10. Andrea Micocci, *The Metaphysics of Capitalism* (Lanham, MD: Lexington Books, 2009), 26. Such defensiveness is an integral part of capitalism, hence "A mode of production like capitalism can be described as an intellectually flawed, self-enclosed, and defensive metaphysics."

11. Jacques Derrida, *Limited Inc,* trans. Samuel Weber and Jeffrey Mehlman (Evanston, IL: Northwestern University Press, 1988), 9. He notes again, "iterability [is] a structural characteristic of every mark" (15).

12. Michael C. Corballis, *The Recursive Mind: the Origins of Human Language, Thought, and Civilization* (Princeton, NJ: Princeton University Press, 2011), 10, https://doi.org/10.1515/9781400851492

13. Corballis, 10.

14. Corballis, 11.

15. Corballis, 5.

16. Ray Jackendoff and Steven Pinker, "The Nature of the Language Faculty and Its Implications for Evolution of Language (Reply to Fitch, Hauser, and Chomsky)," *Cognition* 97, no. 2 (September 1, 2005): 211–25, https://doi.org/10.1016/j.cognition.2005.04.006. My sense is that Chomsky points to recursion as the language faculty unique to human animals, which Jackendoff and Pinker argue against here. My argument is that fully recursive structures are alphabetic, not simply "linguistic."

17. Steven Pinker and Ray Jackendoff, "The Faculty of Language: What's Special about It?," *Cognition* 95, no. 2 (March 2005): 203, https://doi.org/10.1016/j.cognition.2004.08.004

18. Corballis, *The Recursive Mind*, 5.

19. Marx, *Capital*, 104.

20. Marx, *Capital*, 104.

21. Marx, *Capital*, 107.

22. Marx, *Capital*, 106.

23. Gilles Deleuze et al., *Anti-Oedipus: Capitalism and Schizophrenia* (London; New York: Continuum, 2004), 288. They write, capital is "continually repelling and exorcising" its "external limit" while "capitalism itself produces its *immanent limits*, which it never ceases to displace and enlarge."

24. Marx, *Capital*, 108.

25. Deleuze et al., *Anti-Oedipus*, 281.

26. Derrick de Kerckhove, "A Theory of Greek Tragedy," *SubStance* 9, no. 4 (1980): 24, https://doi.org/10.2307/3684038

27. Lotman, "The Place of Art among Other Modelling Systems," 253.

28. Kerckhove, "A Theory of Greek Tragedy," 30.

29. Lotman, "The Place of Art among Other Modelling Systems," 250. Emphasis mine.

30. Keir Elam, *The Semiotics of Theatre and Drama* (New York: Routledge, 2002), 8–9.

31. Elam, 10.

32. Elam, 10.

33. See Andrew Sofer, *The Stage Life of Props* (Ann Arbor: University of Michigan Press, 2003).

34. Elam, *The Semiotics of Theatre and Drama*, 10–11. He adds, "In the classical Chinese and Japanese Noh theatres, the semantic units are so strictly predetermined that the denotation-connotation distinction virtually disappears: all meanings are primary and more or less explicit. In the West, the second-order significations of any

particular element are less tightly constrained, and will even vary from spectator to spectator, although always within definite cultural limits."

35. Elam, 10.

36. Mary C. English, "Reconstructing Aristophanic Performance: Stage Properties in 'The Acharnians,'" *Classical World* 100, no. 3 (2007): 201, https://doi.org/10.13 53/clw.2007.0026

37. Lotman, "The Place of Art among Other Modelling Systems," 256.

38. Petr Bogatyrev, "Theatrical Signs," in *Theatre Theory Reader: Prague School Writings*, ed. David Drozd, Don Sparling, and Tomáš Kačer, trans. Eva Daníčková, Ivan Kolman, and Marta Filipová (Prague, CZ: Karolinum Press, 2016), 100.

39. Jean Baudrillard, *Simulacra and Simulation*, trans. Sheila Glaser (Ann Arbor, MI: University of Michigan Press, 1995), 1, https://doi.org/10.3998/mpub.9904

40. Walter Benjamin, *Illuminations*, ed. Hannah Arendt, trans. Harry Zorn (London: The Bodley Head, 2015), 252.

41. Lotman, "The Place of Art among Other Modelling Systems," 254.

42. Lotman, 251.

43. Lotman, 254.

44. Kerckhove, "A Theory of Greek Tragedy," 30.

45. Kerckhove, 9.

46. Kerckhove, 23. He implies that this is a uniquely Western development.

47. Ferdinand and Isabella, "Privileges and Prerogatives Granted by Their Catholic Majesties to Christopher Columbus: 1492," Documents in Law, History and Diplomacy, Avalon Project, April 30, 1492, https://avalon.law.yale.edu/15th_century/

48. Hugh Thomas, *Rivers of Gold: The Rise of the Spanish Empire, From Columbus to Magellan* (New York: Random House, 2005), 55.

49. Thomas, 55.

50. Thomas, 55.

51. Pope Alexander VI, "The Papal Bull Inter Caetera," May 4, 1493, www.let.rug .nl

52. Ferdinand and Isabella, "Privileges and Prerogatives."

53. Matthew Restall, *Seven Myths of the Spanish Conquest* (Oxford: Oxford University Press, 2004), 12.

54. Restall, 12.

55. Restall, 12.

56. Restall, 36.

57. Enrique Florescano quoted in Matthew Restall, *Seven Myths of the Spanish Conquest* (Oxford: Oxford University Press, 2004), 11.

58. Christopher Columbus, "Christopher Columbus's 'Letter to the Sovereigns': Announcing the Discovery," ed. Margarita Zamora in *New World Encounters*, ed. Stephen Greenblatt (Berkeley: University of California Press, 1993), 5.

59. Columbus, "Letter to the Sovereigns," 5.

60. Columbus, "Letter to the Sovereigns," 7

61. Columbus, 8.

62. Columbus, 6.

63. Columbus, 3.

64. Columbus, 8.

65. Glenn W. Harrison, Ernan Haruvy, and E. Elisabet Rutström, "Remarks on Virtual World and Virtual Reality Experiments," *Southern Economic Journal* 78, no. 1 (July 2011): 87, https://doi.org/10.4284/0038-4038-78.1.87

66. Tzvetan Todorov, *The Conquest of America: The Question of the Other*, trans. Catherine Porter (Norman: University of Oklahoma Press, 1999), 144.

67. Harrison, Haruvy, and Rutström, "Remarks on Virtual World and Virtual Reality Experiments," 87.

68. Todorov, *The Conquest of America*, 144.

69. Todorov, 144.

70. Chinua Achebe, "An Image of Africa," *The Massachusetts Review* 18, no. 4 (1977): 782–94.

71. Lotman, "The Place of Art among Other Modelling Systems," 257. Emphasis mine.

72. Slavoj Žižek, *Less than Nothing: Hegel and the Shadow of Dialectical Materialism* (New York: Verso, 2012), 743.

73. Todorov, *The Conquest of America*, 144.

74. Todorov, 143.

75. Todorov, 145.

76. Todorov, 144.

77. Restall, *Seven Myths of the Spanish Conquest*, 35. Emphasis mine.

78. Diego Durán, "Historia de las Indias de Nueva España e islas de la tierra firme" (1579), http://bdh.bne.es/bnesearch/detalle/bdh0000169486. Durán's illustrations are based on the Ixtlilxochitl Codex and other indigenous sources. See the website of the Biblioteca Nacional de España for the fully digitized work.

79. Todorov, *The Conquest of America*, 121.

80. Inga Clendinnen, "'Fierce and Unnatural Cruelty': Cortés and the Conquest of Mexico," in *New World Encounters*, ed. Stephen Greenblatt (Berkeley: University of California Press, 1993), 28.

81. Clendinnen, 28.

82. Clendinnen, 28.

83. Clendinnen, 28.

84. Clendinnen, 28.

85. De Las Casas quoted in John Erwin Hollitz, *Contending Voices: Biographical Explorations of the American Past* (Australia: Cengage Learning, 2017), 4.

86. Clendinnen, "'Fierce and Unnatural Cruelty,'" 16.

87. Ferdinand and Isabella, "Privileges and Prerogatives."

88. See his article of the same name. Walter J. Ong, "The Writer's Audience Is Always a Fiction," *PMLA* 90, no. 1 (January 1975): 9–21, https://doi.org/10.2307/46 1344

89. Thomas, *Rivers of Gold*, 88.

90. Columbus, "Letter to the Sovereigns," 2–3.

91. Restall, *Seven Myths of the Spanish Conquest*, 66.

92. Durán quoted in Tzvetan Todorov, *The Conquest of America*, 70.

93. Todorov, 96.

94. Florentine Codex quoted in Tzvetan Todorov, *The Conquest of America*, 71.

95. Georges Gusdorf, *Speaking (La Parole)*, trans. Paul T. Brockelman (Evanston, IL: Northwestern University Press, 1979), 114.

96. Ong, *Orality and Literacy*, 55. He explains, "Persons who have interiorized writing not only write but also speak literately, which is to say that they organize, to varying degrees, even their oral expression in thought patterns and verbal patterns that they would not know of unless they could write."

97. Todorov, *The Conquest of America*, 145. Emphasis mine.

98. Anthony Pagden, "Preface," in Tzvetan Todorov, *The Conquest of America*, xi.

CHAPTER 7

1. Walter J. Ong, *Orality and Literacy: The Technologizing of the Word* (London: Taylor & Francis e-Library, 2004), 80.

2. Luther quoted in Elizabeth L. Eisenstein, "Some Conjectures about the Impact of Printing on Western Society and Thought: A Preliminary Report," *The Journal of Modern History* 40, no. 1 (1968): 34.

3. Alfred Sohn-Rethel, *Intellectual and Manual Labour: A Critique of Epistemology*, trans. Martin Sohn-Rethel (Atlantic Highlands, N.J: Humanities Press, 1978), 27.

4. Steven Roger Fischer, *A History of Reading* (London: Reaktion Books, 2003), 14. He goes on to say, "Everyone begins with mediate reading, putting sound to sign. Most learners then progress to immediate reading, or putting sense to sign directly . . . . After several exposures to a word or sign-combination, a reader comes to form a direct pathway between sign and sense, bypassing sound altogether."

5. Alexander R. Galloway, *The Interface Effect* (Cambridge, UK; Malden, MA: Polity, 2012), 31.

6. N. Katherine Hayles, "Cognition Everywhere: The Rise of the Cognitive Nonconscious and the Costs of Consciousness," *New Literary History* 45, no. 2 (2014): 212, https://doi.org/10.1353/nlh.2014.0011

7. Hayles, "Cognition Everywhere," 211. She writes, "some cultural critics are concerned that the 'missing half-second' between perception and conscious awareness may be exploited for capitalistic purposes" and explains with several examples how this is precisely what happens.

8. Hayles, 211.

9. Eric A. Havelock, *The Literate Revolution in Greece and Its Cultural Consequences* (Princeton: Princeton University Press, 2019), 84, https://doi.org/10.2307/j.ctvbc d1d2. Emphasis mine.

10. Esquirol quoted in R. P. Bentall, "The Illusion of Reality: A Review and Integration of Psychological Research on Hallucinations," *Psychological Bulletin* 107, no. 1 (January 1990): 82, https://doi.org/10.1037/0033-2909.107.1.82

11. Juri Lotman, "The Place of Art among Other Modelling Systems," trans. Tanel Pern, *Sign Systems Studies* 39, no. 2/4 (December 1, 2011): 254–55, https://doi.org/10.12 697/SSS.2011.39.2–4.10. Lotman includes a wonderful example from a Tolstoy novel to describe the commitment to play as "real." Otherwise, there is no point in playing. He writes, "An example of a violation of this twofold behaviour, where conventional behaviour wins and the game is taken as pointless, 'non- serious' behaviour that has completely lost its connection to reality, is an episode from L. N. Tolstoy's novel, *Childhood*: 'Woloda's condescension did not please us much. On the contrary, his lazy, tired expression took away all the fun of the game. When we sat on the ground and imagined that we were sitting in a boat and either fishing or rowing with all our might, Woloda persisted in sitting with folded hands or in anything but a fisherman's posture. I made a remark about it, but he replied that, whether we moved our hands or not, we should neither gain nor lose ground—certainly not advance at all, and I was forced to agree with him. Again, when I pretended to go out hunting, and, with a stick over my shoulder, set off into the wood, Woloda only lay down on his back with his hands under his head, and said that he supposed it was all the same whether he went or not. Such behaviour and speeches cooled our ardour for the game and were very disagreeable—the more so since it was impossible not to confess to oneself that Woloda was right. I myself knew that it was not only impossible to kill birds with a stick, but to shoot at all with such a weapon. Still, it was the game, and if we were once to begin reasoning thus, it would become equally impossible for us to go for drives on chairs. . . . If we were always to judge from reality, games would be nonsense; but if games were nonsense, what else would there be left to do?'"

12. Bentall, "The Illusion of Reality," 82.

13. Boris Sidis, *An Inquiry Into the Nature of Hallucinations*, 1904, 15.

14. Manuel Portela, *Scripting Reading Motions: The Codex and the Computer as Self-Reflexive Machines* (Cambridge, MA: MIT Press, 2013), 17.

15. Portela, 17.

16. Angus Stevenson and Christine A. Lindberg, eds., "Gimmick," in *New Oxford American Dictionary* (Oxford: Oxford University Press, 2015).

17. Novalis quoted in Friedrich A. Kittler, *Discourse Networks 1800/1900* (Stanford, CA: Stanford University Press, 1990), 246.

18. E. T. A. Hoffman quoted in Friedrich A. Kittler, *Discourse Networks 1800/1900* (Stanford, CA: Stanford University Press, 1990), 40.

19. "Dyslexia FAQ," The Yale Center for Dyslexia & Creativity, accessed May 23, 2022, dyslexia.yale.edu. According to the site, "Dyslexia is an unexpected difficulty in reading for an individual who has the intelligence to be a much better reader. It is most commonly due to a difficulty in phonological processing (the appreciation of the individual sounds of spoken language), which affects the ability of an individual to speak, read, spell and, often, learn a second language."

20. Kittler, *Discourse Networks 1800/1900*, 53.

21. Sohn-Rethel, *Intellectual and Manual Labour*, 27.

22. Slavoj Žižek, *The Sublime Object of Ideology*, Phronesis (London; New York: Verso, 1989), 17–18.

23. Sohn-Rethel, *Intellectual and Manual Labour*, 27. Emphasis mine.

24. A. R. Luria, *The Mind of a Mnemonist*, trans. Lynn Solotaroff (New York: Avon Books, 1969), 12.

25. Luria, 10.

26. Luria, 67. Luria states, "The big question for him, and the most troublesome, was how he could learn to forget."

27. Luria, 115.

28. S. quoted in Luria, 116.

29. In this instance, the Grand Palace is probably a reference to the Grand Palais des Champs-Élysées, as the novel is set in Paris.

30. Hippolyte Taine, *On Intelligence*, trans. T. D. Haye (Bristol, UK: Thoemmes Press, 1998), 44–45.

31. Oliver Tearle, *Bewilderments of Vision: Hallucination and Literature, 1880–1914* (Brighton, UK: Sussex Academic Press, 2013), 11.

32. Edmund Gurney, "Hallucinations," *Mind* 10, no. 38 (1885): 163.

33. Ludwig Wittgenstein, *Philosophical Investigations*, ed. P. M. S. Hacker and Joachim Schulte, trans. G. E. M. Anscombe, Rev. 4th ed (Chichester, West Sussex, U.K.; Malden, MA: Wiley-Blackwell, 2009). Is this not in part Wittgenstein's conclusion in the private language argument? If I have no means of external corroboration other than my own memory—i.e., if my sensations remain entirely private—then I can never truly establish whether I "followed my rule" about hallucinating or not-hallucinating with any certainty, even if I take recourse to alphabetic markings "outside myself," such as in a notebook, in order to try to become oriented. One facet of Wittgenstein's point is that I cannot rely on my private intuition about whether or not I am hallucinating, not hallucinating, remembering, misremembering, dreaming, fabricating, and so on, with anything like verifiable accuracy.

34. Jacques Lacan, *The Four Fundamental Concepts of Psycho-Analysis*, ed. Jacques-Alain Miller, trans. Alan Sheridan, Reprinted (London: Karnac Books, 2004), 203.

35. Lacan, *The Four Fundamental Concepts of Psycho-Analysis*, 81. Emphasis mine.

36. Lacan, 80–81. Lacan points out how phenomenologists on the contrary argue that perception is not happening "in me" but rather outside me: "[they] have succeeded in articulating with precision, and in the most disconcerting way, that it is quite clear that I see outside, that perception is not in me, that it is on the objects that it apprehends. And yet I apprehend the world in a perception that seems to concern the immanence of the I see myself seeing myself . . . ."

37. Lacan, 81.

38. Taine, *On Intelligence*, 222.

39. Taine, 262.

40. Taine, 44.

41. Laura Ashe, "The 'Short Charter of Christ': An Unpublished Longer Version, from Cambridge University Library, MS Add. 6686," *Medium Aevum* 72, no. 1 (2003): 32.

42. Margaret Aston, *Lollards and Reformers: Images and Literacy in Late Medieval Religion*, History Series 22 (London: Hambledon Press, 1984), 104.

43. Aston, 104.

44. Early fourteenth century poem quoted in Margaret Aston, *Lollards and Reformers*, 104.

45. Elizabeth L. Eisenstein, *The Printing Press as an Agent of Change: Communications and Cultural Transformations in Early Modern Europe* (Cambridge, UK: Cambridge University Press, 1979), 428.

46. Frederick Richmond Goff, *The Permanence of Johann Gutenberg* (Austin: Humanities Research Center, University of Texas at Austin: Distributed by University of Texas Press, 1970), 10.

47. Goff, 10.

48. Ong, *Orality and Literacy*, 120.

49. Mary Raschko, "Review of Holy Scripture and the Quest for Authority at the End of the Middle Ages by Ian Christopher Levy," *The Journal of Medieval Religious Cultures* 40, no. 1 (January 1, 2014): 105, https://doi.org/10.5325/jmedirelicult.40.1.0104

50. Raschko, 105.

51. Mark U. Edwards, *Printing, Propaganda, and Martin Luther* (Berkeley: University of California Press, 1994), 109.

52. Karl Marx, *Capital: A Critique of Political Economy*, ed. Friedrich Engels, trans. Edward Aveling and Samuel Moore, vol. I (Moscow: Progress Publishers, 1887), 47.

53. Ong, *Orality and Literacy*, 116.

54. Ong, 116.

55. Ong, 116.

56. H. G. Haile, "Luther and Literacy," *PMLA* 91, no. 5 (October 1976): 817, https://doi.org/10.2307/461557

57. Harvey J. Graff, *The Legacies of Literacy: Continuities and Contradictions in Western Culture and Society*, 1. Midland Book ed., 598 (Bloomington: Indiana University Press, 1991), 143.

58. Henri-Jean Martin, *The History and Power of Writing*, trans. Lydia G. Cochrane (Chicago: University of Chicago Press, 1994), 334.

59. Georges Gusdorf, *Speaking (La Parole)*, trans. Paul T. Brockelman, Studies in Phenomenology and Existential Philosophy (Evanston, IL: Northwestern University Press, 1979), 113.

60. Eisenstein, *The Printing Press as an Agent of Change*, 428.

61. Joseph Th. Leerssen, *Mere Irish & Fíor-Ghael: Studies in the Idea of Irish Nationality, Its Development, and Literary Expression Prior to the Nineteenth Century*, Utrecht Publications in General and Comparative Literature, v. 22 (Amsterdam; Philadelphia: John Benjamins Publishing Company, 1986), 326–27. Reading itself, quite apart

from the content one imbibes, has additional effects. One might even call them "civilizing effects." Within other parts of Europe, the impetus to root out heathens—as amongst the Celts, for example—largely took the form of a literacy campaign. The first book ever printed in Ireland was a Protestant catechism in the Irish language (*Aibidil gaoidheilge & caiticiosma*, 1571). The first strategy of the missionaries in the non-European colonies was to render indigenous languages into the alphabet using its phonemic principles. Once they created an indigenous alphabet, they would translate the Bible into languages which had had no previously written forms at all and then, alphabetize the populations in turn.

62. Luther quoted in J-F. Gilmont, "Protestant Reformations and Reading," in *A History of Reading in the West*, ed. Guglielmo Cavallo and Roger Chartier, trans. Lydia G. Cochrane (Boston, MA: University of Massachusetts Press, 1999), 218.

63. Louis Althusser, *On Ideology*, Radical Thinkers 26 (London; New York: Verso, 2008), 52.

64. Althusser, 48.

65. Althusser, 48.

66. Giuseppe Mantovani, "Virtual Reality as a Communication Environment: Consensual Hallucination, Fiction, and Possible Selves," *Human Relations* 48, no. 6 (June 1995): 673, https://doi.org/10.1177/001872679504800604

67. Allucquere Roseanne Stone, "Will the Real Body Please Stand Up?: Boundary Stories about Virtual Cultures," in *Cyberspace: First Steps*, ed. Michael Benedikt (Cambridge, MA: MIT Press, 1991), 106.

68. Nigel Thrift, "Remembering the Technological Unconscious by Foregrounding Knowledges of Position," *Environment and Planning D: Society and Space* 22, no. 1 (February 2004): 175–90, https://doi.org/10.1068/d321t

69. Steve Mann and Hal Niedzviecki, *Cyborg: Digital Destiny and Human Possibility in the Age of the Wearable Computer* (Toronto: Doubleday Canada, 2001), 7.

70. N. Katherine Hayles, "Traumas of Code," *Critical Inquiry* 33, no. 1 (September 2006): 140, https://doi.org/10.1086/509749

71. Mantovani, "Virtual Reality as a Communication Environment," 679, https://doi.org/10.1177/001872679504800604. Emphasis mine.

72. See Nick Bostrom, "Are You Living in a Computer Simulation?," *Philosophical Quarterly* 53, no. 211 (2003): 243–55.

73. Thomas Metzinger, *Being No One: The Self-Model Theory of Subjectivity*, A Bradford Book (Cambridge, MA: MIT Press, 2004), 1.

74. Samo Tomšič, *The Capitalist Unconscious: Marx and Lacan* (London; New York: Verso, 2015), 33.

75. Alain Badiou, *The Meaning of Sarkozy*, trans. David Fernbach (London; New York: Verso, 2008), 115. See also his work on the "communist hypothesis," including Costas Douzinas, Slavoj Žižek, and Alex Taek-Gwang Lee, eds., *The Idea of Communism*, vol. I (London; New York: Verso, 2010).

Bibliography

Achebe, Chinua. "An Image of Africa." *The Massachusetts Review* 18, no. 4 (1977): 782–94.

Ahl, Frederick. *Sophocles' Oedipus: Evidence and Self-Conviction.* Ithaca: Cornell University Press, 1991.

Althusser, Louis. *Lenin and Philosophy, and Other Essays.* Translated by Ben Brewster. New York: Monthly Review Press, 2001.

Althusser, Louis. *On Ideology.* New York: Verso, 2008.

Althusser, Louis. *On the Reproduction of Capitalism: Ideology and Ideological State Apparatuses.* Edited by Jacques Bidet. Translated by G. M. Goshgarian. New York: Verso, 2014.

Ariès, Philippe. *Centuries of Childhood: A Social History of Family Life.* Translated by Robert Baldick. London: Jonathan Cape Ltd., 1962.

Ashe, Laura. "The 'Short Charter of Christ': An Unpublished Longer Version, from Cambridge University Library, MS Add. 6686." *Medium Aevum* 72, no. 1 (2003): 32–48.

Aston, Margaret. *Lollards and Reformers: Images and Literacy in Late Medieval Religion.* History Series 22. London: Hambledon Press, 1984.

Austin, J. L. *How To Do Things With Words.* Edited by J. O. Urmson and Marina Sbisà. 2nd ed. Cambridge, MA: Harvard University Press, 1975.

Badiou, Alain. *The Meaning of Sarkozy.* Translated by David Fernbach. New York: Verso, 2008.

Bandopadhyay, Gita. "Bengal's Nonsense Rhymes." *India International Centre Quarterly* 17, no. 3/4 (1990): 263–69.

Bardin, Jon. "Neurodevelopment: Unlocking the Brain." *Nature* 487, no. 7405 (July 4, 2012): 24–26. https://doi.org/10.1038/487024a

Barthelemy, Tiphaine. "Patronymic Names and *Noms de Terre* in the French Nobility in the Eighteenth and the Nineteenth Centuries." *The History of the Family* 5, no. 2 (2000): 181–97. https://doi.org/10.1016/S1081–602X(00)00041–5

Barthes, Roland. *Mythologies*. Translated by Annette Lavers. London: Jonathan Cape Ltd, 1972.

Bassett, Samuel Eliot. *The Poetry of Homer*. Lanham, MD: Lexington Books, 2003.

Baudrillard, Jean. *Simulacra and Simulation*. Translated by Sheila Glaser. Ann Arbor, MI: University of Michigan Press, 1995. https://doi.org/10.3998/mpub.9904

Benjamin, Walter. *Illuminations*. Edited by Hannah Arendt. Translated by Harry Zorn. London: The Bodley Head, 2015.

Bentall, R. P. "The Illusion of Reality: A Review and Integration of Psychological Research on Hallucinations." *Psychological Bulletin* 107, no. 1 (January 1990): 82–95. https://doi.org/10.1037/0033–2909.107.1.82

Bizzocchi, Aldo. "How Many Phonemes Does the English Language Have?" *International Journal on Studies in English Language and Literature (IJSELL)* 5 (October 1, 2017): 36–46. https://doi.org/10.20431/2347–3134.0510006

Bloom, Harold, ed. *Sophocles' Oedipus Rex*. New York: Chelsea House, 2007.

Bogatyrev, Petr. "Theatrical Signs." In *Theatre Theory Reader: Prague School Writings*, edited by David Drozd, Don Sparling, and Tomáš Kačer, translated by Eva Daníčková, Ivan Kolman, and Marta Filipová. Prague, CZ: Karolinum Press, 2016.

Bolton, Doug. "Why It's Impossible for You Not to Read This Sentence." *The Independent*, February 18, 2016. www.independent.uk

Bostrom, Nick. "Are You Living in a Computer Simulation?" *Philosophical Quarterly* 53, no. 211 (2003): 243–55.

Burnet, John. *The Socratic Doctrine of the Soul*. London: Humphrey Milford, Oxford University Press, 1916.

Cajori, Florian. *A History of Mathematical Notations*. New York: Cosimo Classics, 2011.

Changeux, Jean-Pierre. *Neuronal Man: The Biology of Mind*. Translated by Laurence Garey. New York: Oxford University Press, 1986.

Chappell, Mike. "Delphi and the 'Homeric Hymn to Apollo.'" *The Classical Quarterly* 56, no. 2 (December 2006): 331–48. https://doi.org/10.1017/S000983880600036X

Chebet-Choge, Susan. "The Case of Dead and Non-Used Nandi Anthroponyms." *AlterNative: An International Journal of Indigenous Peoples* 6, no. 1 (August 1, 2010): 38–53. https://doi.org/10.1177/117718011000600104

Chion, Michel. *Kubrick's Cinema Odyssey*. London: British Film Institute, 2001.

Clarke, Arthur C. *The Sentinel: Masterworks of Science Fiction and Fantasy*. New York: Berkley Books, 1983.

Clendinnen, Inga. "'Fierce and Unnatural Cruelty': Cortés and the Conquest of Mexico." In *New World Encounters*, edited by Stephen Greenblatt, 12–47. Berkeley: University of California Press, 1993.

Cohen, Edward E. *Athenian Prostitution: The Business of Sex*. Oxford: Oxford University Press, 2015.

Columbus, Christopher. "Christopher Columbus's 'Letter to the Sovereigns': Announcing the Discovery." In *New World Encounters*, edited by Margarita Zamora and Stephen Greenblatt, 1–11. Berkeley: University of California Press, 1993.

Corballis, Michael C. *The Recursive Mind: The Origins of Human Language, Thought, and Civilization*. Princeton, NJ: Princeton University Press, 2011. https://doi.org/10.15 15/9781400851492

Cowan, Nelson. "What Are the Differences between Long-Term, Short-Term, and Working Memory?" In *Progress in Brain Research*, edited by Wayne S. Sossin, Jean-Claude Lacaille, Vincent F. Castellucci, and Sylvie Belleville, 169: 323–38. Elsevier, 2008. https://doi.org/10.1016/S0079-6123(07)00020-9

Cowan, Nelson. *Working Memory Capacity*. New York: Psychology Press, 2016.

Davidson, Andrew. "Writing: The Re-Construction of Language." *Language Sciences* 72 (March 2019): 134–49. https://doi.org/10.1016/j.langsci.2018.09.004

De Saussure, Ferdinand. *Course in General Linguistics*. Edited by Charles Bally and Albert Sechehaye. Translated by Wade Baskin. New York: Philosophical Library, 1959.

Deleuze, Gilles, and Félix Guattari. *Anti-Oedipus: Capitalism and Schizophrenia*. Translated by Robert Hurley, Mark Seem, and Helen R Lane. London; New York: Continuum, 2004.

Deleuze, Gilles, and Félix Guattari. *A Thousand Plateaus: Capitalism and Schizophrenia*. Translated by Brian Massumi. London: Continuum, 2011.

Dennett, D. C. *Consciousness Explained*. London: Penguin Books, 1993.

Derrida, Jacques. *Limited Inc*. Translated by Samuel Weber and Jeffrey Mehlman. Evanston, IL: Northwestern University Press, 1988.

Derrida, Jacques. *Of Grammatology*. Translated by Gayatri Chakravorty Spivak. 1st American ed. Baltimore: Johns Hopkins University Press, 1976.

Dodds, E. R. "On Misunderstanding the 'Oedipus Rex.'" *Greece & Rome* 13, no. 1 (1966): 37–49.

Dodds, E. R. *The Greeks and the Irrational*. Berkeley: University of California Press, 1951.

Douzinas, Costas, Slavoj Žižek, and Alex Taek-Gwang Lee, eds. *The Idea of Communism*. Vol. I. New York: Verso, 2010.

Drozd, David, Tomáš Kačer, and Don Sparling, eds. *Theatre theory reader: Prague school writings*. Translated by Eva Daníčková, Marta Filipová, and Ivan Kolman. Prague: Karolinum Press, 2016.

Durán, Diego. "Historia de las Indias de Nueva España e islas de la tierra firme," 1579. Biblioteca Nacional de España; Biblioteca Digital Hispánica. http://bdh.bne.es /bnesearch/detalle/bdh0000169486

"Dyslexia FAQ." The Yale Center for Dyslexia & Creativity. Accessed May 23, 2022. dyslexia.yale.edu

Edwards, Mark U. *Printing, Propaganda, and Martin Luther*. Berkeley: University of California Press, 1994.

Eisenstein, Elizabeth L. "Some Conjectures about the Impact of Printing on Western Society and Thought: A Preliminary Report." *The Journal of Modern History* 40, no. 1 (1968): 1–56.

Eisenstein, Elizabeth L. *The Printing Press as an Agent of Change: Communications and Cultural Transformations in Early Modern Europe.* Cambridge, UK: Cambridge University Press, 1979.

Elam, Keir. *The Semiotics of Theatre and Drama.* New York: Routledge, 2002.

English, Mary C. "Reconstructing Aristophanic Performance: Stage Properties in 'The Acharnians.'" *Classical World* 100, no. 3 (2007): 199–227. https://doi.org/10.1353/clw.2007.0026

Felsenthal, Julia. "Give Me Your John Hancock: When Did We Start Signing Our Names to Authenticate Documents?" *Slate.com*, March 18, 2011.

Ferdinand and Isabella. "Privileges and Prerogatives Granted by Their Catholic Majesties to Christopher Columbus: 1492." Documents in Law, History and Diplomacy. Avalon Project, April 30, 1492. https://avalon.law.yale.edu/15th_century/

Finley, M. I. *The World of Odysseus.* New York: New York Review Books, 2002.

Fischer, Steven Roger. *A History of Reading.* London: Reaktion Books, 2003.

Flusser, Vilém, and Mark Poster. *Does Writing Have a Future?* Minneapolis: University of Minnesota Press, 2011.

Foucault, Michel. *Discipline and Punish: The Birth of the Prison.* Translated by Alan Sheridan. New York: Vintage Books, 1995.

Foucault, Michel. "What Is an Author?" In *The Foucault Reader*, edited by Paul Rabinow, 101–21. New York: Penguin Books, 1984.

Freedman, Carl. "Superman among the Stars." Review of *Kubrick's 2001: A Triple Allegory*, by Leonard F. Wheat. *Science Fiction Studies* 28, no. 2 (2001): 296–99.

Freud, Sigmund. *Three Contributions to the Theory of Sex.* Translated by A. A. Brill. New York: Nervous and Mental Disease Publishing Company, 1916, 64.

Galloway, Alexander R. *The Interface Effect.* Malden, MA: Polity, 2012.

Gasché, Rodolphe. "The 'Violence' of Deconstruction." *Research in Phenomenology* 45, no. 2 (September 2, 2015): 169–90. https://doi.org/10.1163/15691640-12341307

Gaur, Albertine. *Literacy and the Politics of Writing.* Bristol, UK: Intellect Books Ltd, 2000. http://ebookcentral.proquest.com/lib/tamucc/detail.action?docID=283015

Gilmont, J-F. "Protestant Reformations and Reading." In *A History of Reading in the West*, edited by Guglielmo Cavallo and Roger Chartier, translated by Lydia G. Cochrane, 213–33. Boston: University of Massachusetts Press, 1999.

Goff, Frederick Richmond. *The Permanence of Johann Gutenberg.* Austin: Humanities Research Center: University of Texas Press, 1970.

Graeber, David. *Debt: The First 5,000 Years.* Brooklyn, N.Y: Melville House, 2011.

Graff, Harvey J. *The Legacies of Literacy: Continuities and Contradictions in Western Culture and Society.* Bloomington: Indiana University Press, 1991.

Gurney, Edmund. "Hallucinations." *Mind* 10, no. 38 (1885): 161–99.

Gusdorf, Georges. *Speaking (La Parole)*. Translated by Paul T. Brockelman. Evanston, IL: Northwestern University Press, 1979.

Gustafson, Sandra. "Orality and Literacy in Transatlantic Perspective." *19: Interdisciplinary Studies in the Long Nineteenth Century* no. 18 (May 9, 2014). https://doi.org /10.16995/ntn.687

Haile, H. G. "Luther and Literacy." *PMLA* 91, no. 5 (October 1976): 816–28. https://doi .org/10.2307/461557

Harris, Roy. *Signs of Writing*. New York: Routledge, 1995.

Harrison, Glenn W., Ernan Haruvy, and E. Elisabet Rutström. "Remarks on Virtual World and Virtual Reality Experiments." *Southern Economic Journal* 78, no. 1 (July 2011): 87–94. https://doi.org/10.4284/0038-4038-78.1.87

Harvey, David. "Greeks and Romans Learn to Write." In *Communication Arts in the Ancient World*, edited by Eric A. Havelock and Jackson P Hershbell, 63–80. New York: Hastings House, 1978.

Havelock, Eric A. *The Literate Revolution in Greece and Its Cultural Consequences*. Princeton, NJ: Princeton University Press, 2019. https://doi.org/10.2307/j.ctvbcd1d2

Havelock, Eric A. "Oral Composition in the Oedipus Tyrannus of Sophocles." *New Literary History* 16, no. 1 (1984): 175. https://doi.org/10.2307/468781

Havelock, Eric A. *Origins of Western Literacy: Four Lectures Delivered at the Ontario Institute for Studies in Education, Toronto, March 25, 26, 27, 28, 1974*. Toronto: Ontario Institute for Studies in Education, 1976.

Havelock, Eric A. *Preface to Plato*. Cambridge: Belknap Press, Harvard University Press, 2010.

Hawhee, Debra. *Bodily Arts: Rhetoric and Athletics in Ancient Greece*. Austin: University of Texas Press, 2005.

Haworth, Michael. "Bernard Stiegler on Transgenerational Memory and the Dual Origin of the Human." *Theory, Culture & Society* 33, no. 3 (May 2016): 151–73. https://doi.org/10.1177/0263276415620474

Hayles, N. Katherine. "Cognition Everywhere: The Rise of the Cognitive Nonconscious and the Costs of Consciousness." *New Literary History* 45, no. 2 (2014): 199–220. https://doi.org/10.1353/nlh.2014.0011

Hayles, N. Katherine. *My Mother Was a Computer: Digital Subjects and Literary Texts*. Chicago: University of Chicago Press, 2010.

Hayles, N. Katherine. "Traumas of Code." *Critical Inquiry* 33, no. 1 (September 2006): 136–57. https://doi.org/10.1086/509749

Heidegger, Martin. "Who Is Nietzsche's Zarathustra?" Translated by Bernd Magnus. *The Review of Metaphysics* 20, no. 3 (1967): 411–31.

Hey, David, ed. *The Oxford Companion to Local and Family History*. Oxford: Oxford University Press, 1996.

Hobbes, Thomas. *Leviathan*. Edited by Crawford B. Macpherson. London: Penguin Books, 1972.

Hollitz, John Erwin. *Contending Voices: Biographical Explorations of the American Past*. Australia: Cengage Learning, 2017.

Huhtamo, Erkki, and Jussi Parikka, eds. *Media Archaeology: Approaches, Applications, and Implications*. Berkeley: University of California Press, 2011.

Huttenlocher, Peter R. *Neural Plasticity: The Effects of Environment on the Development of the Cerebral Cortex*. Cambridge, MA: Harvard University Press, 2002. https://doi .org/10.4159/9780674038936

Jackendoff, Ray, and Steven Pinker. "The Nature of the Language Faculty and Its Implications for Evolution of Language (Reply to Fitch, Hauser, and Chomsky)." *Cognition* 97, no. 2 (September 1, 2005): 211–25. https://doi.org/10.1016/j.cognit ion.2005.04.006

Jaynes, Julian. *The Origin of Consciousness in the Breakdown of the Bicameral Mind*. Boston: Houghton Mifflin, 1990.

Johnson, Christopher. "Lévi-Strauss: The Writing Lesson Revisited." *The Modern Language Review* 92, no. 3 (1997): 599–612. https://doi.org/10.2307/3733388

Kamuf, Peggy. "Chris Johnson's Writing Lesson." *Paragraph* 43, no. 1 (March 2020): 114–21. https://doi.org/10.3366/para.2020.0324

Kerckhove, Derrick de. "Theatre as Information-Processing in Western Cultures." *Modern Drama* 25, no. 1 (1982): 143–53. https://doi.org/10.1353/mdr.1982.0000

Kerckhove, Derrick de. "A Theory of Greek Tragedy." *SubStance* 9, no. 4 (1980): 23–36. https://doi.org/10.2307/3684038

Kittler, Friedrich. "Universities: Wet, Hard, Soft, and Harder." *Critical Inquiry* 31, no. 1 (September 1, 2004): 244–55. https://doi.org/10.1086/427310

Kittler, Friedrich. *Discourse Networks 1800/1900*. Translated by Michael Metteer. Stanford, CA: Stanford University Press, 1990.

Kittler, Friedrich. *Gramophone, Film, Typewriter*. Translated by Geoffrey Winthrop-Young and Michael Wutz. Stanford, CA: Stanford University Press, 1999.

Kittler, Friedrich A. "In the Wake of the Odyssey." In *The Truth of the Technological World: Essays on the Genealogy of Presence*, translated by Erik Butler, 286. Redwood City, CA: Stanford University Press, 2013.

Klein, Melanie. "The Rôle of the School in the Libidinal Development of the Child." *The International Journal of Psycho-Analysis* 5 (January 1, 1924): 312–31.

Koch Piettre, Renée. "Claude Lévi-Strauss." École Pratique des Hautes Études, January 14, 2018. https://prosopo.ephe.psl.eu/claude-l%C3%A9vi-strauss

Kolb, Bryan, and Robbin Gibb. "Brain Plasticity and Behaviour in the Developing Brain." *Journal of the Canadian Academy of Child and Adolescent Psychiatry = Journal de l'Academie canadienne de psychiatrie de l'enfant et de l'adolescent* 20, no. 4 (November 2011): 265–76.

Lacan, Jacques. *Écrits*. Translated by Bruce Fink. New York, NY: Norton, 2006.

Lacan, Jacques. *The Four Fundamental Concepts of Psycho-Analysis*. Edited by Jacques-Alain Miller. Translated by Alan Sheridan. London: Karnac Books, 2004.

Leerssen, Joseph Th. *Mere Irish & Fíor-Ghael: Studies in the Idea of Irish Nationality, Its Development, and Literary Expression Prior to the Nineteenth Century*. Philadelphia, PA: John Benjamins Publishing Company, 1986.

Leroi-Gourhan, André. *Gesture and Speech.* Translated by Anna Bostock Berger. Cambridge, MA: MIT Press, 1993.

Lévi-Strauss, Claude. *Structural Anthropology.* Translated by Claire Jacobson and Brooke Grundfest Schoepf. New York: Basic Books, Inc., 1963.

Lévi-Strauss, Claude. *Tristes Tropiques.* Translated by Doreen Weightman and John Weightman. New York: Penguin Books, 2012.

Littleton, C. Scott. "The Pneuma Enthusiastikon: On the Possibility of Hallucinogenic 'Vapors' at Delphi and Dodona," *Ethos* 14, no. 1 (1986): 77.

Liu, Lydia H. "Scripts in Motion: Writing as Imperial Technology, Past and Present." *PMLA* 130, no. 2 (2015): 375–83.

Logan, Robert K. *The Alphabet Effect: The Impact of the Phonetic Alphabet on the Development of Western Civilization.* New York: St. Martin's Press, 1986.

Lotman, Juri. "The Place of Art among Other Modelling Systems." Translated by Tanel Pern. *Sign Systems Studies* 39, no. 2/4 (December 1, 2011): 249–70. https://doi.org/10.12697/SSS.2011.39.2–4.10

Luria, A. R. *The Mind of a Mnemonist.* Translated by Lynn Solotaroff. New York: Avon Books, 1969.

Luria, Alexander Romanovich. *Cognitive Development: Its Cultural and Social Foundations.* Edited by Michael Cole. Translated by Lynn Solotaroff and Martin Lopez-Morillas. Cambridge, MA: Harvard University Press, 1994.

MacKellar, C., ed. *Cyborg Mind: What Brain-Computer and Mind-Cyberspace Interfaces Mean for Cyberneuroethics.* New York: Berghahn, 2019.

Malabou, Catherine. *Plasticity at the Dusk of Writing: Dialectic, Destruction, Deconstruction.* Translated by Carolyn Shread. New York: Columbia University Press, 2010.

Malabou, Catherine. "The End of Writing? Grammatology and Plasticity." *The European Legacy* 12, no. 4 (July 1, 2007): 431–41. https://doi.org/10.1080/1084877070 1396254

Mann, Steve, and Hal Niedzviecki. *Cyborg: Digital Destiny and Human Possibility in the Age of the Wearable Computer.* Toronto: Doubleday Canada, 2001.

Mantovani, Giuseppe. "Virtual Reality as a Communication Environment: Consensual Hallucination, Fiction, and Possible Selves." *Human Relations* 48, no. 6 (June 1995): 669–83. https://doi.org/10.1177/001872679504800604

Marinescu, Constantin A., Sarah E. Cox, and Rudolph Wachter. "Paideia's Children: Childhood Education on a Group of Late Antique Mosaics." In *Constructions of Childhood in Ancient Greece and Italy,* edited by Ada Cohen and Jeremy B. Rutter, 101–14. Princeton, NJ: American School of Classical Studies at Athens, 2007.

Martin, Henri-Jean. *The History and Power of Writing.* Translated by Lydia G. Cochrane. Chicago: University of Chicago Press, 1994.

Marx, Karl. *Capital: A Critique of Political Economy.* Edited by Friedrich Engels. Translated by Edward Aveling and Samuel Moore. Vol. I. Moscow: Progress Publishers, 1887.

Mayall, Berry. "Children's Lived Bodies in Everyday Life." In *Sociology of the Body: A*

Reader, edited by Claudia Malacrida and Jacqueline Low, 198–204. Ontario, Canada: Oxford University Press, 2008.

McClure, Laura. *Courtesans at Table: Gender and Greek Literary Culture in Athenaeus.* New York: Routledge, 2014.

McLuhan, Marshall. *The Gutenberg Galaxy: The Making of Typographic Man.* Toronto: University of Toronto Press, 2008.

McLuhan, Marshall. *Understanding Media: The Extensions of Man.* Cambridge, MA: MIT Press, 1994.

Metzinger, Thomas. *Being No One: The Self-Model Theory of Subjectivity.* Cambridge, MA: MIT Press, 2004.

Micocci, Andrea. *The Metaphysics of Capitalism.* Lanham, MD: Lexington Books, 2009.

Mumford, Lewis. *Technics and Civilization.* Chicago: The University of Chicago Press, 2010.

Neel, Jasper P. *Plato, Derrida, and Writing.* Carbondale: Southern Illinois University Press, 1988.

Nellhaus, Tobin. "Literacy, Tyranny, and the Invention of Greek Tragedy." *Journal of Dramatic Theory and Criticism* 3, no. 2 (1989): 53–72.

Nietzsche, Friedrich. "A Genealogy of Morals." In *The Works of Friedrich Nietzsche*, edited by Alexander Tille, translated by William A. Hausemann, Vol. X. New York: Macmillan, 1897.

Nietzsche, Friedrich. *Thus Spake Zarathustra.* Translated by Thomas Common. New York: Modern Library, 1917.

Nussbaum, Martha C. "The 'Oedipus Rex' and the Ancient Unconscious." In *Sophocles' Oedipus Rex*, edited by Harold Bloom, 155–82. New York: Chelsea House, 2007.

Olson, David R., and Nancy Torrance. "Conceptualizing Literacy as a Personal Skill and as a Social Practice." In *The Making of Literate Societies*, edited by David R. Olson and Nancy Torrance, 3–18. Malden, MA: Blackwell, 2001.

Ong, Walter J. *Orality and Literacy: The Technologizing of the Word.* London: Taylor & Francis e-Library, 2004.

Ong, Walter J. "The Writer's Audience Is Always a Fiction." *PMLA* 90, no. 1 (January 1975): 9–21. https://doi.org/10.2307/461344

Ong, Walter J. "Writing Is a Technology That Restructures Thought." In *The Written Word: Literacy in Translation*, edited by Gerd Baumann. Oxford: Oxford University Press, 1986.

Ornan, Uzzi. "Phonemes and Their Realization in Hebrew." *Hebrew Studies* 57 (2016): 225–38.

Parry, Milman, and Adam Parry. *The Making of Homeric Verse: The Collected Papers of Milman Parry.* Oxford: Oxford University Press, 1987.

Patterson, David W. "Music, Structure and Metaphor in Stanley Kubrick's *2001: A Space Odyssey.*" *American Music* 22, no. 3 (2004): 444–74. https://doi.org/10.2307/3592986

Pinker, Steven, and Ray Jackendoff. "The Faculty of Language: What's Special about It?" *Cognition* 95, no. 2 (March 2005): 201–36. https://doi.org/10.1016/j.cogniti on.2004.08.004

Plato. "Cratylus." In *Plato in Twelve Volumes*, translated by Harold North Fowler, Vol. 12. Cambridge, MA: Harvard University Press, 1921.

Plato. "Phaedo." In *The Collected Works of Plato*, translated by Hugh Tredennick, 41–67. Princeton, NJ: Princeton University Press, 1980.

Plato. *Plato in Twelve Volumes*. Translated by R. G. Bury. Vol. 10 & 11. Cambridge, MA: Harvard University Press, 1967.

Plato. *Plato in Twelve Volumes*. Translated by Harold North Fowler. Vol. 1. Loeb Classical Library 36. Cambridge, MA: Harvard University Press, 2005.

Plato. "Republic." In *Plato in Twelve Volumes*, translated by Paul Shorey, Vol. 5 & 6. Cambridge, MA: Harvard University Press, 1969.

Plutarch. "The Obsolescence of Oracles." In *Moralia, Volume V*, translated by Frank Cole Babbitt. Loeb Classical Library 306. Cambridge, MA: Harvard University Press, 1936.

Pope Alexander VI. "The Papal Bull Inter Caetera," May 4, 1493. www.let.rug.nl

Portela, Manuel. *Scripting Reading Motions: The Codex and the Computer as Self-Reflexive Machines*. Cambridge, MA: MIT Press, 2013.

Quine, W. V. O. *Ontological Relativity and Other Essays*. New York: Columbia University Press, 1969.

Raschko, Mary. "Review of Holy Scripture and the Quest for Authority at the End of the Middle Ages by Ian Christopher Levy." *The Journal of Medieval Religious Cultures* 40, no. 1 (January 1, 2014): 104–7. https://doi.org/10.5325/jmedirelicult .40.1.0104

Restall, Matthew. *Seven Myths of the Spanish Conquest*. Oxford: Oxford University Press, 2004.

Restall, Matthew, and Felipe Fernández-Armesto. *The Conquistadors: A Very Short Introduction*. New York: Oxford University Press, 2012.

Robb, Kevin. *Literacy and Paideia in Ancient Greece*. New York: Oxford University Press, 1994.

Rose, Jacqueline. *The Case of Peter Pan, or, The Impossibility of Children's Fiction*. New Cultural Studies. Philadelphia: University of Pennsylvania Press, 1993, 60.

Rousseau, Jean-Jacques. *Discourse on the Origin of Inequality*. Translated by Donald Cress. Mineola, N.Y: Dover Publications, 2004.

Schaps, David. *The Invention of Coinage and the Monetization of Ancient Greece*. Ann Arbor, MI: University of Michigan Press, 2015.

Schmandt-Besserat, Denise. *Before Writing*. Austin: University of Texas Press, 1992.

Schmitz, Leonhard, and A. S. Wilkins. "Divinatio." In *A Dictionary of Greek and Latin Antiquities*, edited by William Smith, William Wayte, and G. E. Marindin. London: John Murray, 1890.

Scott, Michael. *Delphi: A History of the Center of the Ancient World*. Princeton, NJ: Princeton University Press, 2014.

Seaford, Richard. "Coinage and Early Greek Thought." *Radical Anthropology* 1, no. 5 (2013): 45.

Seaford, Richard. *Money and the Early Greek Mind: Homer, Philosophy, Tragedy.* Cambridge: Cambridge University Press, 2004.

Seidenberg, Mark S. *Language at the Speed of Sight: How We Read, Why So Many Can't, and What Can Be Done About It.* New York: Basic Books, 2018.

Shusterman, Ronald. "Virtual Realities and Autotelic Art." *SubStance* 22, no. 2/3 (1993): 113–25. https://doi.org/10.2307/3685274

Sidis, Boris. "An Inquiry Into the Nature of Hallucinations." *The Psychological Review* 11, no. 2 (March 1904).

Smith-Donald, Radiah, C. Cybele Raver, Tiffany Hayes, and Breeze Richardson. "Preliminary Construct and Concurrent Validity of the Preschool Self-Regulation Assessment (PSRA) for Field-Based Research." *Early Childhood Research Quarterly* 22, no. 2 (April 2007): 173–87. https://doi.org/10.1016/j.ecresq.2007.01.002

Sofer, Andrew. *The Stage Life of Props.* Ann Arbor, MI: University of Michigan Press, 2003.

Sohn-Rethel, Alfred. *Intellectual and Manual Labour: A Critique of Epistemology.* Translated by Martin Sohn-Rethel. Atlantic Highlands, N.J.: Humanities Press, 1978.

Soler, Jean. "Why Monotheism." Translated by Janet Lloyd. *Arion: A Journal of Humanities and the Classics* 14, no. 3 (2007): 41–60.

Sophocles. *Oedipus Tyrannus: A New Translation.* Translated and edited by Luci Berkowitz and Theodore F. Brunner. A Norton Critical Edition. New York: Norton, 1970.

Sophocles. *The Oedipus Casebook: Reading Sophocles' Oedipus the King.* Edited by Mark Rogin Anspach and William Blake Tyrrell. East Lansing, MI: Michigan State University Press, 2020.

St. Augustine. *Confessions.* Peabody, MA: Hendrickson Publishers, 2011.

Steiner, George. *Language and Silence: Essays on Language, Literature, and the Inhuman.* New York: Atheneum, 1972.

Steven Roger Fischer. *History of Writing.* Globalities. London: Reaktion Books, 2001.

Stevenson, Angus, and Christine A. Lindberg, eds. *New Oxford American Dictionary.* Oxford: Oxford University Press, 2011.

Stiegler, Bernard. *Technics and Time, 1: The Fault of Epimetheus.* Translated by Richard Beardsworth and George Collins. Stanford: Stanford University Press, 1998.

Stone, Allucquere Roseanne. "Will the Real Body Please Stand Up?: Boundary Stories about Virtual Cultures." In *Cyberspace: First Steps,* edited by Michael Benedikt, 81–118. Cambridge, MA: MIT Press, 1991.

Svenbro, Jesper. *Phrasikleia: An Anthropology of Reading in Ancient Greece.* Translated by Janet Lloyd. Ithaca, NY: Cornell University Press, 1993.

Taine, Hippolyte. *On Intelligence.* Translated by T. D Haye. Bristol, UK: Thoemmes Press, 1998.

Tearle, Oliver. *Bewilderments of Vision: Hallucination and Literature, 1880–1914.* Brighton, UK: Sussex Academic Press, 2013.

Thomas, Hugh. *Rivers of Gold: The Rise of the Spanish Empire, From Columbus to Magellan*. New York: Random House, 2005.

Thomas, Rosalind. "Literacy in Ancient Greece: Functional Literacy, Oral Education, and the Development of a Literate Environment." In *The Making of Literate Societies*, edited by David R. Olson and Nancy Torrance, 68–81. Malden, MA: Blackwell, 2001.

Thrift, Nigel. "Remembering the Technological Unconscious by Foregrounding Knowledges of Position." *Environment and Planning D: Society and Space* 22, no. 1 (February 2004): 175–90. https://doi.org/10.1068/d321t

Todorov, Tzvetan. *The Conquest of America: The Question of the Other*. Translated by Catherine Porter. Norman: University of Oklahoma Press, 1999.

Tomšič, Samo. *The Capitalist Unconscious: Marx and Lacan*. New York: Verso, 2015.

Uexküll, Jakob von. *A Foray into the Worlds of Animals and Humans*. Translated by Joseph D. O'Neil. Minneapolis: University of Minnesota Press, 2010.

Veracini, Lorenzo. *The Settler Colonial Present*. Basingstoke: Palgrave Macmillan, 2015.

Von Dassow, Eva, ed. *The Egyptian Book of the Dead: The Book of Going Forth By Day*. Translated by Raymond O. Faulkner and Ogden Goelet. San Francisco: Chronicle Books, 2015.

Wade-Gery, H. T. *The Poet of the Iliad*. Cambridge: Cambridge University Press, 2013.

Watts, David P. "Meat Eating by Nonhuman Primates: A Review and Synthesis." *Journal of Human Evolution* 149 (December 2020): 102882. https://doi.org/10.10 16/j.jhevol.2020.102882

White, Susan. "Kubrick's Obscene Shadows." In *Stanley Kubrick's 2001: A Space Odyssey: New Essays*, edited by Robert Phillip Kolker, 127–46. Oxford: Oxford University Press, 2006.

Whitman, Cedric H. "Jocasta." In *Oedipus Tyrannus: A New Translation. Passages from Ancient Authors. Religion and Psychology: Some Studies. Criticism*, edited by Luci Berkowitz and Theodore F. Brunner, 165–70. New York: Norton, 1970.

Willis, Susan. *A Primer for Daily Life*. New York: Routledge, 1991.

Wittgenstein, Ludwig. *Philosophical investigations*. Edited by P. M. S. Hacker and Joachim Schulte. Translated by G. E. M. Anscombe. Malden, MA: Wiley-Blackwell, 2009.

Žižek, Slavoj. *Less than Nothing: Hegel and the Shadow of Dialectical Materialism*. New York: Verso, 2012.

Žižek, Slavoj. *The Sublime Object of Ideology*. New York: Verso, 1989.

Index

Printed and bound by CPI Group (UK) Ltd, Croydon, CR0 4YY

13/04/2025

14656534-0002